WORLD AFLAME

OTHER BOOKS BY BILLY GRAHAM

Peace with God
   Cloth $3.50   Paperback 75c
Secret of Happiness
   Cloth $2.95   Paperback 50c
My Answer
   Cloth $3.50

BOOKS ABOUT BILLY GRAHAM

Billy Graham *by John Pollock*
   Cloth $4.95   Paperback 95c
Those Who Came Forward *by Curtis Mitchell*
   Cloth $3.95
The Making of a Crusader *by Curtis Mitchell*
   Cloth $3.95
The London Crusade Story *by Curtis Mitchell*
      $1.50

THE BILLY GRAHAM EVANGELISTIC ASSOCIATION

Box 779 (1300 Harmon Place), Minneapolis, Minnesota 55440
Box 841 (414 Graham Avenue), Winnipeg 1, Manitoba, Canada
Bush House, Aldwych, London, W.C. 2, England
820 Caltex House, Sydney, New South Wales, Australia
Box 870, Auckland, New Zealand
Decision, 102 Avenue des Champs-Elysees, Paris 8, France
Entscheidung, Postfach 16309, 6 Frankfurt/M, Germany
Casilla 5055, Buenos Aires, Argentina
Decimex, Apartado 10742, Mexico 1, D.F., Mexico
Apartado 13098, Santurce, San Juan, Puerto Rico

WORLD AFLAME

By Billy Graham

Special Crusade Edition
THE BILLY GRAHAM EVANGELISTIC ASSOCIATION
Box 779, Minneapolis, Minnesota 55440

WORLD AFLAME

Doubleday edition published September, 1965

Grateful acknowledgment is made to the following for permission to use copyrighted material:

Benziger Brothers, Inc., for material from *The Truth of Christianity Series* by Fathers Doyle, Chetwood, and Herzog, © by Benziger Brothers, Inc., and used by permission of the publishers.

Fleming H. Revell Company for quotations from *Christ is God* by Archibald Rutledge.

Harcourt, Brace & World, Inc., and Faber and Faber Ltd., for lines from *The Hollow Men* by T. S. Eliot, which appears in *Collected Poems 1909-1962*.

This Crusade edition includes every word contained in the original clothbound edition.

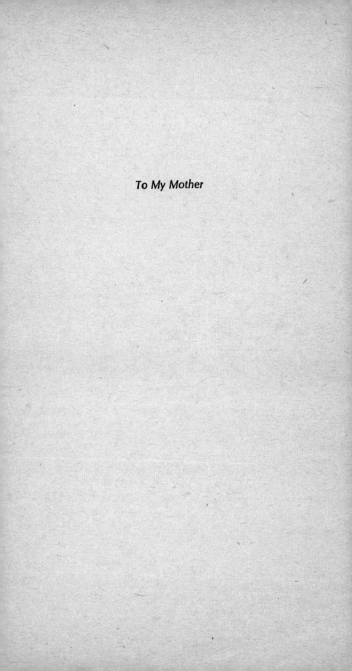

To My Mother

Preface

WORLD AFLAME has been witten in the heat of a multitude of other responsibilities. There have been hundreds of interruptions—from Ned and Franklin running into my study wanting to play ball, to a week spent in the hospital. It seemed that every time I had a few days to work on the book, a new outside challenge would present itself or a new emergency would demand my time and attention. But the message of this book kept burning in my soul; it had to be written!

Pascal said: "Certain authors, when they speak of their work, say: 'My book, my commentary, my history' . . . They would do better to say 'our book, our commentary, our history,' since their writings generally contain more of other people's good things than of their own."[1]

This is our book! I wish to thank all who have helped with WORLD AFLAME. Special appreciation goes to the following who read the manuscript and made valuable suggestions:

The Reverend Frank Colquhoun
The Reverend Lee Fisher
Dr. Frank E. Gaebelein
Dr. Carl F. H. Henry
Dr. Roy L. Laurin
Dr. Wilbur M. Smith
The Reverend Calvin Thielman

Finally, it was read by my wife Ruth, my most valued critic.

[1]Blaise Pascal, *Pensées,* trans. with introduction by J. M. Cohen (Baltimore: Penguin Books, Inc., *Penguin Classics,* 1961), p. 42.

I am grateful to Wanda Ann Mercer who coordinated the material and supervised the typing, which was done by Martha Warkentin and Elsie Brookshire.

Over the years I have gathered ideas and even quotations from sources long since forgotten. To every one whose books and articles I have read, to every man with whom I have talked or prayed about man's need for God and God's plan of redemption, to every minister of the Gospel whose sermons I have heard, I express my gratitude, for each has contributed in some measure to this book. I regret that it is not possible to list each one by name.

It is my sincere hope and prayer that God will bless "our" book.

Montreat, North Carolina
June 1, 1965

                              BILLY GRAHAM

Contents

Contents

Introduction

At 5:30 A.M. on July 16, 1945, a light brighter than a thousand suns illuminated the desert sands of New Mexico. One scientist who was watching wept. "My God," he exclaimed, "we have created hell." From that day on, our world has not been the same. We entered a new era of history—perhaps the last era.

This book attempts to describe our modern world on fire. Fire can either purify or destroy.

The world has been in flames before, but only in a limited sense. Today our world is a common neighborhood, all of it reachable in mere hours by physical flight and in seconds over the airways. This accessibility increases the spread of tension and dissension. Thus when the fires of war and lawlessness break out, they leap the national boundaries and cultural differences to become major conflagrations. The whole world is filled with riots, demonstrations, threats, wars, and with a rebellion against authority that threatens civilization itself.

It is not the purpose of these pages to identify all the different fires that change and shift with kaleidoscopic speed, but rather to examine the cause of the tensions and conditions feeding them. Newspapers, television screens, and radios portray the unfolding crises of our times. Over and over we ask ourselves, Why? What is the cause? What has happened to our world? Can we do anything about it?

It is the assumption of some *economists* that the cause of a world aflame is to be found in monetary inequities. Redistribute the wealth, they say, and we shall solve our problems. But as Justice Whittaker has pointed out: "Even the distribution of wealth would not solve or long alleviate the human problems that plague us."

It is the assumption of some *diplomats* that the cause of world tension is political and that if we could attain good will and friendship with all nations, we should solve our problems. In the United Nations we have tried desperately to do just that. Yet the United Nations is proving to be almost as ineffectual as the old League of Nations. The diplomat ignores the evidence that international diplomacy is a record of broken dreams, broken promises, and broken treaties.

It is the assumption of some *educators* that the cause of world tension lies in the lack of knowledge and that if we can only educate every man, peace will come to the world. They say that if man knows better, he will do better. In *The Suicide of the West,* which purports to explain the meaning and destiny of liberalism, James Burnham says that this plea of the educator overlooks entirely certain facts—that Germany, long one of the great cultured nations of the world, produced a Hitler and a Himmler and that Joseph Goebbels had a Doctor of Philosophy degree. Burnham contends that highly educated people have inward drives, greeds, compulsions, passions, and a lust for power that are not eliminated by any known process of education.

It is the assumption of some *sociologists* that bad environment, in the form of poor living conditions such as urban slums and rural poverty areas, is the breeding ground of evil and trouble. Here again Burnham is right when he says that these bad environmental conditions will continue to exist because their substitutes will inevitably turn bad. A slum is not composed simply of run-down buildings. Skid rows can be torn down, but the same people remain to create new ones. Indeed, some of the greater social problems we now face are found in the more affluent areas of suburbia. We are beginning to realize that the problem is deeper than bad environment.

In this book, my thesis is based on the Biblical philosophy of man and of history. The more I have traveled around the world the more convinced I have become that the Biblical revelation of man, his origin, his present predicament, and his destiny is true. This book is intentionally controversial. I hope that something of what I have written will shock readers out of apathy into the reality of our desperate condition individually and socially.

Christians must never fall into the trap of thinking that a Bible-based philosophy of world events and world destiny will parallel the world's philosophies. For example, there are few philosophers, politicians, economists, or sociologists who accept Jesus' prophetic account of history as recorded in the twenty-fourth chapter of Matthew. To one who accepts the Biblical account, it is exciting to pick up a newspaper in one hand and the Bible in the other hand and to watch the almost daily fulfillment of prophetic events. Man is precisely what the Bible says he is. Human nature is behaving exactly as the Bible said it would. The course of human events is flowing just as Christ predicted it would.

As a Christian, I am under no obligation to attempt to reconcile the Bible's teachings with modern philosophy. Biblical truth does not parallel human opinion of any generation; it usually opposes it! We are to be witnesses, not imitators. The prophets who spoke to their generations for God did not please and conform; they irritated and opposed.

The Bible's philosophy of man in history begins with God as the Creator of the universe. The Bible presents man as being in rebellion against God. This began when, in an overt act of self-will, our first parents rebelled against divine law. In this experience man ruined his divine image, became alienated from God, and started on a course of action that produced civilizations and cultures saturated with crime, lust, hate, greed, and war. The earth is a planet in rebellion.

The Bible reveals that in spite of man's rebellion God loves him. Thus God undertook the most dramatic rescue operation in cosmic history. He determined to save the human race from self-destruction, and He sent His Son Jesus Christ to salvage and redeem us. The work of man's redemption was accomplished at the Cross.

Ultimately, the Bible looks into the future to foresee a new world in which peace and righteousness prevail. There is to be world peace. There is to be a new social order. There is to be a new age. There is to be a completely new man in whom will be no false pride, hate, lust, greed, or prejudice.

This will be the climax of human history. This age will be unlike anything the world has ever known. The Kingdom of God will triumph. The Scripture says: "Nevertheless we, according to his promise, look for new heavens and a new earth, wherein dwelleth righteousness" (II Pet. 3:13).

Until the coming of the new social order by God's direct intervention, the world will continue to plunge from crisis to crisis. In the midst of these trials and tribulations, we must determine which way God is moving in history—and then get in step with God!

In WORLD AFLAME I can touch only the high spots. I could have written an entire book on the subject of each chapter, especially in those chapters where I discuss the end of the world. I have left much unsaid. Someday I hope to write a book on the subject of "The End."

In theory, the people of the West have various forms of democracy based on a belief in God as well as on a general acceptance of moral law. However, in practice we are beginning to resemble the Marxists, who have little respect for moral law or religion. Our interests are centered in ourselves. We are preoccupied with material things. Our supreme god is technology; our goddess is sex. Most of us are more interested in getting to the moon than in getting to heaven, more concerned about conquering space than about conquering ourselves. We are more dedicated to material security than to inner purity. We give much more thought to what we wear, what we eat, what we drink, and what we can do to relax than we give to what we are. This preoccupation with peripheral things applies to every area of our lives.

WORLD AFLAME is an attempt to speak to man in his present situation, to show him how he can find victory over his environment and conquer the downward pull into the infernos of our time.

Today the whole world is on fire! These pages present what I believe to be the Biblical answer to world conflagration.

1

Flames Out of Control

A few years ago the trees on the mountains behind our home caught fire. The flames were discovered by forest rangers who keep a twenty-four-hour lookout from a nearby mountain. The fire was already out of control and moving rapidly toward our home when we were told to be ready to evacuate. Fire fighters came, and we fought the fire all night until it was brought under control.

Our world is on fire, and man without God will never be able to control the flames. The demons of hell have been let loose. The fires of passion, greed, hate, and lust are sweeping the world. We seem to be plunging madly toward Armageddon.

Not long before he was killed in a plane crash several years ago, I visited with Mr. Dag Hammarskjöld in his office at the United Nations. He seemed deeply depressed during our conversation. Looking from his window across New York, he said quietly: "I see no hope for permanent world peace. We have tried so hard and we have failed so miserably." Then he paused a moment, looked at me, and said: "Unless the world has a spiritual rebirth within the next few years, civilization is doomed."

This is the generation that will pass through the fire. It is the generation, *Holiday* magazine said, "under the gun." This is the tormented generation. This is the generation destined to live in the midst of crisis, danger, fear, and death. We are like a people under sentence of death, waiting for the date to be set. We sense that something is about to happen. We know that things cannot go on as they are. History has reached an impasse. We are now on a collision course. Something is about to give.

Jean-Paul Sartre, the French Existentialist, said: "There is no exit from the human dilemma." Sir Winston Churchill spoke of the world's dilemma in these words: "Our problems are beyond us." The flames are licking all around our world—the roof is about to cave in—man is caught in a fire raging out of control.

What are some of these flames that are threatening to destroy us?

The Demographic Flame

This is the current population explosion, which baffles our finest minds. The population increase is frightening. This dilemma is analyzed by the eminent British historian Arnold Toynbee, who believes that if we have a nuclear war, too few people will be left alive to maintain civilization; but if we do not have such a war, too many people will make life on this planet both intolerable and impossible. Statistics overwhelm us when we take into account the rapidity with which births are exceeding deaths.

The population of the world at the beginning of recorded history is estimated to have been 125,000. At the time of Christ there were only about two-thirds as many people on the whole earth as live in the United States alone today. So fast has the population grown since then that three percent of all human beings who ever lived since the dawn of history are on the earth today. By the end of this century in 2000 A.D., the world's population will have exceeded six and a half-billion people. From the year 2000 on, the statistics go berserk.

The results of this explosion are fantastic. In six generations, if the current rate of increase is continued, the United States will have nine billion people, three times the present population of the whole world today. It will result in the United States becoming a single metropolitan city. Scientists are now talking in terms of an ecumenopolis, or worldwide metropolis! Thus we can imagine, human nature being what it is, what frightening prospects lie ahead if this explosion continues unabated.

The world now faces a biological problem as well as a political one. Are we capable of mustering the will, the wisdom, and the compassion to cope with this mounting problem of overpopulation? No present or future schemes of socialistic or altruistic welfare to share the wealth can mean much if there are more people than there is wealth to be shared. Thus people themselves have become a weapon which could ultimately destroy them. Sexual energy is one of the flames out of control.

The Flame of Lawlessness

The Bible teaches that sin is transgression of the law (I Jn. 3:4). This word "transgression" could be translated "lawlessness." Jesus indicated that as men approached the end of history there would be a worldwide rebellion against law and order. Rebellion and lawlessness are already present on a scale such as the world has never known. Children rebel against their parents until many parents are actually afraid of their children. Young people rebel against their teachers. University students rebel against administrative authorities. There is an organized attempt to downgrade the policeman, to make fun of him and despise him. All this is part of a general disrespect for law and order.

It ought to shock us that in many countries organized crime is the biggest business of all. In fact, one of America's leading racketeers casually boasted a short time ago: "Organized crime is bigger than the United States Government."

Crime grosses close to 10 percent of the American national income and forms virtually a state within a state. It costs us more than all our educational and welfare programs combined. Organized crime, with its syndicates, underworld, racketeering, and the Mafia, almost controls some of the world's major cities. In addition, there is unorganized crime, and it is just as bad if not worse.

Crime is increasing with such rapidity that we are now close to open rebellion and anarchy. It is dangerous to walk the streets of almost any city in America after dark. In some areas people live in fear and terror. It is as though some sinister, supernatural force were loose. Our city streets are turned into jungles of terror, mugging, rape, and death. The blight of criminality threatens to engulf our society; as the crime rates rise, the moral foundations of the nation crumble. The chief of police of one of our larger cities confided in me recently: "Crime definitely pays." He said that more than half of all criminals in his city eventually go free. Most of them are undetected; as for those who are caught, the police have a difficult time proving anything to the satisfaction of the courts.

What is the answer to the problem of crime? Is it more police work, more education, stricter punishment? Why is it that in the most affluent society in history our nation leads the world in crime?

We have taught during the past few decades that morals are relative, and now we are reaping the harvest. The tendency of the educational system, the courts, and the mass communications media is often to ignore the victim of a crime and to coddle the criminal. In some cases, we even make the criminal a hero. I find that law enforcement officers throughout the country are discouraged. They feel that the courts are not giving them cooperation. The crime statistics are astronomical. Law enforcement agencies do not have the money or the personnel to apprehend even a fraction of the criminals. No one seems to have the answer. It is another flame out of control!

The Racial Flame

Premier Chou En-lai of China said recently in an English broadcast from Peking: "The colored people of the world outnumber the white 12 to 1. Let's wipe them out." An eminent sociologist confided recently that he believes we will be involved in a bitter racial war within the next few years. Men of the stature of Dr. Martin Niemöller, one of the presidents of the World Council of Churches, and Sir Hugh Foote, a member of the British Labor Government, have joined in warning about the possibility of race war.

In New York City a Negro boy of seventeen was arrested recently for murder. He was called "Big Giant." His mother said he used to be such a wonderful boy, but that the black nationalists made him hate the white man. She said he was brainwashed.

There is no doubt that racial tension is increasing throughout the world. In some areas it is already flaming into underground warfare.

Being born black in some parts of the world—or Jewish in other parts—or Oriental in others—or white in some places—imposes intolerable burdens, while those who are accidentally born to the ruling majority enjoy advantages they have not always earned and of which they seem to have little appreciation. To hate, to discriminate against, and to restrict those who look different, who talk differently, who have different national backgrounds, or who act differently from the dominant group is a consistent and universal trait of human nature extending beyond national barriers. Racial prejudice is not limited to the southern part of the United States or to South Africa. I have observed it almost everywhere. Wherever two races live side by side, there exists prejudice. It is found among the Israelites and the Arabs, the French and the Algerians, the Indonesians and the Malaysians, the white South Africans and the coloreds.

I was in one country that claimed to have solved its race problem. Indeed, on the surface it looked like a racial paradise. However, I found that the darker a man's skin, the less advantage and opportunity he had. There were certain clubs he could not get into, and he could not serve as an officer in the Armed Forces of that country.

I went to another country where they claimed that their race problem was solved, and it did seem that they had no racial prejudice. They constantly condemned racial strife in the United States, British Guiana, and South Africa. Then I realized they had only one race, for they adhere strictly to an "all-white" policy.

Great Britain has always prided itself on being free of racial prejudice. However, when thousands of colored peoples moved into the British Isles, the Britons found that they had plenty of prejudice. Even British elections are affected by racial prejudice. The same is true in the Soviet Union. Even though there were relatively few African students studying in the Soviet Union, many of them have left, complaining of racial discrimination. Thus racial prejudice is a worldwide problem.

There is so much hypocrisy on the subject of racial prejudice that it is difficult to know where to start. Christ has taught the dignity of man and the possibility of the brotherhood of man in Himself. Wherever there is discrimination, Christ is at work with His sword cutting out hatred and intolerance. The Bible says plainly that God is no respecter of persons. This cuts across the theory of racial supremacy and makes all men equal in the sight of God. This Biblical position tends to create dissatisfaction among those who feel they are discriminated against. It also creates a guilt complex among those who do the discriminating.

We are not told in the Bible where the various colors of skin began. There are some who think the races began from the three sons of Noah, but there is no proof as to which one of these sons was dark and which one was white.

The Christian faith is often in conflict with tradition. Jesus' greatest concern was with the Pharisees, who were motivated not by love but by regard for their traditions. Likewise bound by tradition are those areas where discrimination is greatest.

How can we solve this great national and world problem? Even a fool can see that we cannot settle the racial problem by legislation alone.

A day or two after the 1964 Civil Rights Bill was passed, the then Senator Hubert Humphrey came over to the table where I was sitting in Washington and said: "Billy, legislation alone can't do it. It must ultimately come from the heart." How right he was! It takes love, understanding, forbearance, and patience on the part of both races.

There is only one possible solution to the race problem and that is a vital personal experience with Jesus Christ on the part of both races. In Christ the middle wall of partition has been broken down. There is no Jew, no Gentile—no black, white, yellow, or red. We could be one great brotherhood in Jesus Christ. However, until we come to recognize Him as the Prince of Peace and receive His love in our hearts, the racial tensions will increase, racial demands will become more militant, and a great deal of blood will be shed. The race problem could become another flame out of control!

The Red Flame

Communism is a dangerous threat, not only to the West but to Christianity everywhere. George Meany, America's great labor leader and president of the AFL-CIO, said: "The conflict between Communism and freedom is the problem of our time. It overshadows all other problems. This conflict mirrors our age—its toils, its tensions, its troubles, and its task. On the outcome of this conflict depends the future of all mankind."

In the great debate currently raging in the West concerning the Communist peril there are two concepts. One of these concepts views the Communist peril as something almost entirely external, coming from either Chinese or Russian military aggression and territorial expansion. This view is strengthened by the rapid and frightening advance that China is making in nuclear and missile developments. Some experts believe that when the Chinese have the capability of delivering nuclear warheads by missiles, they will strike. The other concept views the Communist peril as something internal, a danger from subversion and infiltration. Both perils are real. And if our missile stalemate reveals anything and if historical evidence teaches any practical lessons, it would seem that the Communist conquest might come through nonmilitary aggression. Many Communist leaders have said openly that they intend to have the whole world under their control by 1975. It would seem that their present plan is to try to take it by infiltration and subversion, while maintaining military pressure, and they are gaining in many countries.

Whatever the method, Communism is real and it is dangerous! The Communists believe in, they plan toward, and they work for ultimate triumph. This is what we might call the eschatological aspect of Communism. It is the feature that binds them together and helps them endure the frowns and grimaces from the West. Their sense of destiny has almost a religious aura about it, a faith in their ability to triumph. Motivated by such a fanatical, burning desire to win, the Communists find no sacrifice too great to make for their cause.

Theirs is an "end justifies the means" philosophy. Wrong though they are, they have a goal, a purpose, and a sense of destiny. It is clear that we can never cope with Communism simply by fearing it and hating it. We must recapture our own national sense of purpose, our devotion to a great cause, and a vital faith, if we are to vie successfully with a foe who is making plans to bury us.

We speak of Communism being a great challenge to Christianity, and ideologically it is; but no system can be seriously threatened by an enemy "without" until it has been weakened by some enemy "within." While I am diametrically opposed to Communism *per se*, I am more concerned about the lack of zeal for Christianity than I am about the zeal and purposes of the Communists.

Communism can never succeed unless Christianity fails. Lenin once said: "Religion is a kind of a spiritual gin in which slaves of capital drown their human shape and their claims to any decent human life." The mistake that Lenin made was to ignore history and to remain ignorant of the teaching of the Bible. The Russian church under the Czars had given Lenin and his followers only a caricature of true Christianity. Thus what he said was in part right when viewed in the context of the place and the times in which he lived.

How many professing Christians in America and Europe consider Christ and the church not as a central loyalty but as a shot in the arm, administered in a brief visit to the church on Sunday morning? It becomes a duty, and often a painful one, like going to the dentist, and the patient heaves a sigh of relief when the pastor says, "Amen" and the weekly treatment is over. Though Lenin by no means presented the whole picture, he was right when he said that for many people religion is a spiritual cocktail that helps to dull the pain of living. Unless we can prove Lenin wrong by an awakened sense of consecration that can equal or excel the dedication of the Communists, we are fighting a losing game.

The Communists' goal is to liquidate religion, for they hold the concept that religion is a product of the capitalist system. Here is another error of Communist reasoning. The Christian religion was begun by Jesus Christ, who was by no stretch of the imagination a wealthy American or European. He was a poor, Middle Eastern carpenter. The Bible says: "Though he was rich, yet for your sakes he became poor, that ye through his poverty might be rich" (II Cor. 8:9). He was born in a borrowed stable. He had no home to call His own. He said: "Foxes have holes, and birds of the air have nests; but the Son of man hath not where to lay his head" (Lk. 9:58). He celebrated His last supper in a borrowed room. He rode into Jerusalem on a borrowed donkey. He was crucified on a borrowed Cross and buried in a borrowed tomb.

Although He refused to set class against class, we read that the common people heard Him gladly. Yet He was as concerned for the bourgeois as He was for the proletariat. He had as much time for the rich young ruler as He had for the blind beggar, and He was as concerned for Nicodemus as He was for the poor lame man at Siloam's pool. An East German pastor told me about the suffering of Christians in East Germany. He said: "Many of us have memorized the Thirty-seventh Psalm." This Psalm says: "For evildoers shall be cut off: but those that wait upon the Lord, they shall inherit the earth . . . The wicked plotteth against the just, and gnasheth upon him with his teeth. The Lord shall laugh at him: for he seeth that his day is coming . . . I have seen the wicked in great power, and spreading himself like a green bay tree. Yet he passed away, and, lo, he was not."

While the Communist peril is real, the Christian prospect is also real. Communism does not have the ultimate answer or the final hope. With whatever vigor and effort Communism may attack the problems of the world's disinherited masses, it has no answer for man's real problem—the problem of the human spirit in search of God. This is one of the reasons why Communism will ultimately fail.

There is comfort in Christ's words: "Upon this rock I will build my church; and the gates of hell shall not prevail against it" (Matt. 16:18). If the church remains strong, vital, warm, and Spirit-filled, we have the promise of our Lord that even the gates of hell shall not prevail against it; but if we allow our Christian faith to be adulterated with materialism, watered down by secularism, and intermingled with a bland humanism, we cannot stand up to a system that has vowed to bury us.

Is the church to turn its preaching and teaching facilities over to an all-out fight against Communism? This is not the church's mission or task. In the time of Christ and the early church, the great peril of Christianity was imperial Rome and the succeeding threats of the Goths and Mongols, but this did not mean that the church was to marshal all its forces simply to fight these enemies. It had a distinctive mission to the world that was neither national, ideological, nor political. It was to bear witness to Jesus Christ. This witness was not to employ any kind of state power or to receive any

measure of state support. It was not to take the sword
and employ force. It was to preach the transforming
Gospel of the grace of God and to use such means of
social relief as would minister to the present needs of
man. As Christians, we are to live and minister under
all forms of government—and to die for our faith if
necessary.

It is my opinion that God may be using Communism
as a judgment upon the West. The sins of the West are
now so great that judgment is inevitable, unless there is
national repentance. God has done this before. The
Bible says: "And the Lord God of their fathers sent to
them by his messengers, rising up betimes, and sending;
because he had compassion on his people, and on his
dwelling place: but they mocked the messengers of
God, and despised his words, and misused his prophets,
until the wrath of the Lord arose against his people, till
there was no remedy. Therefore he brought upon them
the king of the Chaldees" (II Chron. 36:15-17). Here
we have a picture of God's allowing a wicked, godless,
atheistic government to bring judgment upon His own
people. His people had sinned against great light, and
judgment was inevitable.

We see a similar situation in the world today. America and Western Europe are on a moneymaking, pleas-
ure-mad spree unparalleled in the history of the world.
God is generally ignored or ridiculed. Church members
in many cases are only halfhearted Christians. Judgment is coming. God *could* use atheistic Communism
to bring about this judgment. Thus the greatest threat
of Communism is not Communism itself, but the
spiritual apathy of the people of the West. Meanwhile
the Communist flame becomes ever more dangerous—
and in some areas of the world it is out of control!

The Flame of Uncontrolled Science

It is an ironic fact that science, dedicated to solving
our problems, has itself become a problem. Science has
given us the electric light, the automobile, the airplane,

television, and the computer, but science has also given us the hydrogen bomb. We can use automobiles profitably for transportation and pleasure, but the other side of the coin is that tens of thousands of people in America alone die by automobile accidents every year. When scientists first split the atom and released the power of its nucleus, the first use of this great scientific achievement was to rain suffering and death on Hiroshima and Nagasaki.

The problem of science lies in its misuse. The blessing of knowledge becomes a curse when we pervert it. Because man is what he is, scientific achievements are often used destructively rather than constructively. Because our morality does not match our intellectuality, the misuse of science can be greater than the use. Not until man's moral progress catches up with his intellectual progress can we hope to solve the problems posed by science. While science has achieved the ultimate in destruction, it still lies prone and helpless before the really great problems of life.

Our Western civilization may die in spite of all of its political, economic, social, and scientific achievements. Indeed, the latter may be the cause of its death. This is the generation that produced DDT to kill bugs, 2-4-D to kill weeds, formula 1080 to kill rats, and $E = MC^2$ to wipe out populations.

"Advances in the sciences are doubling accumulated information every ten years. As the experts contemplate the future, they are disturbed by the potentialities of evil that might arise from the application of their findings. Already biological research is in a ferment, creating and promising methods of interference with natural processes which could destroy or transform nearly every aspect of human life which we value."[1]

Compounding our problems is the worldwide longing for peace, which is constantly threatened by nuclear war. General Omar Bradley said: "Our plight is critical, and with each effort we have made to relieve it by further scientific advance, we have succeeded only in aggravat-

[1]Gordon Wolstenholme, ed., *Man and His Future* (Boston: Little, Brown, 1963). From the jacket.

ing our peril. Missiles will bring antimissiles and anti-missiles will bring anti-missile missiles, but inevitably this whole electronic house of cards will reach a point where it can be constructed no higher . . . have we already gone too far in the search for peace through the accumulation of peril?" He concluded: "If we are going to save ourselves from the instruments of our own intellect, we had better soon get ourselves under control and begin making the world safe for living."

It has come to pass, as Guy D. Newman, president of Howard Payne College, has observed, that "Man's knowledge has surpassed his wisdom. He is afraid of what he knows." The age of automation threatens every phase of man's dignity, personality, and individuality. It, too, has become a flame out of control.

The Flame of Political Dilemma

A European statesman said recently: "If the devil could offer a panacea for the problems of the world, I would gladly follow the devil." This is precisely what the Bible predicts will someday happen. When the world can no longer solve its problems, the great Anti-Christ will appear with a charm and a cleverness never before known. The whole world will follow him and even worship him.

Meanwhile the modern political era is dominated by the events and changes that took place as a result of the First World War of 1914-1918. This marked the era of crashing crowns and toppling thrones. Democracy began to blossom, but so did dictatorship. We all remember when President Franklin Roosevelt promised the four freedoms for the entire world, yet today there is less freedom than ever. Instability has entered into the changing political climate of the entire world until to-day the world is a seething political cauldron. Riots, demonstrations, and revolutions occur somewhere almost every day. Even in Britain and America the people have become addicted to sitting, squatting, demonstrating, and striking for what they want!

History speaks with thundering words to say that no state or government devised by man can flourish forever. It is also true, as Will Durant said: "No great nation has ever been overcome until it has destroyed itself." Republics, kingdoms, and empires all live their uncertain lives and die. In America we are now on the verge of seeing a democracy gone wild. Freedom has become license. Moral law is in danger of being abandoned even by the courts. To what degree can we expect immunity from the inevitable law of regress that sets in when nations defy the laws of God?

This, then, is the modern international scene with its problems of population, crime, racism, Communism, science, and politics. These are complicating modern existence and making the world into which our young men and women are going one where personal liberties are hedged about by all sorts of limiting regulations. As the world gets smaller, our problems grow larger. Our freedoms disappear and our danger increases! Trouble and danger lie ahead. This present generation of young people can expect nothing but crisis, bloodshed, war, hate, greed, lust, and struggle as the world tries to readjust without the climate of peace.

The modern world moves amidst its baffling dilemmas. While we know more economics than ever before, the world has more poverty and hunger than ever before. With our space program readying a flight to the moon, we have not yet solved the basic problems of earth. The threat of war and revolution hangs over our heads like the sword of Damocles. While psychiatry and psychotherapy promise us a whole personality, there are more nervous disorders and mental illnesses than ever before.

What is the trouble? What is the answer to our problems? Without God, man is worse off than a flower severed from its stem. We forget that we are finite. We have paraded our arrogance to the very precipice of a tragic end. The problem now is: Can we recover ourselves, clear our minds, regain our composure, and change our direction before it is too late?

Most of the current experts, analysts, historians, scientists, philosophers, and statesmen agree that man is sick. But the crucial question is: Are we beyond saving? Are we beyond hope? Some of our greatest minds privately agree that we have already passed the point of no return.

The people who ask these questions and express these forebodings are the experts, not the rank and file of the people. In a declining culture, one of its characteristics is that the ordinary people are unaware of what is happening. Only those who know and can read the signs of decadence are posing the questions that as yet have no answers. Mr. Average Man is comfortable in his complacency and as unconcerned as a silverfish ensconced in a carton of discarded magazines on world affairs. Man is not asking any questions, because his social benefits from the government give him a false security. This is his trouble and his tragedy. Modern man has become a spectator of world events, observing on his television screen without becoming involved. He watches the ominous events of our times pass before his eyes, while he sips his beer in a comfortable chair. He does not seem to realize what is happening to him. He does not understand that his world is on fire and that he is about to be burned with it.

Into this cacophony of the voices of doom comes the Word of God. The Bible says that it is *not* too late. I do not believe that we have passed the point of no return. I do not believe that all is black and hopeless. There is still time to return to the moral and spiritual principles that made the West great. There is still time for God to intervene. But there is coming a time when it will be too late, and we are rapidly approaching that time!

2

The Old Immorality

Some time ago a friend and I were walking down Oxford Street in London, when we saw what appeared to be an actress or model getting into a chauffeured limousine while a small crowd gathered to watch. Several photographers begged her to get out of the car so that they could get better pictures. When she complied, they began to yell: "Pull your dress down at the top. The editors won't use the pictures unless you do."

Today every area of our lives is invaded by this immoral flare, which leaves no one untouched. In many of our publications and in most of our entertainment, the emphasis is on sex appeal. Even churchmen, having failed to locate the cause or to produce a remedy for this disease of man, now talk about a "new morality" to fit the times; but their so-called new morality is nothing more than the old immorality brought up to date.

Evidence of the moral disintegration of our society appears everywhere we look. A senator told me recently: "Every time we appoint an investigating committee to investigate anything, it turns up snakes!" It seems that we have gone back to the days of Noah and come full cycle to what Jesus prophesied would take place when He said: "But as the days of Noah were, so shall also the coming of the Son of man be" (Matt. 24:37). He reaffirmed the Old Testament account of a social and moral disintegration so bad that God allowed the world to be destroyed by a flood in the days of Noah. He said also that moral history would repeat itself and that this same moral disintegration would be characteristic of the era just preceding the end of history as we know it.

The concern for Western man's moral dissolution is not confined to sociologists, psychologists, preachers, and professors. It is the concern of political leaders, military leaders, business and professional people, and trade union leaders. It is the concern of newspaper editors such as Jenkins Lloyd Jones of the Tulsa *Tribune,* who declared in an address to a convention of newspaper editors that our people have decided that sin is largely imaginary. We have become enamored of a psychology that holds that man is a product of his heredity and a victim of his environment. Mr. Jones said: "We have sown the dragon's teeth of pseudoscientific sentimentality, and out of the ground has sprung the legion bearing switchblade knives and bicycle chains. Clearly something is missing."

Taking a look at Hollywood, editor Jones said: "Can anyone deny that movies are dirtier than ever? But they don't call it dirt. They call it 'realism.' Why do we let them fool us? Why do we nod owlishly when they tell us that filth is merely a daring art form, that licentiousness is really social comment?"

In the face of this legalized pornography, the conscience of America seems to be paralyzed. More serious than our fakery in art, literature, and pictures is the collapse of our moral standards and the blunting of our capacity as a nation for righteous indignation. We seem to be insensible to the rowdiness of the stage, the glorification of burlesque, the drowning of our youngsters in the violence, cynicism, and sadism that is piped into the living room and even the nursery via television. We are struck dumb in the presence of bawdy-house literature, which fills our best-seller lists with risqué novels that belong in the brothel. One newspaper executive had the courage to ask his book department to quit advertising morally objectionable literature in the list of best sellers. We are accused of tampering with the facts. But what facts? There are the facts of immorality, degeneracy, and whoremongering. These are not only American facts. They are facts that should put a blush on the flags of almost every nation under the sun.

Sex

It has always been a mark of decaying civilization to become obsessed with sex. When people lose their way, their purpose, their will, and their goals, as well as their faith, like the ancient Israelites, they go "a whoring." It is a form of diversion that requires no thought, no character, and no restraint. One of the world's great historians told me: "The moral deterioration in the West will destroy us by the year 2000 A.D. even if the Communists don't!"

Pornography

Our Western society has become so obsessed with sex that it seeps from all the pores of our national life. Formerly, novelists wove the subject subtly into their stories as a part of life. But today from the pens of D. H. Lawrence, Norman Mailer, Henry Miller, and a hundred lesser lights pours a stream of perverse, vulgar, and even obscene writings like the drippings from a broken sewer. Sex is front page copy everywhere.

The question is, does freedom of speech and the press imply the freedom to corrupt the minds of the people through mass media, thus inciting every form of sexual perversion and immorality? We have laws in our cities forbidding open sewers and cesspools. Why shouldn't we have laws forbidding pornography and obscenity? Many heroic leaders have tried, but they have stumbled over even the definition of the word "obscenity." If we cannot agree on the length of a foot, it is because we have lost our yardstick. No one has ever improved upon the moral yardstick given to man in the Ten Commandments. Pornography is anything that depicts lewdness in such a way as to create impure thoughts and lusts. However, the sewers continue to flow, destroying the moral fabric of our society, until they have become the greatest threat to our security.

So-called artistic realism, which is both the goal and guiding star of some parts of the motion picture industry in Europe and America, adds up to filth, rottenness, dirt, and animated pornography that is feeding our youth with poison. No wonder young people are sexually sophisticated at sixteen.

We are corrupting the imagination and taste of a whole generation. Love is perverted to Sodom lust. Sensibilities are so hardened that domestic crimes and international atrocities are accepted as matters of course.

No one can doubt that dirty appetites are becoming the principal satisfaction of life. In this way we are permitting the diabolic to triumph. Jeremiah the prophet warned: "Were they ashamed when they had committed abomination? nay, they were not at all ashamed, neither could they blush; therefore they shall fall among them that fall: at the time that I visit them they shall be cast down, saith the Lord" (Jer. 6:15).

Dr. P. A. Sorokin, one of the most astute observers of America's sex scene and former professor of sociology at Harvard University, says: "There has been a growing preoccupation of our writers with the social sewers, the broken homes of disloyal parents and unloved children, the bedroom of the prostitute, a cannery row brothel, a den of criminals, a ward of the insane, a club of dishonest politicians, a street corner gang of teen-age delinquents, a hate-laden prison, a crime-ridden waterfront, the courtroom of a dishonest judge, the sex adventures of urbanized cavemen and rapists, the loves of adulterers and fornicators, of masochists, sadists, prostitutes, mistresses, playboys. Juicy loves, id, orgasms, and libidos are seductively prepared and served with all the trimmings."

Ancient historians tell us that one of the symptoms of a declining civilization is a desexualization of the human race, with men becoming more effeminate and women becoming more masculine, not only in physical characteristics but in their basic characters.

Perversion

Hand in hand with this desexualization appears the sinister form of perversion so increasingly evident in our society today, of such a nature that the old-fashioned sins look almost wholesome in contrast. Nothing can alter the fact that God calls perversion sin. "There is therefore no possible defence for their conduct . . . God has given them up to shameful passions. Their women have exchanged natural intercourse for unnatural, and their men in turn, giving up natural relations with women, burn with lust for one another; males behave indecently with males, and are paid in their own persons the fitting wage of such perversion" (Rom. 1:20-27, NEB).

The immutable law of sowing and reaping has held sway. We are now the hapless possessors of moral depravity, and we seek in vain for a cure. The tares of indulgence have overgrown the wheat of moral restraint. Our homes have suffered. Divorce has grown to epidemic proportions. When the morals of society are upset, the family is the first to suffer. The home is the basic unit of our society, and a nation is only as strong as her homes. The breaking up of a home does not often make headlines, but it eats like termites at the structure of the nation.

As a result of the mounting divorces, separations, and desertions, about twelve million of the forty-five million children in the United States do not live with both parents. A vicious circle is set in motion. As the Bible says: "The fathers have eaten a sour grape, and the children's teeth are set on edge" (Jer. 31:29).

In every area of our social life we see operating the inevitable law of diminishing returns in our obsession with sex. Many do something for a thrill only to find the next time that they must increase the dose to produce the same thrill. As the kick wears off, they are driven to look for new means, for different experiences to produce a comparable kick. The sex glutton is tormented by feelings of guilt and remorse. His mode of living is saturated with intense strain, unnatural emotions, and inner conflicts. His personality is thwarted in its search for development. His passions are out of control, and the end result is frustration. In his defiance of God's law and society's norm, he puts a death-dealing tension on his soul. His search for new thrills, for new kicks, for exciting experiences keeps him in the grip of fear, insecurity, doubt, and futility. Dr. Sorokin says: "The weakened physical, emotional, and spiritual condition of the sex glutton usually makes him incapable of resisting the accompanying pressures, and he eventually cracks under their weight. He often ends by becoming a psychoneurotic or a suicide."

The warning of the Bible is clear. In Hebrews 13:4 the Scripture says: "Whoremongers and adulterers God will judge." Those who scoff at the idea of judgment would do well to study the latest statistics on illegitimate births and venereal diseases. Illegitimate births are at an all-time high; venereal disease rages at epidemic proportions throughout the nation; and all this in the face of the latest in contraceptives and antibiotics. The Scripture says: "Be not deceived: neither fornicators, nor idolators, nor adulterers, nor effeminate, nor abusers of themselves with mankind . . . shall inherit the kingdom of God" (I Cor. 6:9).

One of the most disturbing features of the situation is the attitude of certain Protestant clergymen. *Time* magazine says: "Protestant churchmen are beginning to change their attitude. They are no longer shaking their finger because boys and girls give in to natural biological urges and experiment. They don't say 'Stop, you are wrong!' but 'Is it meaningful?'" Many pastors and university chaplains now openly condone premarital sex.

Ours is an age of moral relativism. However, there are certain areas in which the Scriptures do not allow us to negotiate. In all of these centuries there has not been the slightest shadow of change in the nature of God or in His attitude toward sin. The Bible teaches from beginning to end that adultery and fornication are sin, and the attitude of certain modern churchmen does not alter its character.

Dishonesty

But we must not leave the impression that sexual

immorality is the only sphere of moral danger in our civilization. Dishonesty has increased in our society to alarming proportions. I sat in a federal court to hear the case of a highly respected member of the medical profession who had willfully and deliberately falsified his income tax. He was sentenced to ten years in a federal prison.

The disease of dishonesty invades every profession, and its spread into our society is alarming even to the most apathetic among us. The sports scandals shocked the nation as young amateur athletes sold out their ideals and ethics to the hoodlums and gangsters. It has been known for years that professional boxing is deeply infiltrated by the rackets, and the investigations which revealed that the throwing of fights is common practice came as no surprise to many. In a recent survey on a college campus, it was found that seventy-five percent of the students admitted to cheating sometime during their college careers.

Recently as I rode from the airport of a major city in a taxi, I engaged in conversation with the taxi driver. He said: "Payoffs are the practice at every level in the city. If the business house does not pay off, they will just dig up the street in front of the house and keep it that way for a year. When I get my cab inspected, I have to pay twenty-five dollars under the table. The man who collects says he only gets to keep five." He said: "If you took the payoff out of the city, the economy of the city would collapse."

John Steinbeck wrote a letter to Adlai Stevenson in which he said: "There is a creeping all-pervading gas of immorality which starts in the nursery and does not stop until it reaches the highest offices both corporate and governmental." Walter Lippmann says: "America is beginning to accept a new code of ethics that allows for chiseling and lying."

Why is there all this dishonesty in every phase of our life? Russell Kirk tells us why: "All this century, this columnist suspects, honesty in great things and small has been diminishing in most of the world. Public and private honesty is produced in part by religious convictions . . . when religious sanctions decay . . . the average sensual man tends to cheat."

A Dying Culture

That moral and spiritual decadence is upon us today becomes evident at the turn of every page of our daily newspaper. We live in a day when old values are rejected and the sense of significance and purpose has disappeared from many people's lives. The Western world's sole objective seems to be success, status, security, self-indulgence, pleasure, and comfort. If we can judge our times by the paintings produced by some modern artists, we see indiscriminate splashes of color with no recognizable pattern or design. A child throwing paint on the canvas could do as well. As a matter of fact, at one art exhibit a chimpanzee won first prize for his painting. The incomprehensible mixture of pigment merely denotes the confused minds and values of our day. The playwright, the novelist, and the movie scriptwriter all give us unadulterated doses of violence, sex, and murder. This would indeed seem to be a sick generation in need of salvation. The cause of our trouble was revealed recently in a statement by Tennessee Williams, one of the most widely read playwrights of our day, when he said: "We have very little conviction of our own essential dignity, or even of our essential decency."[1]

With all this evidence of decadence in view it is no wonder that May Craig, Washington correspondent, says: "Unless there is a change deep down in the American people, a genuine crusade against self-indulgence and immorality, public and private, then we are witnesses to the decline and fall of the American Republic."

Yes, we need to cry out to be saved—saved from ourselves, for it is the soul of a nation and a culture that is dying! Hosea the prophet urged the people of his day: "Sow to yourselves in righteousness, reap in

---

[1] *Missions,* January 1962.

mercy; break up your fallow ground: for it is time to seek the Lord, till he come and rain righteousness upon you" (Hos. 10:12).

The crack in the moral dam is widening, but like the people of Noah's day before the flood, life goes on as usual with only a few concerned and scarcely anyone alarmed. However, apathy will not deter catastrophe. The people of Noah's day were not expecting judgment—but it came! We have become soft and comfortable. Watching television, I notice that when almost any crisis arises on the screen, the actor usually says: "Give me a drink." When the headlines get black and foreboding, the sale of alcohol and barbiturates rises in the country, as millions try to escape from the grim realities of our dangers.

In a seminar on a university campus a student asked me: "Is our society in the process of dying, or is it committing the hypocrisy of being dead without knowing it?" I answered: "I am not sure; but I am alarmed, and I feel the burden and compulsion of the prophets of old to warn the people. Whether they listen or not is really not my responsibility." Time after time the prophets warned the people of old, but the Scriptures say that their hearts became hardened and their ears deaf. They were deliberately deaf to the Word of God.

This we do know, our decaying morals do not surprise God. They add to the pile of inflammable tinder that shall someday be ignited by the fires of God's judgment. The words of the Apostle Paul in the first chapter of Romans, addressed to the decadent Roman society, might well apply to us: "Because that, when they knew God, they glorified Him not as God, neither were thankful" (Rom. 1:21). If ever a generation was bequeathed the knowledge of God, we were. Yet we are throwing away this glorious heritage on our lust and passions.

Again Paul said: "But became vain in their imaginations, and their foolish heart was darkened. Professing themselves to be wise, they became fools" (Rom. 1:21, 22). The word "became" suggests deterioration and decay. In a decadent society, the will to believe, to resist, to contend, to fight, to struggle is gone. In place of this will to resist, there is the desire to conform, to drift, to follow, to yield, and to give up. This is what happened to Rome, but it applies to us. The same conditions that prevailed in Rome prevail in our society. Before Rome fell, her standards were abandoned, the family disintegrated, divorce prevailed, immorality was rampant, and faith was at a low ebb. As Gibbon said: "There was much talk of religion but few practiced it." Today our churches are filled, but how many are actually practicing Christianity in daily life?

Again Paul said: "(They) changed the glory of the incorruptible God into an image made like to corruptible man" (Rom. 1:23). Humanism has become the god of our time. Aldous Huxley spoke of "human control by human effort in accordance with human ideals." The modern creed of "I believe in man" is a complete reversal of Biblical theology.

The great Apostle again said: "Wherefore God also gave them up to uncleanness, through the lusts of their own hearts, to dishonor their own bodies between themselves" (Rom. 1:24). It does not say that God gave up, only that God gave man up to unclean and unrighteous practices. When this happens, we are in terrifying danger!

Thus three times in this passage from Romans it tells that God gave man up. In one instance, God gave them up when man turned to immoral lust and practices. In another instance, God gave them up when man turned to vile affections and to immoral deviations. In yet another instance, God gave them up when man turned to a reprobate mind and became filled with all unrighteousness, fornication, covetousness, and maliciousness.

When God gives man up, there is only one thing left—judgment! Here it is: "Who, knowing the judgment of God, that they which commit such things are worthy of death, not only do the same, but have pleasure in them that do them" (Rom. 1:32). When Sodom and Gomorrah became guilty of the same sins that we commit, God judged them with fire and brimstone. The Bible says: "God spared them not." When the people of Noah's day became guilty of these same sins, the Bible says: "God spared them not."

We cannot claim to be God's pets. We have no special dispensation from judgment. If we continue on our present course, the moral law that says "the wages of sin is death" (Rom. 6:23) will mean ultimate death to our society.

How ironic it is that a civilization that has produced the best automobiles, the best refrigerators, and the best television sets is at the same time producing some of the worst human beings. The total answer to our dilemma in this debacle is that we have forsaken God. God's indictment of man is summed up in four words: "They are without excuse" (Rom. 1:20). We as a nation are without excuse, because we have bartered our birthright for a mess of immoral delights. We are finding out that what de Tocqueville said is true: "When America ceases to be good, it will cease to be great."

In our knowledge, which has become foolishness, we are setting the stage for personal and national dissolution and ultimate judgment. We are heaping high for conflagration. We are building for destruction. We are begging for judgment. Thomas Jefferson said: "I tremble for my country when I remember God is just." "Verily I say unto you, it shall be more tolerable for the land of Sodom and Gomorrah in the day of judgment," said Jesus (Matt. 10:15).

In the King Tut museum in Cairo there is a grain of wheat five thousand years old taken from the tombs of the Pharaohs. It is said that if the seed were planted, it would grow. The seeds of integrity, reverence, and righteousness are not dead; but we are not allowing them to germinate. There is still time. The day is far spent, it is true; but it is not too late for us to stay the catastrophic fires of God's judgment. The Bible declares: "(God is) not willing that any should perish" (II Pet. 3:9). And again the Bible declares: "To-day if ye will hear his voice, harden not your hearts" (Heb. 3:7, 8).

3

Our Psychological Jitters

One of the world's leading mathematicians visited me in my hotel room recently. I could sense that the weight of his personal problems had become so heavy that he was on the verge of a breakdown. The strain of modern living had become too great. He was in danger of becoming another statistic in the alarming growth of mental illness.

The intellectual climate in which modern man lives is a paradox. Our technology creates miracles of science, but fails to satisfy our deepest needs. It puts wheels under our feet, but fears and apprehensions in our hearts. We are able to live longer, but not better. We are able to live more comfortably, but not more contentedly.

According to a United States Public Health Service report, eight million persons are suffering from some form of mental illness. Out of this number, one million are treated in the hospitals of the United States each year. Over fifty percent of the nation's hospital beds are occupied by patients suffering from some form of mental or psychological problem. One out of every ten babies born today will be confined to a hospital with some form of mental illness at some time during his lifetime.

Many of the mentally ill are literally sick at heart and soul. Their maladies do not involve corrupted or damaged brains. People do not lose their minds or break their nerves in so-called nervous breakdowns; they lose themselves! They disappear into worlds of their own creation in their attempt to escape the real world.

...t about mental and emotional illness
...ng alarming inroads into this present
...ing people. A recent magazine article
...of today "the tormented generation."[1] It
say... ...University of Pennsylvania, twenty percent of t... ...dents require help from the mental health
service during their college years. At Harvard, twenty-
five percent of the undergraduates consult a psychiatrist
or a social worker." These percentages reflect no dis-
credit on the Universities of Pennsylvania and Harvard.
A recent poll of 600 college psychiatrists revealed that
about fifteen percent of the students in their schools
seek psychiatric help, while thirty percent should do so.

Escapism

Millions are busy burying their heads in the sand
pretending that the devastating events of our times are
not really happening. They are desperately trying to
escape the realities of the pressures of modern living.

Escapism is not in itself a condition of mental sickness, but a subconscious mechanism to escape reality. It
is a mode of behavior adopted to evade unpleasant facts
and realities. It can take many forms. The harassed
housewife goes on a shopping spree, while someone else
may take refuge in a clandestine love affair or a Watusi
session. One of the most conspicuous modes of escape
is alcoholism, which is now a national catastrophe.

Each week in our Minneapolis office we receive
thousands of letters, more than half of which have to
do with domestic problems; and half of these are related to problems of drinking. Drinking has become one
of our most serious social problems. It is basically the
result of an attempt to escape from the responsibilities
and realities of life. "Every time my husband and I
have a disagreement, he dashes for the corner bar,"
writes a woman from Iowa.

Volumes could be written on the problem of dope

[1]*The Saturday Evening Post,* 1963.

addiction. Millions of barbiturates are swallowed every night to help the nation sleep. Millions of tranquilizers keep us calm during the day. Millions of pep pills wake us up in the morning after the hangovers of the night before.

The Bible warns that these flights from reality bring no lasting satisfaction. "Whose end is destruction, whose God is their belly, and whose glory is in their shame, who mind earthly things" (Phil. 3:19).

Anxiety

Historians of the future may label this present time "The Age of Anxiety." Although in some ways we have less to worry about than previous generations, we seem to do more worrying. Although we have it easier than our forefathers, we have more uneasiness. Although we have less cause for anxiety, we are more anxious. Calloused hands were the badge of the pioneer, while furrowed brows are the insignia of modern man.

The pioneers complained that they were "run down" from physical exhaustion, but the trouble with us is that we are "wound up" from hypertension. Much of this is due to a shift of emphasis. A century ago, man's chief concern was his spiritual life; today his chief concern is with his physical and temporal affairs. Vast numbers of people actually believe that if we give man enough food, shelter, clothing, education, and recreational facilities, then we will have reached Utopia.

Psychoanalyst Erich Fromm asserts that modern living turns men into anxious, loveless shadows. He says: "Most Americans believe that our society of consumption . . . happy, fun-loving, jet-traveling people creates the greatest happiness for the greatest number. Contrary to this view, I believe that our present life leads to anxiety, helplessness, and eventually to the disintegration of our culture. Could it be that our dream that material welfare *per se* leads to happiness is just a pipe dream?"

Leisure

Another problem facing millions in the Western world is leisure. We may not think of it as a problem, but psychologists, psychiatrists, and sociologists are beginning to realize that it may become the foremost psychological problem of the next generation. Realizing the importance of the growing prospects and consequence of leisure as a result of automation, *Life* magazine devoted a two-part series of articles to the subject.

In societies where leisure is already a reality, boredom is the big new problem. Some time ago I was visiting in a welfare state where one of the church leaders said to me: "We in the church have fought for better living conditions and a higher standard of living. In this country, we now have security from the cradle to the grave; but we are faced with psychological problems, such as boredom, which are just as great and devastating as the old social problems of a century ago."

With more leisure and less responsibility, the problem of "what to do" assumes major proportions. The proposed twenty-hour week and ten-week vacations, together with accelerating automation which will increase the numbers of the jobless, are becoming the causes of one of the most serious social problems in our century. The rapid growth of leisure could produce more crime, more home breakups, more psychological problems than we can deal with. It could breed discontent and restlessness, which could lead to greater unhappiness than we now have with our great prosperity.

We see this potential of crime already among us in the vandalism of unoccupied youth. We see it in the cocktail lounges where the bored and restless while away the tedious hours of leisure. We see it in the nightclubs where jaded and frustrated businessmen watch sensual performers go through their frenzied routines, leaving their audiences empty and frustrated. All of us have read stories of the boredom suffered at the average cocktail party. I have had more than one wealthy person tell me: "If I have to go to one more cocktail party, I'll blow my brains out." A senator once confided to me that the greatest need in Washington was the elimination of the cocktail party. He said: "It consumes so much of our time that we don't have time for matters of state."

In an interview Arnold J. Toynbee was asked: "Would the abolition of poverty ensure that America's civilization would continue to grow and be dynamic?" He replied: "No. There is more to it than that in the age of automation. I think the essential question is what Americans do with their leisure. In time people will have to work only a few hours a day, and they will have more and more leisure. If they spend it staring at television or playing pinball machines, then the future of American civilization would not be very healthy."[2]

The future course of America's civilization will depend at least in part on whether her people use their leisure constructively. This has become one of our greatest challenges. Tomorrow's prospect of leisure may be a greater problem than today's problem of work. One psychiatrist has said: "A great majority of our people are not emotionally or psychologically ready for free time." An economist has said that by the year 2000 A.D. it may be possible for two percent of our population, working in factories and on farms, to produce all the goods and foods that the other ninety-eight percent can possibly consume.

If these forecasts and calculations should prove correct, life would soon be virtually all play and no work. What then will we do with this leisure? Shakespeare said: "If all the years were playing holidays, to sport would be as tedious as to work." Carlyle said: "A life of ease is not for any man nor for any god." And the Bible says: "The Lord God took the man, and put him into the garden of Eden to dress it and to keep it" (Gen. 2:15). God's plan for the human race was for man to be occupied. This was for man's good—psychological, physiological, and spiritual. If, through our

---

2*U. S. News and World Report*, March 30, 1964.

technological progress we succeed in forsaking this principle, it will be to our own peril. Already we see foreshadowings of what that peril may be.

"Double-Thinking"

How does a society develop the kind of psychosis that plagues us today? It is the product of many things, including the loss of religious faith, faulty education, and too much softness. In his book *1984*, George Orwell describes what he calls "doublethink." This is not an original idea, for the Bible says: "A double-minded man is unstable in all his ways" (Jas. 1:8). Nationally we are in a state of double-mindedness that could endanger our very survival. "Doublethink," or double-mindedness, means the faculty of holding two contradictory beliefs in one's mind and accepting both of them. The whole world has become familiar with the Communists' double-talk. When they speak of peace, they mean "peace on our terms." But we, too, talk out of both corners of our mouths at once. We say we are a Christian nation, but much of our literature, our social practices, our deep interests are not Christian at all. They are totally secular.

Erich Fromm, in his book *Will Man Prevail?*, says: "While people believe in God, they are not concerned with God. That is, they do not worry or lose sleep over religious or spiritual problems. Most people of the West say they believe in God, hence in God's principles of love, justice, truth, and humility. Yet these ideas have little influence on our behavior. Most of us are motivated by the wish for greater material comfort, security, and prestige."

We say we believe in the church, and yet many of us without conscience can drive by the church to go golfing, boating, swimming, or even nightclubbing.

Ideals can easily be turned into shibboleths—mere catchwords. The ideal becomes alienated. It ceases to be an authentic experience and becomes instead an idol, outside of self, to which we pay homage and which we use to cover up dishonesty and immorality.

Freud learned what the Bible teaches, that a person can be fully sincere and at the same time be in error in his thought. Sincerity can even be a cover, a disguise for the real impulse that motivates him. This can be true with a nation as well. We can employ the "double-think" and be unaware of any wrong.

"Group-Thinking"

Besides the "doublethink" we are beset with a new method of thought called "group-think." The allure of identity, security, and acceptance drives us into patterns of thought, action, and behavior. We tend to think, act, and talk like those around us. And one of our most deep-seated fears is that we might be called an "out-sider."

This fear has led us down the road to conformity, has put the imprint of "the organization man" on our souls, and has robbed us of originality of thought, individuality of personality, and constructive action. It has invaded not only our secular life but our religious life as well.

In *The Status Seekers,* Vance Packard observed: "For the vast majority of American Christians, going to church is the nice thing that proper people do on Sunday. It advertises their respectability, gives them a warm feeling that they are behaving in a way their God-fearing ancestors would approve, and adds a few cubits to their social stature by throwing them with a social group with which they wish to be identified. And even those who take their worship seriously often prefer to do it while surrounded by their own kind of people."

It is not easy to break away from the "group-think" of our times, with the television hucksters downgrading your brand of aspirin and dramatizing its devastating effects on your stomach with clanging bells and eerie sounds of your "innards" disintegrating if you do not run out immediately to buy their brand.

The "group-think" pressure affects our voting at the polls, the brands of food we buy at the grocery, the makes of cars we drive, the brands of gasoline we burn, as well as our patterns of religious belief.

It is almost terrifying to note the way in which crowds can be swayed to believe almost anything, provided it is put in a form that travels the avenues along which they are accustomed to receive their knowledge, whether it be true or false. For example, several years ago when a certain actor ordered pink champagne in a movie, he started a minor revolution in the wine industry. Immediately, restaurants all over the country were amazed by the demand for this exotic beverage. From one end of the nation to the other, movie and television stars lay down the law of fashions, manners, speech, and even moral behavior. The elaborate bathroom, the one-hand telephone, and the Venetian blind were all inspired by Hollywood and later became essentials for almost every American home. However, these are only the superficial symptoms of Madison Avenue's and Hollywood's power of suggestion. The movies and television with equal ease lead and change the nation's thoughts on politics, morals, and social questions of great importance. In the darkness of a living room or theater, where people sit relaxed to give undivided attention to the flashing pictures, psychological conditions are perfect for insinuating ideas into the mind. In test after test among high school and university students, it has been proven that a movie or a television program can brainwash.

The Lie

We are in the midst of a generation whose minds have been prepared for THE LIE. The Bible speaks in II Thessalonians of the coming of the great Anti-Christ: "It will be attended by all the powerful signs and miracles of the LIE, and all the deception that sinfulness can impose on those doomed to destruction" (II Thess. 2:9, 10, NEB). The movies, television, radio, the sensual novel, the cheap magazine all have combined to make it almost impossible for the masses to do any real individual thinking. With the breakdown of discipline in the home and with every source of amusement and instruction pouring poison into daily life, it is not to be wondered at that the minds of people are ready to receive anything but the truth and that they are ready to believe lies and ultimately THE LIE.

It is possible that "group-think" has made individual action passé in our country. Are we becoming a robot civilization, manipulated by mass media, pressurized by conformity, and pushed by political maneuvers? Have we developed a department-store mind, where we shop for name brands of faith, politics, and a way of life? Are we collectivizing the mentality of America? In the 1964 election the polltakers predicted to the very percentage point what the American people would do at the polls, and less than an hour after the polls had closed the computers had predicted who would win and what the majority would be. One columnist said later: "In the future we might as well let the pollsters tell us who the American people are for, and it would save all the expense of a campaign." It seems that as a nation we are in danger of losing our individuality and our personal identity. The student has become only an IBM card. He is a statistic. The personal relationship between teachers and students that used to prevail has broken down. The student is now only a part of the "mass."

When we look for a remedy for a condition that produces an unhealthy national psychosis, we should remember what was said by Bernard Iddings Bell: "All human predicaments are not to be resolved by tinkering with the symptoms, because our disorders are not those of mere housekeeping. It is the whole sewer system that is out of whack."

In times of national problems we should be hearing the voice of God in His effort to have us think His thoughts after Him. Many times we miss the purpose of national catastrophes. Charles C. West says: "We turn to God for help when our foundations are shaking, only to learn that it is God who is shaking them."

Perhaps out of all this God is speaking to the nation

and to the individual. We are not made for emptiness. We are not made for boredom. We were not created to cringe in fear. Our anxiety, our mental anguish, our concern all reach upward for purpose and fulfillment. There are signs in the sky. They portend a better life, a better way, a better day.

You and I were made for the heights. The Bible says of man: "Thou has made him a little lower than the angels, and hast crowned him with glory and honor. Thou madest him to have dominion over the works of thy hands; thou hast put all things under his feet" (Ps. 8:5, 6).

It is Jesus Christ who gives dignity and worth to the individual. He says: "For what shall it profit a man, if he shall gain the whole world, and lose his own soul?" (Mk. 8:36). Christ taught that in the sight of God one soul is worth the entire materialistic world! In God's sight the individual is all-important. When Christ calls a man to follow Him, He calls him "out" from the "group." Christ can fill the vacuums. He can restore your personal identity. He can become THE TRUTH to your generation.

The question is: Where can we find Christ? Where can we find this new life? How can we become the men and women God meant us to be?

4

The National Idolatry

Some time ago I asked a student at the University of North Carolina if he believed in God. "Yes," he said, "I have my own private gods."

The idolatry of Western man is humanism, materialism, and sex. Idolatry has an almost automatic connotation of superstition, magic, sorcery, and physical idols; but our modern gods are sophisticated, cultured, fashionable, and intellectual.

When a nation turns from the true and living God of its Christian heritage, then it substitutes false gods. Man is innately religious. He must have a god of some kind. Russell Kirk has well observed: "In the final test, the power of a nation or a civilization will be weighed not in missiles or divisions, but in faith, whether false or true." This condition of false faith, as well as nominal religion, is reflected in a statement by Carl Henry, editor of *Christianity Today* magazine: "Although modern man zestfully explores outer space, he seems quite content to live in a spiritual kindergarten and to play in a moral wilderness." Acutally, he plays with the gods of his own fashioning.

Modern Western culture has become a mixture of paganism and Christianity. We are a blend of both. We talk of God, but we often act as though we are atheists. We have developed a sort of dual personality, a schizophrenia. We have "In God We Trust" on our coins, but "Me First" engraved on our hearts. The fact is, while theoretically we believe in God, we have made unto ourselves graven images and have come to worship them. We have almost a new kind of polytheism wherein we attempt to worship both the God of the Bible and the gods of our own making at the same time.

Campus Gods

The chasm between a working relationship with the God of the Bible and our present idolatry is seen in the student attitudes of our generation. Otto Butz of Princeton University, in his book *The Unsilent Generation,* quoted from essays written by eleven members of the class of 1957. Their statements about God are quite revealing. One said: "I figure I can be indifferent to an indifferent God . . . it is this world, not the next one, that I am concerned with." Another wrote: "I seldom think of God as such, and only pray when I am exceptionally troubled. Even when I pray, I don't consider myself asking for help or advice. I simply find that I discover a measure of assurance."

The majority of today's college students profess faith in God, but theirs is not faith in a personal God. To them a personal God is not relevant: He does not matter. They have, therefore, a tendency to manufacture a god or gods of their own—what Chad Walsh calls campus gods in his book entitled *Campus Gods on Trial.*

Part of the difficulty has been the church's tragic neglect of its youth during the critical years when they most need spiritual guidance. The average university student has a caricature of God in his mind. He has done little or no real Bible study and has little concept of the Biblical teaching of God or of our moral responsibilities to Him. He therefore rejects the Biblical God. But since he must have a god of some kind, he creates one for himself on campus. His chief object may be the best grades, the conquest of beautiful girls, athletic prowess, or rebellion, as one student said, "just for the hell of rebelling." Such things become his substitutes for God. They actually become gods in the lives of thousands of students, and to one or more of these gods a student will commit his life. Therefore, thousands of students lack any genuine belief in God or in the moral values that sustain human society.

The Idolatry of the Masses

Turning from campus gods to the idolatry of the masses, consider first of all the god of humanism, or the worship of man. The true humanist sings with Swinburne: "Glory to man in the highest." This is the new idolatry of our age, intellectual and sophisticated; and it is becoming highly organized. David Winter, editor of *Crusade* magazine in London, says: "No more subtle enemy has ever faced the Christian church than this one which dethrones her God and replaces Him with His creature." The humanists, especially in Great Britain, are becoming militant. They are dedicated to attacking Christianity. Julian Huxley said that if humanism is to acquire a wider appeal, it must become a religion; while another humanist, L. F. J. Ross, suggests that "a simple humanist bible and humanist hymns must be adopted, a ten commandments for humanists could be added, as could humanist confessional practices for group or individual . . . the use of hypnotic techniques . . . music and other devices . . . during humanist services would give the audience their deep spiritual experience, and they would emerge refreshed and inspired with their humanist faith." In an enlightening series of articles in *Crusade* magazine, Edward Atkinson says: "Humanism may slowly be developing into a mystery cult, complete with its own odd superstition, confused thinking, and obscure jargon. And like all such cults it primarily appeals to the mystic. It is most ironic that humanism, for all its absurd charges that Christianity derives its origin from mystery cults, should develop into one itself."

Thus we see that humanism has become for many a polite name for a vocal, aggressive, influential crusade against religion in the name of social and moral advance. There is nothing new about humanism. It is the yielding to Satan's first temptation of Adam and Eve: "Ye shall be as gods" (Gen. 3:5)

Second, in America we have an idolatry called the "adulation of youth" in a recent article in *Look* magazine. Apparently distressed by their inability to communicate with the younger generation, many adults simply imitate it. Increasingly, women who follow the trends of the new age strive to look like teen-age girls.

Man Worships Science

Third, out of the new age of science and technology there has been emerging a new faith of scientism that displaces Biblical faith. This nuclear age has greatly reduced the faith that was woven deeply into the culture of the past. One scientist said: "The world picture of the nuclear age does not include God. The cultivated man today finds no God in his reactor, and he finds none through his telescope. God is not among the rushing electrons, and He is not visible in outer space." There is no doubt that there are new powers of science that respond to the touch of a button at the shrine of computers, rather than at the word of our prayers or at the altars of our churches. In our hands is a power that seems to our finite minds as great as that we once attributed to God. To many this is the power of a god, and in a new way we hear again the words of the serpent to our first parents: "Ye shall be as gods" (Gen. 3:5).

Yet, like the other gods of our generation, science does not satisfy the deep longings of the human soul. The more man learns, the less he knows. Thus many of our leading scientists have come to express their faith in God.

Man Worships Things

Fourth, another of our idolatries is the worship of things. I leave it to the psychologist to discover what our deeper motivation is—whether it is immaturity, boredom, pride, or a genuine sense of need that sends us out in quest of material things to the exclusion of all else. A leading magazine carries an advertisement with this revealing paragraph: "Is automation, the use of electronics to run machines, going to fill your home with pleasant surprises? Will magic eyes light each room? Will you own a portable piano, cordless electric clocks, and a telephone you can answer without lifting the receiver? Discover how this exciting new development can make your life happier." Has happiness been reduced to portable pianos and the blinking of magic eyes?

In Pat Frank's book, *Alas Babylon,* he imagines Florida under the pall of a fictional atomic attack. All electricity was cut off, gasoline supplies were exhausted, and life settled down to the basics. Cadillacs were traded for fat hens, and power boats for a shaker of salt. If and when a nuclear war strikes our world, the survivors will suddenly realize that most of the things we have been striving for and racking our brains to acquire are worse than useless. If we could only discover this in time, perhaps the fate of Sodom and Gomorrah toward which we are moving could be averted.

Madison Avenue has found it profitable to direct the main thrust of advertising at that inherent trait of human nature—creature pride. Leaf through our slick magazines and note the lavish full-color advertisements. They often appeal to the pride of the buyer rather than stressing the usefulness of the object. "Think how proud you will feel when your friends gaze with envy on your new bathroom, new car, or new yacht." And the illustrations depict the look of envy on the faces of friends being shown a new house with its fine furnishings and built-in appliances. Bacon once wrote: "The happiness of the great consists not in feeling that they are happy, but in realizing how happy other people think they must be."

Thus we see bored people riding in sleek cars, looking not for opportunities to make a contribution to society but rather for people to admire them. Pride consists not in wanting to be rich, but in wanting to be richer than your neighbor. It is not in wanting to be noticed but in wanting to be the most noticed. It is not in wanting to have things but in wanting more things than others.

Man Worships Himself

Man has rejected the revelation of the Bible concerning the true and living God of his fathers, and he has substituted gods of his own making. In actuality, modern man has decided to dethrone God and to enthrone himself in all his nuclear glory. Many intellectuals have come to believe that the human mind can understand everything eventually. Kintner says: "The epitome of this point of view is developed in the doctrines of Marx, Engels, and Lenin." And, as Carl Henry says: "In his desire to control the universe, man repeatedly puts himself in God's place; but the idea of God's Son as substitute in man's place he dismisses as incredible nonsense." Thus man has thrown aside the pagan deities of past civilizations, such as the sun, the moon, fire, water, and beasts—and the living God as well. Today he worships himself.

From many university classrooms come these conclusions:

First, man is only an animal.

Second, existence is a chemical accident.

Third, the struggle for survival has made man what he is.

Fourth, morality and standards of conduct are derived only from a sociological context.

Fifth, man lives in and for this world only, and any other thought is unscientific.

As a result of such premises, man's failure to cope with his new world has brought futility and pessimism into every area of his life. Joy has gone out of living. The wonder of living, the uplifted face, the smile of gladness, and the thrill of romance have somehow escaped us. Since we have made a god of man, our eyes are no longer lifted up to the sky but are turned inward, distorting our whole world.

The Little Deities Have Failed

Man no longer accepts the standards of behavior handed down in our Biblical teaching. We have become pragmatists, content with existential and situational ethics. We are no longer concerned with doing what is right but with getting along and adjusting. We are losing our moral balance. America, Britain, and Western Europe are becoming nations of sitters, squatters, and malcontents, fed up and bored with all the nonsense that has been handed them. Whether they realize it or not, they are sick and tired of their man-made gods. Their little deities have utterly failed them. The joy, peace, security, and happiness these deities were supposed to bring are not there.

Even a quick reading of the Bible would have taught them that their little gods would fail. The Scripture says: "Turn ye not unto idols . . . I am the Lord your God" (Lev. 19:4). This is a warning. It is a challenge from the true and living God. In fact, the Bible teaches in Psalm 59:8 that, as God looks upon these little gods of our own fashioning, He laughs.

The Apostle Paul warned us not to change the truth of God into a lie (Rom. 1:25). He warned us that we are not to worship and serve the creature more than the Creator. Yet this is precisely what has been happening in much of the Western world. The Bible warns that "idolaters . . . shall not inherit the kingdom of God" (I Cor. 6:9, 10). The Apostle John wrote: "Keep yourselves from idols" (I Jn. 5:21). Again he warned: "Idolaters . . . shall have their part in the lake which burneth with fire and brimstone: which is the second death" (Rev. 21:8).

In the sight of God, idolatry is a grave sin. "Thou shalt have no other gods before me" (Exod. 20:3). Judgment will fall upon all idolaters. Millions of Americans are guilty, and many of the guilty are churchgoers who serve God with their lips, while their hearts are far from Him. They are more guilty of idolatry than the savage in the jungle who bows before an image made with his own hands.

All the way through the Scriptures, God is urging the people to "turn." When the city of Nineveh had committed its immoralities and served other gods, Jonah was sent to warn them. He preached repentance in the streets, and the people did repent. They were spared from the judgment of God. It is not too late for us to repent. There is still time.

5

The Searchers in a Flaming World

In the early dark hours before dawn on December 7, 1946, a raging fire engulfed the Winecoff Hotel on Atlanta's Peachtree Street. Before the last flames had been brought under control, scores of men, women, and children had died. Most were not actually burned to death. Instead, they died as they searched desperately for escape. Many jumped in panic from high windows to perish on the pavements below. Others were overcome by smoke and heat as they searched for one safe exit after another. But for all of them it was too late. They simply woke up too late to escape the horror of that fifteen-story holocaust of flames, and they died searching for a way out.

Today with the world in flames on every continent and in every country, there are those who search for a way out. Indeed this is the Age of the Search. In every area of life man is searching for truth. Recently the United States sent into outer space a rocket called "The Discoverer" to search for scientific truth. Just as man is searching for scientific truth, so he is searching for answers, for panaceas, for meanings, for remedies for his deepest spiritual needs. To this search, man brings the accumulated wisdom of the past.

The President of the United States recently established a unique office in the government in which he installed a "think man," whose sole function is to offer new ideas for consideration. Industry realizes that tomorrow begins today. Change occurs so fast that men must project their thinking a decade or more in advance in order to keep abreast of progress. To bring this about, industry depends on "the corporate planner," whose job it is to search and probe, to discover and plan. His chief responsibility is to answer the question: "What is this business all about?"

All of this planning, thinking, and idea-making is well and good. But what about the great issues of life and death? Are there not deep moral and spiritual questions that must be answered? Man has always thought so, and this is why we have philosophers, psychologists, and theologians. However, today much of our quest is materialistic, naturalistic, and humanistic. A professor at the University of Michigan said to me: "As soon as we create life in a test tube, we won't need God any more." I answered: "This happened once before when man ruled God out and proposed the Tower of Babel. It ended in frustration, confusion, and judgment."

In a bull session at Harvard a student observed: "Does it not seem strange that millions should be spent trying to create life or to discover its origin? Is not our number-one problem to care for the life we already have?"

Either man began nowhere and is looking for some place to go, or he began somewhere and has lost his way. In either case, he is looking and searching. The Bible tells us that man began in the image of God and lost his way. A good indication of the human predicament today is a sign on the rear window of an automobile: "Don't follow me. I'm lost." Carl Jung, the eminent psychologist, once said: "Man is an enigma to himself."

There is within every man a certain sense of frustration. Voices echo from within the inner chambers of his soul: "I ought not to be the way I am. I was made for something higher. There must be a supreme being. Life was not meant to be this empty." These voices, often unconscious and unarticulated, cause man to struggle onward toward some unknown, unnamed goal. We may try to evade this quest; we may detour into fantasy; we may revert to the lower levels of life and seek escape from this laborious truth. Indeed, we may even give up temporarily, throw up our hands, and say: "What's the use?" But always some inner compulsion drives us back, and invariably we take up the quest again.

Men in every culture are engaged in this eternal search. I took some of my college work in anthropology, where we studied primitive societies. We never found a tribe anywhere in the world, no matter how primitive, that was not engaged in this search. It is a search to find purpose and meaning in life. It is a search to find truth and reality. It may be crude, primitive, or even vulgar; but it is still part of the search!

It is my conviction that the riots, pranks, escapades, and often the crimes of young people are symptoms of this search. The chaplain of a great eastern university told me about a group of students who came to him one day and said: "We want to demonstrate for something, but we don't have a cause." As I have observed demonstrations for various causes around the world, I have seen "the search" written on the faces of the demonstrators.

In the lobby of the Ukraine Hotel in Moscow I sat beside a man of some obvious importance. One of the friendliest men I met in Russia, he spoke fairly good English. We began to chat first about the weather, then about Sputniks, and finally he said to me: "I have lived through two wars, I have seen a lot of changes, but there is one thing unchanged." Curious, I asked: "And what is that?" "The human heart," he said, patting his chest. "No matter what form of government or ideology we embrace, the heart always seeks peace."

From the jungle to the campus, I have talked with people on every continent, from merchants to soldiers; and always in every place there is the age-old phenomenon, the mystery of *anthropos,* the "upward-looking one," searching, probing, inquiring for life's deeper and often hidden meaning.

The owner of a luxurious resort hotel in Miami Beach confided in me: "Billy, I have everything a man could have materially. I thought I had it made, but lately I have been fed up with it all. I have always wanted these things, but now that I have them they seem less than I thought they would be, I believe life is more than this." He was right. Jesus said: "A man's life consisteth not in the abundance of the things which he possesseth" (Lk. 12:15).

In India a professing Hindu said to me: "I need something here," as he patted his heart. This is the cry of all men of all times: "I need something here!"

At the end of the First World War we thought we had found the answers. Science had come into its own. The "war to end war" was finished. The League of Nations was formed. Progress became a god of the age. Optimism reigned everywhere. But we did not get far into the twenties before it seemed that history had been thrown into reverse. Crime increased, morals declined, faith waned. Then the Depression came. Fascism and Nazism sprang up, the atomic bomb exploded—and millions had died in the bloodiest war of history. When the spree was over, we woke up with a hangover called "the balance of terror."

Man's Self-Examination

While the West had lulled itself to sleep with the comforting doctrine of man's achievements, a great revolution had been in progress in Russia. The hammer pounded and the sickle gleaned until a new social order called Communism emerged as one of the most powerful ideologies of all time. It challenged every concept man had ever held. It threatened the life of the whole world. It became the greatest challenge Christianity had faced in 2,000 years. Soon it was recognized that Communism was far more than economic determinism. It was a fanatic religion that asked questions and demanded answers. Throughout the world, students began to ask questions as never before.

Once again man has been forced to examine his soul. The questions we thought were answered are being raised once more. What is man? Where did he come from? What is his purpose on this planet? Where is he going? Is there a God? If there is a God, has He revealed Himself to man? Can man know God? Is God relevant to daily life? Does God really matter?

Dr. Jung has said that "The central neurosis of our time is emptiness." Putting his words into action, he himself embraced Christianity to fill the void in his own life. Here and there, other intellectuals, disillusioned with the shallow goals of a materialistic society, began to examine their souls. Many turned to the ancient book called the Bible. Thousands flocked to various messiahs, and still others turned to the escapist drugs, such as DMT, UM-491, LSD-25, and CI-395. Others went into strange cults. Nevertheless, many began to find an answer in a renewal of the faith of their fathers.

Everywhere people are searching for something that works. We would like to save ourselves, for this would feed our egos and our pride. It nourishes our self-esteem to believe that we can manage independently of God. Like Lucifer, we say: "I will be like the Most High" (Isa. 14:14). The destructive power of pride is that it countenances nothing higher than itself. Because of an inherent fault in our nature, man's bias is on the side of error. In our willful desire to live independently of God, we have severed the lifeline that flows from the source of all life. We have cut ourselves off from the one hope.

Never has a generation been called upon to experience more intense suffering, trouble, heartache, and despair than ours. Paralyzing fear, benumbing pain, devastating war, tragic death, intellectual pessimism— all because man in his pride refuses to turn to God! We are reminded of the words of Jesus, who said: "Man shall not live by bread alone" (Matt. 4:4). Man is so constituted that he cannot subsist without God. Material prosperity alone will not suffice. We must have God. To penetrate space, to land on the moon or on Mars, as thrilling and as exciting as that may be, will not satisfy man's inner hunger. He must have God! To have more leisure time, to live in split-level homes, to drive high-powered cars, to watch color television— these are not the answer. Man must have God!

At the end of his life Buddha said: "I am still searching for truth." This statement could be made by countless thousands of scientists, philosophers, and religious
leaders throughout all history. However, Jesus Christ
made the astounding claim: "I am the truth" (Jn.
14:6). He is the embodiment of all truth. The only
answer to man's search is found in Him.

Faith versus Prideful Intellectualism

Nor will an analytical attitude toward God suffice.
We live in a day when the emphasis is on prideful
intellectualism. The Bible teaches that man by wisdom
cannot find God. Job asked the question: "Canst thou
by searching find out God?" (Job 11:7). Notice that
Job did not ask: "Canst thou by searching find God?"
Job was saying that a man, with his limited mental
capacity, cannot even measure and comprehend the
immensity of God. It is possible to find God; but it is
impossible to "find out" the infinitude of God's immensity. In other words, man would like to put God in a
laboratory. We would like to contain Him in the con-
fines of our little brains. This is, of course, impossible.
We cannot even prove the existence of God, but we
know that He does exist.

Christianity can never be reduced to reason alone.
This is one of the differences I have with some theologians who try to reduce the whole content of the Christian faith to an intellectual gymnastic exercise. If man
is to find God, he must come in simple childlike faith
and in complete dependence on His revealed Word. The
word "faith" is used ninety-two times in the Gospel of
John alone, indicating something of the great emphasis
the Bible puts on faith.

I have a friend who vowed in college that he would
be a millionaire before he was twenty-five years old,
and he achieved that goal with little effort. He became
a successful businessman. He had arrived. He married a
beautiful woman. He could say: "Soul . . . take thine
ease, eat, drink, and be merry" (Lk. 12:19). However,

they were both miserable in the midst of their affluence. Out of curiosity they came to one of our meetings and responded to the appeal to receive Jesus Christ. Christ demanded a decision, a plunge, a choice! They took that plunge, and today they are two of the most radiantly happy people I know.

The Bloodless Revolution

There is going on in the world today a quiet, bloodless revolution. It has no fanfare, no newspaper coverage, no propaganda; yet it is changing the course of thousands of lives. It is restoring purpose and meaning to life as men of all races and nationalities are finding peace with God.

Dr. Fred Smith was one of the world's great biochemists. Educated in Great Britain and, until his recent death, a professor at the University of Minnesota, Dr. Smith came to one of our meetings "to see the show." Through science he had been searching for the answers to the deepest questionings of his heart, and that night after a simple message he found the answer.

It is at this point that the account of the Atlanta hotel fire ceases to serve as an illustration, because there is a way of escape. Safety and security are available for everyone who searches. Man need never plunge recklessly into certain destruction to escape the problems of this world. For despite the modern philosophers who tell us that there is no way out, Jesus Christ still beckons to all who search. He still says: "I am the way, the truth, and the life" (Jn. 14:6).

My friend, Dr. Kenneth L. Pike, Professor of Linguistics at the University of Michigan, has written an incisive little book entitled *With Heart and Mind*. In it is a chapter called "Prescription for Intellectuals" in which Dr. Pike says: "The down-and-outer who wants to be cleansed, forgiven, and straightened out does not need extensive understanding of how help comes; he only needs help and needs it quickly." If you are about to drown, you simply yell "Help!" At that moment you do not try to reason out how you got into your dangerous predicament. You know you need help, you shout it, and you grab anything in sight. And that is all the person who is "down" does. He is one who is helpless and knows it. You don't have to know about the philosophy of Christianity to get help. The Scripture says: "Whosoever shall call upon the name of the Lord shall be saved" (Rom. 10:13).

However, Dr. Pike points out that the same thing is not true for the intellectual who already has his mental outlook logically formed into a coherent system with all of the pieces fitting together in a neat mosaic, so that the removal of one piece destroys the pattern. The intellectual thinks he must be able to understand before he comes to Christ. The intellectual just cannot reach out and grasp a helping hand because he must have the situation explained in terms of his system of thought. He wants to know the source of that help, the manner of that help, because he has already committed himself to a set of assumptions that are rigid and all-inclusive. From his point of view, his system is complete.

Nicodemus was an intellectual. He, too, had a rigid philosophical and theological system worked out, and it was a good system. He had even included a belief in God. The intellectual structuring of his philosophical religious system excluded Jesus as the Son of God.

But what did Jesus tell this intellectual? He said something like this: "Nicodemus, I am sorry that I cannot explain it to you. You have seen something that troubles you. You have seen something that does not fit your system. You have seen me to be good, and you have heard me say that I am God, that I act with the power of God. This does not fit your system, but I cannot explain it to you because your assumptions do not allow for a starting point. Nicodemus, to you it is not logical. Nothing in your system permits it. I am sorry I cannot explain. You will just have to be born again" (Jn. 3:1-5).

In other words, Nicodemus had to start without even being logical from his own point of view. He had to start without fitting what Jesus said into his system. He had to take a leap of faith into a new system.

If you are to find the answer to your search, you too may have to reject much of your old system and plunge into this new one. As Dr. Pike says: "The intellectual needs to be told that his system as a whole must be replaced . . . that he must be born again. Christianity is not an accretion, it is not something added. It is a new total outlook which is satisfied with nothing less than penetration to the furthest corners of the mind and the understanding."

6

Who Am I?

Late one night in a discussion at Yale, a student suddenly asked: "Who am I?" Some of the other students, not catching the depth of the meaning of this question, laughed. I did not laugh because I knew that this inquiring student had asked one of the most profound questions ever asked. A long time ago, Socrates said: "Know thyself." Modern man is even more perplexed by the quest to know himself than the philosophers of the past. Many of our modern thinkers wonder if man is knowable. Where did I come from? Why am I here? Where am I going? What is the reason for my existence? These questions plague every thoughtful man.

It was only a few years ago that man thought he could rule the world by his scientific achievements, and so he threw God out the window. However, man is beginning to realize that he also threw himself out. While man has achieved brilliant success in science, he has made little advance in understanding himself. Dr. Fred H. Klooster says: "True, man has come to a more realistic awareness of himself, but this experience merely shadowed his old myths and left him in skepticism or despair. Stupendous manifestations of evil in industrial society and distilled violence in world wars have shattered the liberal myth of man's innate goodness."[1]

---

[1] "The Nature of Man" in Carl F. H. Henry, ed., *Christian Faith and Modern Theology* (New York: Channel Press, 1964), pp. 147-48.

Pessimism

Modern writers depict the pessimism of our times. Many have thrown up their hands in despair and said there is no answer to man's dilemma. Ernest Hemingway, in *Death in the Afternoon,* says: "There is no remedy for anything in life . . . death is a sovereign remedy for all misfortunes." Millions agree with Mr. Hemingway's words: "I live in a vacuum that is as lonely as a radio tube when the batteries are dead and there is no current to plug in to." Eugene O'Neill, in *Long Day's Journey into Night,* typifies the philosophical attitude of our day, that life is a search for the meaning of life. "Life's only meaning is death," he says, "so face it with courage and even love of the inevitable. Death becomes like a blanket on a cold night." A film such as *The Misfits,* which was the last film Clark Gable and Marilyn Monroe were to make, is the story of "lost people." Arthur Miller's *After the Fall* is the story of the hopelessness of existence. This is an age of spiritual emptiness in which man is desperately searching, but few seem to be finding.

Thus, man has become secularized. He is now in danger of entering a state of spiritual nihilism. He negates spiritual values. He has lost his faith and denies any higher ideals than the satisfaction of his appetites.

"While Nietzsche asserted that God died in the nineteenth century, some now add that man died in the twentieth. Since the relationship between God and man is so close, when faith in God fades, then man's knowledge of himself is also impossible."[2]

Modern man's dilemma is that he does not know who he is or what the significance of his life implies.

In my travels throughout the world, some truths have made a great impact on me. One of them is the truth that man is the same all over the world. His hopes, dreams, problems, difficulties, and longings are essen-

---

2 Ibid.

tially the same whether he is in the heart of Africa or in the heart of America. Another truth that has impressed me as I have studied man on every continent is that man is essentially no different today from what he was a thousand years ago. His circumstances change, but human nature remains essentially the same. As Goethe said: "Mankind is always advancing. Man remains ever the same."

Thus the problem facing the world today is the anthropological problem. What is man? What is his purpose for existence? There is only one book in the world that gives an adequate answer, and that is the Bible. Man's nature and destiny are revealed in the Scriptures.

Man Made for God

The Scriptures tell us that God made man in His image. The present condition of man is not his original condition. The Scriptures tell us that God made man after His likeness. This was not a physical image, for God is a spirit and does not have a body. Man bears the image of God in his rational and moral faculties and in his social nature. God gave to man freedom of the will. Man differs from all other creatures in the world. He belongs to the same order of being as God Himself. Thus because we are made in God's likeness, we can know Him. If we were not like God, we could not know Him.

Adam and Eve were perfect. Ecclesiastes 7:29 says: "God hath made man upright." Genesis 1:31 indicates that man was morally perfect. There was no such thing as lust, greed, and hate in the beginning.

Because man was mentally, morally, and socially like God, he was also free. He thought, he understood, he was good, he had affections, and he could make choices. With regard to moral choices, his will was absolutely free. He had the ability always to choose the right, but he had also received the power to choose evil. Adam's freedom is implied in the commandment of God. "Of every tree of the garden thou mayest freely eat: But of the tree of the knowledge of good and evil, thou shall not eat of it: for in the day that thou eatest thereof thou shalt surely die" (Gen. 2:16, 17). If man *could* not do evil, then why warn him? If he could not but sin, then why punish him? Man had the ability not to sin and he had the ability to sin.

There is no conclusive scientific evidence that man is "up from the ape." While the animals were created "after their kind," we are told that "God created man in his own image" (Gen. 1:27). The Bible does not tell us exactly how God created man. There is no use speculating any further. We know only that man is unique, different, and special. As far as we know, there were no other creatures in the universe comparable to man. He was the crowning act of God's creation. An animal is conscious, but man is self-conscious. The animal does not objectify self. If a dog could once say, "I am a dog," it would cease being a dog. The animal does not distinguish "self" from its sensations. Man is a self-conscious and self-determining being, made in the image of his Creator and capable of free moral decisions between good and evil.

Man's Partnership with God

In the beginning, God and man were friends. They walked together and talked together. They made great plans as to how this planet was to be populated and developed. The planet earth was to show God's glory to the entire universe. It was to be the center of God's activities in His partnership with man.

It is quite evident that God desired the fellowship of a creature like man. Thus man was created with a high and exalted purpose, a high and exalted destiny. Man was to be God's closest friend, His partner in cultivation and development of the earth.

God did not create man a piece of machinery so that He could push a button and man would obey Him. Man was no robot. Man was a "self." He had dignity and he had ego. He could choose whether he wanted God's friendship and fellowship or not. God did not want His creature to love Him because he was forced to do so. This would not be true love. He wanted man's love and fellowship because man chose to love God.

Thus from the very beginning God proceeded to test man's love and friendship. This is why He put the tree in the garden. He said: "Of every tree of the garden thou mayest freely eat: But of the tree of the knowledge of good and evil, thou shall not eat of it: for in the day that thou eatest thereof thou shalt surely die" (Gen. 2:16, 17).

God promised to reward man with "the tree of life" if he obeyed, but God invoked the penalty of death for disobedience. We do not know all that "the tree of life" implies, but the reward must have been something far beyond our comprehension. If we accept the Genesis account, which Christ certainly accepted, then all of life has meaning.

Life with Meaning

When students rioted on a Labor Day weekend in Hampton Beach, New Hampshire, some of them were interviewed as to why they did it. Some of the answers were very enlightening. "We have no purpose, nothing to live for." "Life has no meaning." In the midst of the world's crisis and change, there are thousands striving to find the purpose and meaning of life. The question being asked is "What is meaning?" Nietzsche said: "If a man has a *why* for his life he can bear with almost any *how*." Albert Camus said: "Here is what frightens me. To see the sense of this life dissipated. To see our reason for existence disappear. That is what is intolerable. Man cannot live without meaning."

But man made in the image of God has meaning. There is purpose, destiny, and meaning in life. In a book called *From Death Camp to Existentialism*, Victor Frankl, who suffered the worst of Nazi horrors, said: "Has all this suffering, this dying around us, a meaning? For if not, then ultimately there is no meaning to survival."

Jean Paul Richter once said: "Never shall I forget the phenomenon in myself . . . when I stood by the birth of my own self-consciousness, the place and time of which are distinct in my memory. On a certain morning I stood at the door of the house, and looking out toward the woodpile as in an instant the inner revelation 'I am I' like lightning from heaven flashed and stood brightly before me. In that moment I had seen myself as I . . . for the first time and forever."

This "I" was made in the image of God, for fellowship with God. Without God it is miserable, empty, confused, and frustrated. Without God life has no meaning; but with God at its center there is life, an inner strength and peace, a deep satisfaction, an unfading joy known only to those who know Jesus Christ. With Him, even the troubles and sufferings of life can become the means of that inner joy that glories in tribulation.

"Apart from Jesus Christ we know not what our life is, nor our death, nor God, nor ourselves,"[3] wrote Pascal. With Jesus Christ, we can know.

---

3 Pascal, *Pensées.*

7

Man's Fatal Disease

A few years ago, a medical school graduate who had just obtained his M.D. degree began practice in a small village. An old man was his first patient. The young doctor was nervous about trying to make a good first impression. The old man listed all his ailments and waited for the doctor to give him a diagnosis. After a long examination, the young doctor had no clue as to what was wrong with his patient. Finally he asked: "Have you ever had this trouble before?" The old man said: "Yes, many times." The doctor said: "Well, you have it again." As we look at the distress, frustration, confusion, and deep maladies of our age, about all we can say is, "The world has it again." But what does it have?

Every newspaper or magazine that we pick up contains evidence of man's disease—hate, lust, greed, prejudice, manifesting themselves in a thousand ways every day. The very fact that we have policemen, jails, and military forces is an indication that something is radically wrong.

Man is actually a paradox. On the one side there is futility, degradation, and sin; on the other side, there is goodness, kindness, gentleness, and love. As Seneca said: "Men love their vices and hate them at the same time."[1] Wherever we look we meet the paradox of man. On the one hand he is a helpless sinner, and on the other hand he has capacities that would relate him to God. No wonder Paul spoke of man's disease as "the mystery of iniquity."

[1] Seneca, *Letters* 112.3.

Thus we all recognize that the human race is sick, that man has a disease that has affected the whole of life. The Bible calls this disease sin. The Bible teaches that man is a sinner. What is sin? The Westminster Confession defines it as "any want of conformity unto or transgression of the law of God." To put it simply, sin is anything contrary to the will and law of God.

The Origin of Sin

The puzzling question is: Where did evil and sin originate, and why did God allow it? The Bible teaches that sin did not originate with man, but with the angel whom we have come to know as Satan. Yet exactly how sin originated is not fully known. It is one of those mysteries the Bible does not fully reveal. We catch glimpses now and again in the Bible of the answer to this riddle. For example, in the twenty-eighth chapter of Ezekiel there is a description of a great and glorious being of whom the prophet said: "Thou art the anointed cherub that covereth; and I have set thee so: thou wast upon the holy mountain of God . . . Thou wast perfect in thy ways from the day that thou wast created, *till iniquity was found in thee*" (Ezek. 28:14, 15). Here we find a glimpse of where it all started. In some unknown past, iniquity was found in the heart of one of the most magnificent creatures of heaven. How this iniquity got there we are not told. For some reason, it has not pleased God to reveal the full answer to the mystery of where iniquity began. It is enough for us to know that it is in the world and that man has fallen under its power.

In the book of Isaiah we have another hint of the origin of evil: "How art thou fallen from heaven, O Lucifer, son of the morning! how art thou cut down to the ground, which didst weaken the nations! For thou hast said in thine heart, *I will* ascend into heaven, *I will* exalt my throne above the stars of God: *I will* sit also upon the mount of the congregation, in the sides of the north: *I will* ascend above the heights of the clouds; *I will* be like the Most High. Yet thou shalt be brought down to hell, to the sides of the pit" (Isa. 14:12–15). Here we have a picture of Lucifer's sin. It is a description of the iniquity that was found in his heart, but there is no explanation as to how it got there.

From these references we learn that he fell and became Satan because of his excessive ambition. The New Testament gives us a glimpse concerning the sin of pride: "Lest being lifted up with pride he fall into the condemnation of the devil" (I Tim. 3:6). Here the Apostle Paul affirms that the basic sin of Lucifer was pride.

Revolt Against God

Sin is a revolt against God. It is a setting up of a false independence, the substitution of a "life-for-self" for "life-for-God."

When we come to the entrance of sin into the human race, the Bible is much more specific. It teaches that, through one act of one man, sin came into the world, and with it all the universal consequences of sin. This one man was Adam, and this one act was the partaking of the fruit of the tree of the knowledge of good and evil that God had forbidden (Rom. 5:12–19; Gen. 3:1–8). God gave to man the gift of freedom. Man could choose either to serve and love God or to rebel and attempt to build his world without God. The tree of the knowledge of good and evil served as a test.

The immediate cause of man's rebellion was the "lust of the flesh, and the lust of the eyes, and the pride of life" (I Jn. 2:16). "And when the woman saw that the tree was good for food, and that it was pleasant to the eyes, and a tree to be desired to make one wise, she took of the fruit thereof, and did eat, and gave also unto her husband with her; and he did eat" (Gen. 3:6). Centuries later Christ faced the same three temptations in the wilderness. He overcame them all, and thereby showed to us that it is possible for man to resist the temptations of Satan (Matt. 4:1–11).

To desire what God has forbidden is to prefer self to God, and this is sin. In the Ten Commandments we are told not to covet or to lust. We are commanded not to desire anything that God has forbidden, but Adam and Eve failed their test. Their act was rebellion against God. However, all moral law is more than a test; it is for man's own good! Every law that God has given has been for man's benefit. If man breaks it, he is not only rebelling against God; he is hurting himself.

God had warned earlier: "But of the tree of the knowledge of good and evil, thou shalt not eat of it: for in the day that thou eatest thereof thou shalt surely die" (Gen. 2:17). As a result of man's breaking this commandment of God, he died spiritually and faced eternal death. Immediate, far-reaching, and fearful were the consequences of the sin of Adam and Eve. Had they obeyed God, we can only imagine the possibilities that man would have realized in the thousands of years that have followed. There would have been no hate, no greed, no prejudice. There would have been no wars. Man would have never known suffering, disease, poverty, or death. God and man together would have built on this planet a glorious social order that is totally unknown to us today.

However, there is no use speculating on what might have been. Sin is the stubborn fact of our world. We must reckon with it.

Thus in the first chapter of Genesis we read the story of man's potential glory as a creature made in God's image, and the effects of man's yielding to temptation with its ensuing tragedy and degradation. By this record we are shown that evil existed before man. It did not originate in him. There already existed a breach and disharmony in creation in the person of Satan, who was an angel-prince or viceroy of God. It was from this evil source that man's temptation came. Yet this does not free man from the responsibility of his own action of rebellion.

Thus the Bible teaches that man's chief problem is spiritual. The basis of the problem is revealed in the Genesis account of man's temptation and fall. God created man free. He was not only free to obey but also free to disobey. If disobedience had not been an option, then obedience would have no meaning.

In this freedom, man was subjected in effect to two options that counteracted each other. God offered man supremacy and power if he submitted to divine law and government. Satan offered man enlightenment and god-likeness if he would disobey God. Although the rewards of obedience far outweighed those of disobedience, man chose to disobey.

What was the result? Satan had promised man the knowledge of good and evil, and in a distorted form he kept his word. But instead of perceiving from the free height of the good, he perceived the "good" from the deep abyss of the evil. According to God's plan, man through victory over temptation should have perceived what good is and what evil would have been. But through sin he actually perceived what evil is and what good would have been. And because he deliberately sinned, he must now also be cut off from the tree of life. Death entered the human race, and hell began in paradise.

The universe we live in is under God's law. In the physical realm, the planets move in split-second pre-cision. In all the universe we see harmony, order, and obedience. God is no less exacting in the higher spiritual and moral order. Although God loves man with an infinite love, He cannot and will not counte-nance disorder. Therefore He has laid down spiritual laws which, if obeyed, bring harmony and fulfillment, but if disobeyed bring discord and unhappiness.

The specific result of Adam's sin followed in a num-ber of ways. Both Satan and Adam had challenged God's law. They did not break it; they broke themselves upon it. As God warned: "In the day that thou eatest thereof thou shalt surely die" (Gen. 2:17). The result was death as predicted. The life of beauty, freedom, and fellowship Adam had known was now gone. His sin resulted in a living death. Nature became cursed and the venom of sin infected the entire human family. The whole of creation was thrown into disharmony.

Paradise gained was now paradise lost! The earth was now a planet in rebellion!

What Is Sin?

There are many words in the New Testament that are translated "sin." One of the commonest is *hamartia*. It means "a missing of the target." Sin is the missing of the target at which life must aim and which life ought to hit. Thus sin is failure to live up to God's standards. Since not one of us is capable of fulfilling all of God's laws at all times, we are all "target missers." The Bible said of the very beginning of humanity: "All flesh had corrupted his way upon the earth" (Gen. 6:12). According to King David: "They are all gone aside, they are all together become filthy: there is none that doeth good, no, not one" (Ps. 14:3). Isaiah the prophet confessed: "All we like sheep have gone astray; we have turned every one to his own way" (Isa. 53:6). And King Solomon declared: "There is no man which sinneth not" (II Chron. 6:36).

We Are Sinners by Choice

While the tendency to sin has been passed on to us from our first parents, we are also sinners by choice. When we reach the age of accountability and are faced by the choice between good and evil, we all at some time or other choose to get angry, to tell a lie, to act selfishly. As David said: "Behold I was shapen in iniquity, and in sin did my mother conceive me" (Ps. 51:5). This does not mean that he was born out of wedlock, but rather that he inherited the tendency to sin from his parents. Thus Jeremiah said: "The heart is deceitful above all things, and desperately wicked: who can know it?" (Jer. 17:9).

A seventeen-year-old boy stabbed an old man to death in Brooklyn. Later at the police station he said:

"I don't know why I did it." "There is," said a great lion tamer, "no such thing in the world as a tamed lion. A lion may be on good behavior today and a whirlwind of ferocity tomorrow." None of us can really trust our hearts. The Bible vividly puts it like this: "Sin croucheth at the door" (Gen. 4:7, RV). Given the right circumstances, most of us are capable of almost any transgression.

This does not mean that every person is devoid of all qualities pleasing to men. Man may have certain moral qualities. He may be a gentleman in every sense of the word. However, the Scriptures teach that every person is destitute of that love for God that is the fundamental requirement of the law. It means that the average man is given to preferring "self" to God.

Because man fails to meet God's requirements, he is guilty and under condemnation. Being guilty means that he deserves punishment. God's holiness reacts against sin, because He is a holy God. Thus there is "the wrath of God" (Rom. 1:18).

The Results of Sin

The Bible teaches that sin affects *the mind*. "The natural man receiveth not the things of the Spirit of God . . . neither can he know them, because they are spiritually discerned" (I Cor. 2:14). While a man may be brilliant in some things, he may be grossly confused about spiritual realities. The Bible teaches that there is a veil over his mind. Before a person can be converted to Christ, this veil must be lifted. This is done by the supernatural power of the Holy Spirit. Without this "veil-lifting" there is no possibility of a man's coming to God. The Gospel of Jesus Christ is not anti-intellectual. It demands the use of the mind, but the mind is affected by sin. It is in the service of a rebellious will. In the final analysis a man must submit his mind to the Lordship of Christ. During recent years, I have seen a number of intellectuals respond to the Gospel. Many of them have tried to come head first, and it will not work! There must be a response of the whole man—intellect, will, and emotions—to the saving initiative of God.

The Bible teaches that sin affects *the will.* Jesus said: "Whosoever committeth sin is the servant of sin" (Jn. 8:34). There are vast numbers of persons living under the tyranny of pride, jealousy, prejudice, or perhaps they are living under the bondage of alcohol, barbiturates, or narcotics. Even some who do not want to do the things they are doing are powerless to quit. They have become slaves. They cry for freedom but there seems to be no escape. But Christ said: "Ye shall know the truth, and the truth shall make you free" (Jn. 8:32). He is the truth. He can set you free.

Sin also affects *the conscience,* until one becomes slow to detect the approach of sin. The Bible talks about the deceitfulness of sin. Psychologists have learned that they can put a frog in hot water and he will jump out. However, if they put a frog in lukewarm water and gradually heat it, they can boil him without his jumping. So it is with sin. There was a time when you were disturbed and conscience-smitten about a certain sin. It may have been immorality. It may have been a lie. It may have been the first time you cheated in school. But now your conscience bothers you hardly at all. Your heart has become hardened. You no longer have a sensitivity to things you know to be wrong. You have built up a rationalistic system to keep your conscience quiet. In the first chapter of Romans, the Apostle Paul said that because men were so given over to their sins, "God gave them up." God once said concerning Ephraim: "Ephraim is joined to idols; let him alone" (Hos. 4:17).

This is one of the most terrifying results of sin. You begin to call black white—and white black. You no longer know the difference between good and evil. I have met men who are habitual liars. They have lied so long that they no longer can distinguish between the truth and a lie. Their sensitivity to sin has been almost completely deadened.

The totality of this infection is reflected in every part of the Scriptures. It is reflected in every newspaper we read. It is reflected in every radio and television newscast. Thus man is described as being totally depraved. This does not mean that man is totally sinful, hopelessly and irreparably bad, without any goodness at all. It means that sin has infected the totality of man's life, darkening his intellect, enfeebling his will, and corrupting his emotions. He is alienated from God and in need of restoration. His natural, instinctive inclinations are away from God and toward sin.

Man in his self-assertion, like his father Adam, would like to believe that he can build his world without God. That is his depravity. He would like to believe that his problems can be solved by more knowledge, by diplomacy, by negotiation, by his own manipulation. That is his depravity. He would like to believe that he can save himself by his own good works and efforts. That, too, is his depravity.

The Threefold Death

Because all men have sinned, all are under the penalty of death. Not only does man suffer as a result of sin in this life, but he must face the judgment to come. As it was with Adam, so it is with all men. God punishes sin with a threefold death—physical, spiritual, and eternal.

First, there is physical death. The Bible says: "It is appointed unto men once to die" (Heb. 9:27). The Bible teaches that there is "a time to be born, and a time to die" (Eccles. 3:2). As Psalm 89:48 asks: "What man is he that liveth, and shall not see death?" Thus the Bible states clearly that God has already made an appointment for each man with death. There is for each man a day, an hour, a minute. The Bible talks in many places about the brevity of life. We are told that our physical lives are "a tale that is told"—a "flower that fades"—"grass that withers." One generation passes and another comes. If God had not given the judgment of physical death on the human race, men would have continued in their sins until the earth would have become hell itself. Each generation has a fresh new start. Thus, although death is a penalty for sin, divinely imposed on individuals, when it comes to successive generations of mankind, death is a blessing.

Because of the brevity of life, the Bible warns that we should be prepared to meet God at all times. "Seeing his days are determined, the number of his months are with thee, thou has appointed his bounds that he cannot pass" (Job 14:5).

The Bible exhorts us: "Prepare to meet thy God" (Amos 4:12). Caesar Borgia said in his last moments: "I have provided in the course of my life for everything except death; and now alas! I am to die entirely unprepared."

Second, there is spiritual death. There are millions of persons here and now who are suffering spiritual death. Almost any day you can pick up a newspaper and read of those whose lives testify that they are empty or lost. They were made for fellowship with God, and they are separated from their Maker. This is spiritual death. It is the separation of the soul from God, the separation of man from the One who said: "I am . . . the life." It is spoken of in Scripture as being "dead in trespasses and sins" (Eph. 2:1).

Third, there is eternal death. The Bible has a great deal to say about hell. No one spoke more about hell than Jesus did, and the hell He came to save men from was not only a hell on earth. It was not only some condition in which men are now living. It was something to come. Jesus never once taught that anyone on earth was living in hell now. He always warned of a hell to come. Whatever He meant by hell, essentially it is the separation of the soul from God as the culmination of man's spiritual death. There are many mysteries here, and we dare not go beyond the teaching of Scripture. It is enough to warn men that Jesus said: "And these shall go away into everlasting punishment" (Matt. 25:46). Jesus also said: "The Son of man shall send forth his angels, and they shall gather out of his kingdom all things that offend, and them which do iniquity; And shall cast them into a furnace of fire: there shall be wailing and gnashing of teeth" (Matt. 13:41-42).

Sir Thomas Scott, the former Lord Chancellor of England, said on his deathbed: "Until this moment I thought there was neither God nor hell. Now I know and feel there are both, and I am doomed to perdition by the just judgment of the Almighty."

Thus the Biblical position is that something happened to man, that he became something other than what God created, and that he continues to be what he was not intended to be. This requires a recovery, and the recovery must be radical and revolutionary. It must turn man around and give him a new direction.

The need for spiritual rebirth is evident to the most casual observer of human nature. Man has fallen. Man is lost. Man is alienated from God. Man's recovery must begin at the point of his fall. He chose self rather than God. If he is to be recovered, he must choose God over self. Man lives under the sentence of death. This condemnation can be lifted only if man, by a free act of his own will, makes a complete reversal of his original choice.

The first hint of the Gospel comes from Genesis 3:15: "I will put enmity between thee and the woman, and between thy seed and her seed; it shall bruise thy head, and thou shalt bruise his heel." This is the first note of the Gospel. The first promise of salvation! For the first time God speaks of His Son, in whose redemptive act Satan's head will be crushed.

Thus God initiates what man is powerless to provide —his own salvation. All the moral powers of the individual and all the social forms of the community will be proved inadequate, for God's salvation in Christ is the only possible plan of man's redemption.

Man has tried desperately to recover his lost fellowship with God. He has tried a thousand ways but to no avail. Through various religions, man has attempted to recover paradise. Western man has now turned to secularism and humanism, hoping that by his own efforts he can build a Utopia on earth. As all other plans have failed, so this one will fail, too.

But there are those who say that the world has tried Christianity and that it, too, has failed. But the fact that the world has not improved morally is not the fault of Christianity. It is the lack of its application. When confronted with the world's problems, we Christians say automatically: "Christianity is the answer." But this is not true! It is the application of Christianity that is the answer. It was G. K. Chesterton who said a generation ago: "The Christian ideal has not been tried and found wanting. It has been found difficult, and left untried."

God's Way versus Man's Way

From the very beginning, all attempts to recover man from his lost estate have been divided into two ways. Adam and Eve had two sons, Cain and Abel. One of them came God's way; he was obedient. The other one, Cain, came his own way; he was disobedient to the plain command of God. Abel was the representative of "the seed of the woman," while Cain was the representative of "the seed of the serpent."

Cain is the architect of modern civilization. He is the self-sufficient materialist and the religious humanist. While he was religious and appeared before God's altar, he denied the implied revelation of salvation given to Adam in the form of clothing provided through the life of another (Gen. 3:21). Cain brought to the altar an expression of his own labors and strength. He became the prototype of all who dare approach God without the shedding of blood.

From this point onward, two ways run through human history. On the one hand, there is the way of Cain with its religion of the flesh, with a human redemption that relies upon man only and rejects God's substitution. His way humanized God and deified man. His way was the way of the materialist, the secularist, the humanist.

On the other hand, there is the way of Abel, with its humble acknowledgment that sin demands death, that the guilty sinner must rely on the sacrifice appointed by God. His offering became a type of the death of Christ.

The Remedy of Redemption

From the time of Cain and Abel until today, man has sought to provide his own remedy for his disease, sin. It did not work for Cain, it has never worked for any man, and it will not work today. Only God can properly diagnose man's disease; only God can provide the remedy. And God chose blood as the means of man's redemption. The Apostle John wrote that Jesus Christ "washed us from our sins in his own blood" (Rev. 1:5).

Blood is the symbol of the life sacrificed for sin. "For the life of the flesh is in the blood; and I have given it to you upon the altar to make an atonement for your souls: for it is the blood that maketh an atonement for the soul" (Lev. 17:11). Throughout the Old Testament it is recorded over and over again that God required the life of a perfect animal, with its blood poured out upon the altar, as a sacrifice for sin. "Without the shedding of blood there is no forgiveness of sins" (Heb. 9:22, RSV). These sacrifices were made in anticipation of the day when a permanent sacrifice would be made. "And it is by the will of God that we have been consecrated, through the offering of the body of Jesus Christ once and for all" (Heb. 10:10, NEB).

When Jesus Christ, the perfect God-man, shed His blood on the Cross, He was surrendering His pure and spotless life to death, as an eternal sacrifice for man's sin. Once for all, God made complete and perfect provision for the cure for man's sins; without the blood of Christ, it is indeed a fatal disease.

When Jesus sat down for the last supper with his disciples, He said: "This is my blood, the blood of the covenant, shed for many for the forgiveness of sins" (Matt. 26:28, NEB).

The apostles affirmed this repeatedly:

Paul wrote: "In whom we have redemption through his blood, the forgiveness of sins" (Eph. 1:7).

Peter wrote: "Forasmuch as ye know that ye were

not redeemed with corruptible things, as silver and gold
. . . but with the precious blood of Christ, as of a lamb
without blemish and without spot" (I Pet. 1:18, 19).

John wrote: "The blood of Jesus Christ his Son
cleanseth us from all sin" (I Jn. 1:7).

Every person must make his choice between the two
ways—man's way or God's way. One is the way of self-
effort and striving to cure one's self and to provide
one's own redemption; the other way is justification
through faith in the blood of Jesus Christ.

At our Crusades we sing this hymn, which illustrates
man's need and God's answer to that need:

> *Just as I am, without one plea*
> *But that Thy blood was shed for me,*
> *And that Thou bidd'st me come to Thee,*
> *O Lamb of God, I come! I come!*
>
> *Just as I am, and waiting not,*
> *To rid my soul of one dark blot,*
> *To Thee whose blood can cleanse each spot,*
> *O Lamb of God, I come! I come!*

8

The Inadequacy of Modern Religion

William James once said that religion is either a dull habit or an acute fever. And John Dewey observed: "Nowhere in the world at any time has religion been so thoroughly respectable with us . . . and so nearly totally disconnected with life." These statements remind us that religion is a word with many meanings. It can mean the frenzied orgies of a jungle tribe, or it can mean the meditative, intelligent worship of the Lord God. As a term, "religion" appears only twice in the King James Version of the New Testament, once in Acts 26:5 and again in James 1:26, 27.

When men speak of religion, they do not always speak of the same thing. For all definitions of religion are governed by two magnetic poles, the naturalistic and the theistic. The naturalistic pole is what the Apostle Paul spoke of when he wrote that men "changed the glory of the uncorruptible God into an image made like to corruptible man, and to birds, and four-footed beasts, and creeping things" (Rom. 1:23). The theistic pole is embodied in the teachings of the Bible with its revelation of man's beginning, fall, and recovery through redemption.

When Cain approached the first altar with his offering of "the fruit of the ground," this was his way of trying to regain paradise without accepting God's plan of redemption. Cain, in his selfishness and arrogance, decided to come his own way. He rejected God's plan. Times have not changed. Millions today want salvation, but on their own terms. They want to come their own way, and so we have hundreds of schemes and plans

devised by men to regain paradise. They have given rise
to many sects, each shouting its own particular plan of
salvation.

The sin of Lucifer was pride. The sin of Adam was
pride. The sin of modern man is pride. He does not
want to admit his weakness and helplessness in the face
of life's insoluble situations. He feels that somehow,
someway, he can make his own salvation. Cain brought
the evidences of his own culture, amounting to a salvation by works, while Abel obeyed God and humbly
offered a sacrifice of blood, thereby acknowledging that
sin deserved death and could be covered before God
only through the substitutionary death of a guiltless
sacrifice. And it was this plan that Cain deliberately
rejected.

Natural Religion versus God's Plan

There, back in the very beginning, was the introduction of natural religion upon the human scene as an
effort to circumvent God's plan. Natural religion, however, is not always a crude invention of early man. Today
it is the full-time effort of many intellectuals to circumvent God's plan. Some of them are professors of religion
in our universities; others are even leaders in the church.

The Apostle Paul said of man's corruption of God's
general revelation into a naturalistic religion: "For the
invisible things of him from the creation of the world
are clearly seen, being understood by the things that are
made, even his eternal power and Godhead; so that
they are without excuse: because that, when they knew
God, they glorified him not as God, neither were
thankful; but became vain in their imaginations, and
their foolish heart was darkened. Professing themselves
to be wise, they became fools . . . who changed the
truth of God into a lie, and worshipped and served the
creature more than the Creator, who is blessed for
ever" (Rom. 1:20-22,25). This is a Biblical picture of
man's perversion of God's revelation, with all its primitive crudity, sensuality, fetishism, superstition, and

magic. It has passed through many refinements and much refurbishing. Today, it presents itself in the forms of intellectual respectability, but in primitive cultures it still exists in the same forms of debasing sensuality and deceit.

Natural religion is opposed to divine revelation, which accepts the Bible as the authoritative source of the ideas of sin and justification by faith in the atoning death of Christ. Natural religion rejects almost everything in the Apostles' Creed.

This is not to say that natural religion does not contain elements of truth, or embody some high ethical standards and moral values. Some of its followers at times employ terms that recall the language of the Bible. While the morality encouraged by natural religion may win the approval of men, it neither secures acceptability with God nor reflects His full moral demands. In fact, some of the crudest immorality in human history has had the sanction of natural religion, as the Apostle Paul reminds us in the Epistle to the Romans.

The Bible teaches that Satan can transform himself into an "angel of light," adapting himself to every culture and every situation, even at times deceiving true believers. Counterfeiters always try to make their counterfeit money look exactly like the real thing. This is how Satan operates today. Thousands of people have even been herded into the church without a vital experience with Jesus Christ. They have substituted good works, community effort, social reform or a religious rite for personal salvation. Many people have just enough natural religion to make them immune to the real thing. Every time I go to the Far East I take cholera shots, and usually I get sick from the shots. Actually, I get a small case of cholera, which makes me immune to the dreaded disease, should I come in contact with it in my travels. This is true of most vaccinations. And it is also true in the realm of religion. There are many people who have just enough religion to be immune from a genuine personal experience with Jesus

Christ. Therein lies the grave danger for thousands of professing Christians.

False Prophets

There is no doubt that naturalistic religion has invaded the church today. Many of our concepts of the church are secular. Even the mission of the church is often changed from a Biblical basis to a secularized one.

There is a strong movement, especially in Protestantism, to recast the Christian message in order to make it acceptable to modern man. These people contend that the intellectuals reject Christianity today because "they cannot accept certain traditional beliefs which were really the envelope in which the message was sent, rather than the message itself."[1] Yet these modern theologians fail to agree among themselves as to which part of the New Testament is to be retained and which part is to be thrown out. Many of them seem to agree that the miracles were myths. They regard the resurrection as a subjective experience of the disciples rather than as an objective historical event. These theologians call God "the ground of being." They deny absolutely that Jesus Christ was supernatural. They say that He was a man who was so good and unselfish that God's love shone through His humanity rather than in the Biblical terms of the Incarnation. Karl Barth, the European theologian, in a scathing denunciation of these demythologizers, says: "They have thrown out the baby with the bath water. In trying to make Christianity plausible for skeptics, they have succeeded only in making it meaningless."

All the way through the Bible we are warned against false prophets and false teachers. In the Sermon on the Mount, Jesus said: "Beware of false prophets, which

---

[1] John A. T. Robinson, *Honest to God* (Philadelphia: Westminster Press, 1963).

come to you in sheep's clothing, but inwardly they are ravening wolves . . . wherefore by their fruits ye shall know them" (Matt. 7:15, 20). Sometimes it is very difficult even for a Christian to discern a false prophet. There is a close resemblance between the true and the false prophet. Jesus spoke of false prophets who "show great signs and wonders; insomuch that, if it were possible, they shall deceive the very elect" (Matt. 24:24). Paul tells of the coming Anti-Christ, whose activity in the last days will be marked by "signs and lying wonders" (II Thess. 2:9). Satan's greatest disguise has always been to appear before men as "an angel of light" (II Cor. 11:14).

Deception

The underlying principle of all Satan's tactics is deception. He is a crafty and clever camouflager. For Satan's deceptions to be successful they must be so cunningly devised that his real purpose is concealed by wiles. Therefore he works subtly and secretly. No Christian, however spiritual, is beyond the seductive assaults of Satan. His deception began in the Garden of Eden. "The woman said, The serpent beguiled me, and I did eat" (Gen. 3:13). From that time to this, Satan has been seducing and beguiling. "But evil men and seducers," Paul warned Timothy, "shall wax worse and worse, deceiving, and being deceived" (II Tim. 3:13). He also warned the church at Ephesus: "Let no man deceive you with vain words" (Eph. 5:6); and again: "That we henceforth be no more children, tossed to and fro, and carried about with every wind of doctrine, by the sleight of men, and cunning craftiness whereby they lie in wait to deceive" (Eph. 4:14). Yes, there will be more and more false teachers and preachers, as the age draws toward its end. As the Apostle Peter said: "There shall be false teachers among you, who privily shall bring in damnable heresies, even denying the Lord that bought them, and bring upon themselves swift destruction. And many shall follow their pernicious ways; by reason of whom the way of truth shall be evil spoken of. And through covetousness shall they with feigned words make merchandise of you: whose judgment now of a long time lingereth not, and their damnation slumbereth not" (II Pet. 2:1–3).

Satan has not built a worldwide church using his name. He is far too clever for that. He invades the Sunday school, the Bible class, and even the pulpit. He even invades the church under cover of an orthodox vocabulary, emptying sacred terms of their Biblical sense. Paul warned that many will follow false teachers, not knowing that in gulping down and feeding upon what these apostates say, they are taking the devil's poison into their own lives. Thousands of uninstructed Christians are being deceived today. False teachers use high-sounding words that seem like the epitome of scholarship and culture. They are intellectually clever and crafty in their sophistry. They are adept at beguiling thoughtless, untaught men and women. Of them the Apostle Paul wrote: "Now the Spirit speaketh expressly, that in the latter times some shall depart from the faith, giving heed to seducing spirits, and doctrines of devils; speaking lies in hypocrisy" (I Tim. 4:1, 2). These false teachers have departed from the faith God revealed in the Scriptures. The Bible states plainly that the reason for their turning away is that they gave heed to Satan's lies and deliberately chose to accept the doctrines of devils rather than the truth of God. So they themselves became the mouthpiece of Satan, speaking lies.

True and False Religions

Because the church, in turning to naturalistic religion, increasingly proclaims a humanistic gospel, thousands of laymen and clergymen alike are asking penetrating questions about the purpose and mission of the church. Thousands of loyal church members, particularly in America, are beginning to meet in prayer groups and Bible study classes. Multitudes of Christians within the church are moving toward the point where they may reject the institution that we call the church. They are beginning to turn to more simplified forms of worship. They are hungry for a personal and vital experience with Jesus Christ. They want a heartwarming, personal faith.

Unless the church quickly recovers its authoritative Biblical message, we may witness the spectacle of millions of Christians going outside the institutional church to find spiritual food.

In order to compete with God for the dominion of the world, Satan, whom Christ called "the prince of this world," was forced to go into the "religion" business. Although expelled from the Garden, man still carried a God-consciousness within his heart. Satan's strategy was to divert this innate hunger from the Lord God. Thus came the advent of what we call false, counterfeit, or naturalistic religion—and its history is long and tragic. The Bible differentiates clearly between true faith and mere religiosity. Nothing could be more wrong than the old cliché that says any religion will do just as long as one is sincere. In no other area of life is there so much error, deception, and charlatanism as in religion.

The two altar fires outside Eden illustrate the difference between true religion and false religion. One belonged to Abel who brought of the firstlings of his flock as the offering to the Lord God. He offered it in love, in adoration, in humility, and in reverence. And the Bible says that the Lord had respect unto Abel and his offering. The other belonged to his older brother Cain, who had brought a bloodless, cheap offering to the altar, and the Bible says that "unto Cain and his offering God had not respect." How could the Lord God be so capricious? After all, did not Cain attempt to please God, and was he not perfectly sincere?

This story was put in the Bible to teach that there is a right way and a wrong way to make contact with God. Abel made his sacrifice humbly, reverently, and sacrificially, bringing his very best to God—and he came in God's way. Cain made his sacrifice grudgingly, selfishly, and superficially—but he also disobeyed God in the way he came, for he came without faith. When God did not sanction and bless his sacrifice, Cain became angry and killed his brother. Abel truly loved God and worshiped Him. Cain's worship was a meaningless religiosity, as empty and hollow as his whole life became. Leaving his family, he walked the earth embittered, crying unto the Lord: "My punishment is greater that I can bear" (Gen. 4:13).

Here we see the emergence of a stream of religiosity, branching off from the mainstream of true worship of the Lord God. Throughout history this stream is destined to become an ever-widening river. Man is eternally torn between the true and the false, the worship of idols and the worship of the Lord God, the lure of religiosity or the recognition of the plain Biblical teaching of the way of salvation.

Even while Moses was on Mount Sinai receiving the tablets of stone "written with the finger of God," humanistic religion was breaking out in the camp of Israel. The people said to Aaron: "Up, make us gods which shall go before us." Aaron submitted to their demands and said: "Break off the golden earrings, which are in the ears of your wives, of your sons, and of your daughters, and bring them unto me. . . . And he received them at their hand, and fashioned it with a graving tool, after he had made it a molten calf: and they said, These be thy gods, O Israel, which brought thee up out of the land of Egypt" (Exod. 32:1–4).

As time moved forward, other idolatrous tributaries flowed into the mainstream of religion—Baal, the god of the tribes of Canaan; Chemosh, the god of the Moabites; Dagon, the god of the Philistines; and Molech, the god of the Amorites. If all the gods of history were listed by name, a good-sized volume would be needed to hold them all.

The inescapable implication of a counterfeit is that the real thing exists. No one ever counterfeited a seventy-five-dollar bill. Every counterfeit bears witness to the reality of the currency it copies. So in the midst of all the plans and programs men have devised to satisfy their religious urge, true religion does exist and is available for all who will come to God on His terms.

9

The Incredible Journey

Shelia Burnford wrote the tale called *The Incredible Journey*, which Walt Disney made into a film. It is the story of two dogs and a cat that searched for their master on a 250-mile trek through Canadian wilderness. For centuries, mankind has been on an incredible journey taking him across every generation and through every conceivable experience in his search for God.

A young man approached a holy man of India sitting on the bank of the Ganges and asked him how he could find God. The holy man seized him and held him under the water until he nearly drowned. As the youth came up sputtering and gasping, he asked: "Why did you do that?" to which the holy man answered: "When you long for God as much as you longed for air when you were under the waters of this river, you will find Him." Ever since man's separation from God in the Garden of Eden, man has been trying desperately to find his way back to paradise.

The Bible begins with the majestically simple words: "In the beginning God." These four words are the cornerstone of all existence and of all human history. Without God there could have been no beginning and no continuing. God was the creating power and the cohesive force that brought cosmos out of chaos. By divine fiat He brought form out of shapelessness, order out of disorder, and light out of darkness. As Alfred Noyes said: "The universe is centered on neither the earth nor the sun . . . it is centered on God."

You Cannot Rationalize God

If you try to rationalize God exhaustively, you will fail. There are mysteries about God that we will never understand in this life. How can the small and finite, limited to time and space, understand an infinite God! We should not think it strange that it is impossible to comprehend God intellectually, when it is equally impossible to explain many mysteries in the realm of matter. Who can explain why objects are always attracted to the center of the earth? Who can fathom the law of gravity? Newton discovered it, but he could not explain it. Who can explain the miracle of reproduction? For years, scientists have tried to reproduce a living cell and solve the mystery of procreation. They believe they are coming close, but as yet they are without success.

There are many arguments we could marshal to give evidence of the existence of God. There is scientific evidence pointing to God's existence. For example, whatever is in motion must be moved by another, for motion is the response of matter to power. In the world of matter there can be no power without life, and life presupposes a being from which emanates the power to move things, such as the tides and the planets.

Or there is the argument that says nothing can be the cause of itself. It would be prior to itself if it caused itself to be, and that is an absurdity.

Then there is the law of life. We see objects that have no intellect, such as stars and planets, moving in a consistent pattern, cooperating ingeniously with one another. Hence it is evident that they achieve their movement not by accident but by design. Whatever lacks intelligence cannot move intelligently. An arrow would be useless without a bow and an archer. What gives direction and purpose and design to inanimate objects? It is God. He is the underlying, motivating force of life.

Thus, many evidences and many arguments could be advanced to indicate that there is a God. Yet the plain truth is this: God cannot be proved by mere rationalization. He cannot be contained in a tiny, man-made test tube or confined to an algebraic formula. If God can be fully proved by the human mind, then He is no greater than the mind that proves Him.

Other Gods

In my travels throughout the world I have met very few atheists. Whatever period of history one studies, whatever culture one examines, the searcher finds man believing in a god of some sort. All peoples, primitive or modern, have acknowledged some kind of deity. During the past two centuries, archaeology has unearthed the ruins of many ancient civilizations, but none has ever been found that did not yield some evidence of a god who was worshiped. Man's concepts of God have been as varied as his moods. He has made gods out of his imaginations in all kinds of multiple forms.

Some men in their frustration give up the pursuit of God and profess to be irreligious, but the vacuum left within them must be filled with some kind of deity. Therefore man makes his own "god." Today many use the nation as an object of worship and espouse the gospel of nationalism. They make the mistake of making a god and a religion out of their nationalism. This takes the place of the true and living God in their lives. Although the Communists deny faith in God, they have made a god of their cause. Thousands willingly lay down their lives, suffer privation and poverty because of their belief in "the cause."

Thus, having failed to find the true God, millions declare their allegiance to lesser gods and causes. This has always been man's way. But these other gods and causes do not bring the ultimate answers or satisfactions. Just as Adam was made for fellowship with God, so are all men. When Jesus, commenting on the First Commandment, said: "And thou shalt love the Lord

thy God with all thy heart, and with all thy soul, and
with all thy mind, and with all thy strength" (Mk.
12:30), He meant that man has the capacity to love
God.

Can Man Know God?

The great questions are: Can we know God? Has God
revealed Himself? Can fellowship with God be restored?

Ultimately you must come to God by faith. Faith is
the link between God and man. The Scriptures say you
must believe that He is. This is why the word "faith" is
used so many times in the Scriptures.

Astounding as it may seem, in spite of man's transgressions and rebellions, God loves man with an everlasting love. God has never forsaken man. The most
dramatic quest of the centuries is God's loving and
patient pursuit of man. God longs for man's return and
recovery. In his poem *The Hound of Heaven,* Francis
Thompson portrays God and His persistent pursuit of
man, chasing him down the corridors of history, relent-
lessly tracking him, graciously stalking him, like a com-
passionate St. Bernard pursuing an imperiled child in
the mountains of Switzerland.

Where does the breakthrough of this revelation of
God occur? How can a blind man see? How can a
deaf man hear? When man chose in the Garden of
Eden to defy God's law, a great tragedy occurred. The
line of communication between God and man was
broken. They could no longer have fellowship. Light
and darkness could not live side by side.

One of the things the average person does not realize
is that God is "holy." God said to Israel long ago: "I
the Lord your God am holy" (Lev. 19:2). In Joshua's
farewell address to the armies of Israel, he said: "He is
a holy God; he is a jealous God" (Josh. 24:19). The
Psalmist said: "God sitteth upon the throne of his
holiness" (Ps. 47:8). In the book of Revelation the cry
in Heaven night and day is: "Holy, holy, holy, Lord

God Almighty, which was, and is, and is to come" (Rev. 4:8).

Because God is holy, He cannot look upon iniquity and sin. Sin is ugly and revolting to God. It is impossible for our finite, sin-dulled minds to comprehend the absolute holiness of God. Because man was stained with sin and iniquity, God could no longer have fellowship with him. Somehow, some way, God must devise a plan to restore fellowship with man in spite of his sin. As a holy God, He could not go back on His word. He had said, in effect: "In the day that you transgress my law . . . you shall die" (cf. Gen. 2:17). Man had to die, or God would be proved a liar, and then He would no longer be God.

Because man still sins, still defies authority, and still acts independently of God, a great gulf exists between God and man. It is across this dark and barren chasm that God beckons, calls, and pleads with man to be reconciled to His heart of love. For as the Apostle John said: "For God is love" (I Jn. 4:8). Jeremiah the prophet quotes God as saying: "Yea, I have loved thee with an everlasting love: therefore with loving-kindness have I drawn thee" (Jer. 31:3). Likewise, Malachi the prophet quoted God as saying: "I have loved you, saith the Lord" (Mal. 1:2). Because God is holy, He could not automatically forgive or ignore man's rebellion. Because God is love, He could not completely cast man aside. This was the great divine dilemma: How could God be just and still justify the sinner? This is the question Job posed: "But how should man be just with God?" (Job 9:2).

Revelation is a means of communication. It means "to make known" or "to unveil." Revelation requires a "revealer," who in this case is God, and it also requires a "hearer." God's hearers were the chosen prophets and apostles who recorded God's revelation. Thus it is a line of communication, at one end of which is God, and at the other end, man.

When I was a boy, radio was just coming of age. We would gather around a crude homemade set and twist the three tuning dials in an effort to establish contact with the transmitter. Often all the sound that came out of the amplifier was the squeak and squawk of static, but we knew that somewhere out there was the unseen transmitter and if contact was established and the dials were in adjustment, we could hear a voice loud and clear. After a long time of laborious tuning, the far distant voice would suddenly break through and a smile of triumph would illuminate the faces of all in the room. At last we were tuned in!

In the revelation that God established between Himself and us, we can find a new life and a new dimension of living, but we must "tune in." There are higher levels of living to which we have never attained. There is peace, satisfaction, and joy that we have never experienced. God is trying to break through to us. The heavens are calling. God is speaking! Let man hear.

10

How Does God Speak?

When a spacecraft returns from its orbital flight, there is a blackout period of about four minutes when all communications are broken. This is due to the intense heat generated by the spacecraft's reentry into the earth's atmosphere.

The Bible teaches that man is in a period of spiritual blackout. Spiritually, he is *blind*. "We grope for the wall like the blind, and we grope as if we had no eyes: we stumble at noonday as in the night; we are in desolate places as dead men" (Isa. 59:10). "The god of this world hath blinded the minds of them which believe not" (II Cor. 4:4).

Spiritually, man is also *deaf*. "They have ears to hear, and hear not" (Ezek. 12:2). Jesus went so far as to say: "If they hear not Moses and the prophets, neither will they be persuaded, though one rose from the dead" (Lk. 16:31).

Spiritually, man is even *dead*. "Who were dead in trespasses and sins" (Eph. 2:1).

All of this means that the communication between God and man is broken. There is a wonderful world of joy, light, harmony, peace, and satisfaction to which millions of persons are blind and deaf, and even dead. They long for serenity, they search for happiness, but they seem never to find it.

Many give up the search and surrender to pessimism. Often their despondency leads to a frantic round of cocktail parties where vast amounts of alcohol are imbibed. Sometimes it leads them to narcotics. It is all part of man's desperate search to find an escape from

the cold realities of a sin-blighted existence. All the
while, God is there speaking and beckoning. The television set may be sitting in your room cold, dark, and
lifeless, but this is not the fault of the television broadcast-
ers. They are sending forth programs from many trans-
mitters, and their sending stations are in perfect order.
But you must turn the dials of your set; you must tune
in on the right channel. God is sending forth His
message of love, but you must tune in. You must be
willing to listen and to receive His message and then to
obey it.

Many persons want to hear what God says just out
of curiosity. They want to analyze and dissect it in their
own test tubes. To these persons God may remain the
great cosmic silence "out there somewhere." He com-
municates to those who are willing to hear and receive
Him and willing to obey Him. Jesus said that we must
become humble as little children, and God has most
often revealed His message to the meek and humble—to a
shepherd boy like David, to a rough desert man like
John the Baptist, to shepherds watching their flocks, to
a girl named Mary.

How does God speak? How can a blind man see?
How can a deaf man hear?

From the beginning, God spoke to man. Adam heard
the voice of the Lord in the Garden of Eden. Adam
had two sons, Cain and Abel, and God spoke to them.
Cain spurned that which was revealed to him, but Abel
was obedient to the Word of God. Abel's response
showed that a man tainted and handicapped by sin
could respond to God's overtures. Thus in the very
beginning God began by revelation to build a bridge
between Himself and man.

Revelation in Nature

God reveals Himself in *nature*. "The heavens declare
the glory of God; and the firmament showeth his
handiwork. Day unto day uttereth speech, and night
unto night showeth knowledge. There is no speech nor

language, where their voice is not heard" (Ps. 19:1–3). There is a language in nature that speaks of the existence of God. It is the language of order, beauty, perfection, and intelligence. Some time ago, a scientist told me that when he gave serious thought to the majestic order of the universe and its obedience to unchanging law, he could not help but believe in God. He had become aware that God was speaking through nature.

God speaks in the certainty and regularity of the seasons; in the precision of the movements of the sun, the moon, and the stars; in the regular coming of night and day; in the balance between man's consumption of life-giving oxygen and its production by the plant life of the earth; and even in the cry of a newborn child with its ever-new demonstration of the miracle of life. When my younger son Ned was born, I had the privilege of being in the delivery room with my wife. Just before the moment of his birth, the doctor looked up at me and said: "I have delivered thousands of babies, and I never cease to be amazed at the miracle of birth. How anyone could deny the existence of God after witnessing this, I do not know."

As man's knowledge leaps forward in our generation, it does not mean the discovery of new things, but only the extension of his understanding and his ability to use that which is already there. Man is ever discovering worlds new to him, but old to God. Even a casual study of the statistics of astronomy causes us to stand in awe. The space density of the universe is so great that it is estimated that there are now more than a thousand million galaxies. These galaxies average twenty thousand light years across, and many of them are more than two million light years apart. It is impossible for our minds to take it in. Many astronomers say there may be no limit to the universe. Old theories and ideas about the beginning of the universe are being thrown out the window. If a scientist lacks a belief in God, he must be baffled indeed by the mysteries of the universe.

To look into a microscope is to see another universe so small that only the electronic microscopes can even find it. For instance, it is revealed that one single snowflake in a snow storm with millions of other snowflakes is the equivalent of twenty billion electrons. Scientists are learning that the miniature world of a single living cell is as astonishing as man himself.

Thus the Apostle Paul said: "For the invisible things of him from the creation of the world are clearly seen, being understood by the things that are made, even his eternal power and Godhead" (Rom. 1:20). God says that we can learn a great deal about Him just by observing nature. Because He has spoken through His universe, all men are without excuse for not believing in Him. This is why the Psalmist said: "The fool hath said in his heart, There is no God" (Ps. 14:1).

Revelation in Conscience

God has revealed Himself also in the *conscience*. Conscience has been described as the light of the soul. What causes this warning light to go on inside me when I do wrong?

Conscience is our gentlest counselor and teacher, our most faithful friend, and sometimes our worst enemy. There are no punishments or rewards comparable to those of the conscience. The Scripture says: "Man's conscience is the lamp of the Eternal" (Prov. 20:27, Moffatt). In other words, conscience is God's lamp within man's breast. In his *Critique of Pure Reason*, Immanuel Kant said there were just two things that filled him with awe—the starry heavens and conscience in the breast of man.

The conscience in its varying degrees of sensitivity bears a witness to God. Its very existence within us is a reflection of God in the soul of man. Without conscience, we would be like rudderless ships at sea and like guided missiles without a guidance system.

Revelation in Scripture

God has revealed Himself also through the *Scriptures*. God has two textbooks, one the textbook of nature and the other the textbook of revelation. The laws of God revealed in the textbook of nature have never changed; they are what they were since the beginning. They tell us of God's mighty power and majesty.

In the textbook of revelation, the Bible, God has spoken verbally; and this spoken word has survived every scratch of human pen. The Bible has withstood the assaults of skeptics, agnostics, and atheists. It has never bowed its head before the discoveries of science. It remains supreme in its revelation of redemption. The more the archaeologist digs and the more the scientist discovers, the greater the confirmation of the truth of the Bible.

The writers of the Bible claim repeatedly that God gave them their material. Two thousand times in the Old Testament they said that God spoke. In the first five books we find such expressions as these:

"The Lord God called unto Adam and said"

"The Lord said unto Noah"

"God spake unto Israel"

"These are the words which the Lord hath commanded"

"God said"

"The Lord spake, saying"

"The Lord commanded"

"The word of the Lord"

Over and over the Old Testament prophets used such expressions as these:

"Hear the word of the Lord"

"Saith the Lord"

"I heard the voice of the Lord saying"

"The word of the Lord came unto me"

"Whatsoever I command thee thou shalt speak"

"I have put my words into thy mouth"

"The Word of the Lord came unto me saying"

Either God did speak to these men as they wrote by inspiration, or they were the most consistent liars the earth ever saw. To tell more than two thousand lies on one subject seems incredible, and more than two thousand times the writers of the Bible said that God spoke these words! Either He did just that, or they lied. If they were mistaken in this emphasis, why should we honor their witness at any point?

Jesus quoted frequently from the Old Testament. He never once indicated that He doubted the Scriptures. The Apostles quoted the Scriptures often. The Apostle Paul said: "All Scripture is given by inspiration of God" (II Tim. 3:16). The Apostle Peter said: "For the prophecy came not in old time by the will of man: but holy men of God spake as they were moved by the Holy Ghost" (II Pet. 1:21).

Thus, God speaks to man through the Scriptures. This is why it is so important to read the Bible for yourself. So many take the Bible secondhand, and they have only a caricature of what the Bible says, only vague ideas about its teachings. When I go to university and college campuses, I am amazed to find how ignorant the students are of the real teachings of the Bible. They think they know, but they don't.

Revelation in Jesus Christ

Finally, God speaks in the person of *His Son Jesus Christ*. "God . . . hath in these last days spoken unto us by his Son" (Heb. 1:1, 2). The idea that God would some day visit this planet is an ancient truth that is no doubt an oral remnant of the original revelation God gave to Adam of a promised salvation (Gen. 3:15). We find crude references to it in most other religions of the world, indicating that man at some time had heard or sensed that God would visit the earth. However, it was not until the "fulness of the time" when all the conditions were right, when all the prophetic considerations were fulfilled, that God "sent forth his Son, made of a woman" (Gal. 4:4).

On that first Christmas night in Bethlehem, "God was manifest in the flesh" (I Tim. 3:16). This manifestation was in the person of Jesus Christ. The Scripture says concerning Christ: "In him dwelleth all the fulness of the Godhead bodily" (Col. 2:9). This manifestation

of God is by far the most complete revelation God ever
gave to the world. If you want to know what God is
like, then take a long look at Jesus Christ. In Him were
displayed not only the perfections that had been
exhibited in the creation—such as wisdom, power, and
majesty—but also such perfections as justice, mercy,
grace, and love. "The *logos* was made flesh, and dwelt
among us" (Jn. 1:14).

To His disciples Jesus said: "Ye believe in God, believe also in me" (Jn. 14:1). This sequence of faith is
inevitable. If we believe in what God made and what
God said, we will believe in the One whom God sent.

The means of understanding these facts of salvation
is faith. We are not always challenged to understand
everything, but we are told to believe. "But these are
written, that ye might believe that Jesus is the Christ,
the Son of God; and that believing ye might have life
through his name" (Jn. 20:31).

Every hope we have of God, every prospect we have
of eternal life, every anticipation we have of heaven,
every possibility we have of a new social order—all
must be linked to Jesus Christ. It is as we come to Jesus
Christ that the unknown becomes known; and not only
that, but as we come to Jesus Christ we experience God
Himself. Our limited, darkened lives receive the light of
the eternal presence of God, and we see that there is
another world beyond the confusion, limitation, and
frustration of this world.

11

The Inescapable Christ

A woman in India had learned that she was a sinner and that God is holy and cannot overlook sin. She often said: "I need some great prince to stand between my soul and God." Eventually she heard that the Bible contains the account of a Savior who had died for sinners, so she asked a pundit to read the Bible to her. He began at the first chapter of Matthew, and as he read the list of names in the genealogy of Christ, the woman thought: "What a wonderful prince this Jesus must be to have such a long line of ancestors." And when the pundit read: "Thou shalt call his name Jesus: for he shall save his people from their sins" (Matt. 1:21), the woman exclaimed: "This is the prince I want! This is the prince I want! The Prince who is also a Savior!"

One of the most crucial questions on any university campus is: "What about Jesus Christ?" The modern student simply cannot escape Him. He must decide whether Christ and the Gospel really matter, whether He is relevant in this modern age. On the one hand, Jesus Christ is the center of opposition; on the other hand, He is the object of devotion and worship. What we think of Christ influences our thinking and controls our actions.

History, philosophy, theology, and, in many centers of learning, even the sciences are being studied to discover what they have to say about Jesus Christ. The records of the early church are being reexamined with minute care for their testimony to Him. Archaeologists are digging to discover new evidence concerning Jesus

Christ. What D. S. Cairns said in the forepart of this century remains true in the closing decades: "The historic personality of Jesus has risen upon the consciousness of the church with the force almost of a new revelation, the ultimate results of which still lie far in the future. It is literally true that this century is face to face with the great figure as no century has been since the first."[1]

Some say that Jesus Christ is a myth, that He never really existed in history. Others say that He was merely a man, that there was nothing supernatural about His birth, and that His resurrection was to the Apostles a hallucination. Others talk about a Christless Christianity. They say that whatever one thinks about Christ does not affect Christianity. They are wrong.

Christianity is forever linked with the person of Christ. Carlyle recognized this when he said: "Had this doctrine of the deity of Christ been lost, Christianity would have vanished like a dream." Lecky remarks: "Christianity is not a system of morals; it is the worship of a person."

When many religious leaders are exploring points of contact between Christianity and the non-Christian religions, the question of the person of Christ becomes all-important to the church. Christianity is now being compared with other religions as never before. Even some Christian leaders advocate syncretism, or the working out of a system of morals, ethics, and religion that would bring together all the religions of the world. Many of these leaders are willing to give up some of the teachings of the Bible in order to harmonize Christianity with the other religions.

The Uniqueness of Christ

Why insist on the uniqueness of Christianity? What is different about Christianity? What did Christianity bring into the world that had not appeared before? The

---

[1]*Christianity and the Modern World* (New York: George H. Doran, 1906), p. 14.

Christian answer is the uniqueness of Christ, the supreme manifestation of God. "God was in Christ, reconciling the world unto himself" (II Cor. 5:19). This is the central fact of our Christian faith.

Some 700 years before Christ was born, Isaiah the prophet had said: "Behold, a virgin shall conceive, and bear a son" (Isa. 7:14). This expression is unparalleled in literature. No man but Christ in all history could say that his mother was a virgin. The Scriptures teach that Jesus Christ did not have a human father. If he had had a human father—"that which is born of the flesh is flesh" (Jn. 3:6)—he would have inherited all the sins and the infirmities that all men have. He would have been conceived in sin and shapen in iniquity even as the rest of us. He was not conceived by natural means but by the Holy Spirit, who overshadowed the virgin Mary; and Christ stands as the one man who came forth pure from the hand of God. He could stand before all of His fellowmen and say: "Which of you convicts me of sin?" (Jn. 8:46, RSV). He was the only man since Adam who could say: "I am pure."

There are mysteries about the incarnation that none of us can ever understand. In fact, Paul speaks of "God . . . manifest in the flesh" as a "mystery" (I Tim. 3:16). In another epistle, he says: "Let this mind be in you, which was also in Christ Jesus: who, being in the form of God, thought it not robbery to be equal with God: but made himself of no reputation, and took upon him the form of a servant, and was made in the likeness of men" (Phil. 2:5-7).

The Deity of Christ

Jesus Christ was uniquely, divinely, and wholly God's only begotten Son. None ever approached the eminence that Jesus reached. None ever became what He was, because none was ever born as He was born or died as He died!

From beginning to end, the New Testament testifies of the deity of Jesus Christ. The Apostle Thomas called

Him, "My Lord and My God" (Jn. 20:28). Since Thomas was not rebuked by Jesus, this is equivalent to an assertion on His own part of His claim to deity. He possesses all the attributes of God Himself.

He has divine life. "In him was life" (Jn. 1:4). "I am . . . the life" (Jn. 14:6).

He is unchanging. "Jesus Christ the same yesterday, and today, and for ever" (Heb. 13:8).

He is the truth. "I am . . . the truth" (Jn. 14:6).

He is holy. "That holy thing which shall be born of thee shall be called the Son of God" (Lk. 1:35). "We know that you are the Holy One of God" (Jn. 6:69, NEB). "Holy, harmless, undefiled, separate from sinners" (Heb. 7:26).

He existed before time began. "Before Abraham was, I am" (Jn. 8:58). "He is before all things" (Col. 1:17). "I am Alpha and Omega, the beginning and the end" (Rev. 21:6).

He knew all things. "Jesus knowing their thoughts" (Matt. 9:4). "He knew all men . . . he knew what was in man" (Jn. 2:24, 25). "Thou knowest all things" (Jn. 16:30). "In whom are hid all the treasures of wisdom and knowledge" (Col. 2:3).

To Him are ascribed all the works of God. "All things were made by him" (Jn 1:3). "One Lord Jesus Christ, by whom are all things" (I Cor. 8:6). "All things were created by him, and for him" (Col. 1:16). "The heavens are the works of thine hands" (Heb. 1:10).

To Him was given worship and honor accorded only to deity. "If ye shall ask anything in my name, I will do it" (Jn. 14:14). "Let all the angels of God worship him" (Heb. 1:6). "That at the name of Jesus every knee should bow . . . and that every tongue should confess that Jesus Christ is Lord" (Phil. 2:10, 11). "Lord and Saviour Jesus Christ. To him be glory both now and for ever" (II Pet. 3:18).

When He forgave sins, He did the work that only God can do. "But that ye may know that the Son of man hath power on earth to forgive sins . . . Arise, take up thy bed, and go unto thine house" (Matt. 9:6).

"Why doth this man thus speak blasphemies? who can forgive sins but God only?" (Mk. 2:7).

William E. Gladstone once said: "All I write and all I think and all I hope is based upon the divinity of our Lord, the one central hope of our poor wayward race."

Jesus calls himself the Son of God. Twice in John's Gospel He identifies Himself as the Son of God, in Chapters 9:37 and 10:30. He does it again in Mark 14:61, 62, as well as many other places either by direct statement or inference. John's Gospel opens with this majestic statement, which parallels Genesis 1:1: "In the beginning was the Word, and the Word was with God, and the Word was God." Here is coequality with God. Again John says: "And I saw, and bare record that this is the Son of God" (Jn. 1:34). Nathaniel said: "Rabbi, thou art the Son of God" (Jn. 1:49). Reference can be made also to John 3:16, 18, and 19:7. It is clearly established that Jesus claimed to be the Son of God, and it was ascribed to Him by God, and claimed for Him by His contemporaries.

When the New Testament prescribes saving faith, it identifies that faith with the deity of Christ. At the conclusion of John's Gospel, the Apostle says: "But these are written, that ye might believe that Jesus is the Christ, the Son of God; and that believing ye might have life through his name" (Jn. 20:31).

Two things are most important at this point. First, the object of faith is Jesus Christ. "These are written that ye might believe that Jesus is the Christ, the Son of God" (Jn. 20:31).

It is specified and emphasized that "Jesus is the Christ, the Son of God." This is the highest revelation of Jesus. Anything less than this level of faith is ineffectual as an act of saving faith.

The object of saving faith is not a body of truth called a creed, although creeds are important. The object of faith is a person—Jesus Christ. This person is not merely the historical person known as Jesus Christ, but the prehistorical and posthistorical person of Jesus Christ known as the Son of God! He is "the same yesterday, and today, and for ever" (Heb. 13:8).

If the Bible is to be our basis of authority, then we must "by faith" accept Him as the Son of the living God. This sounds narrow and intolerant, and in a sense it is! Some of our modern theologians would not go so far as this. However, in my long study of the Bible, I have had to come to the conclusion that the Scriptures teach that we must believe that Jesus is the Christ, the Son of the living God.

When Jesus returned to His home in Nazareth, it is said: "And he did not many mighty works there because of their unbelief" (Matt. 13:58). What was their unbelief? They believed that Joseph was His father, not that He was the Son of God.

Salvation is an act of God. It is initiated by God, wrought by God, and sustained by God. The faith that saves the soul is described as faith in Christ as the Son of God—not as a good man or a great man, but as the uniquely begotten Son of the living God! This is consistent with the witness of the entire New Testament and with the proclamations of the first preachers of the Gospel. All proclaim the necessity of faith in Jesus Christ as deity.

The second important thing about John 20:31 is that the effect of faith in Jesus Christ is "life." "And that believing ye might have life through his name." The result of a well-placed faith of this specific nature is described as "life." The Bible describes man as alive physically, but dead spiritually. A dead man needs life. The whole human race is described as being "dead in trespasses and sins" (Eph. 2:1). This means they are dead to God. They are incapable of producing divine life. This can be done only by God. They are capable only of believing and receiving. The life spoken of in John 20:31 is that with which Adam was created, but which he lost because he sinned. It is the life that Jesus, the eternal Son of God, displayed. It is the life that was subjected in the wilderness temptation to the enticements of the lust of the flesh, the lust of the eye, and the pride of life. It is the life that was submitted to the routine of daily life as we have to live it today, where Christ was "in all points tempted like as we are, yet without sin" (Heb.

4:15). This life was made available to all humanity by
Christ's death on the Cross. He said: "I am come that
they might have life" (Jn. 10:10). This is the life you
can have—now. This is "Christ in you, the hope of
glory" (Col. 1:27).

The Historic Reality of Christ

The life of Jesus has been the object of human
tribute from the greatest of men to the lowest. This is
particularly true of great minds who have recognized
Jesus as the world's unique and superlative character.
Their estimates of Jesus have testified to His historic
reality and have confirmed that what He was and did is
based on solid historic fact. Rousseau said: "It would
have been a greater miracle to invent such a life as
Christ's than to be it." Another has said: "It would take
a Jesus to forge a Jesus." Pascal wrote: "We know God
only by Jesus Christ. Without this mediator all communion with God is taken away; through Jesus Christ
we know God."[2] Men are awed in the presence of the
Savior's life, and their instinctive assessments are ample
witness to the uniqueness of a life to which no other
human being has either approximated or approached. On
the death of Winston Churchill a London newspaper said:
"It might be said that he was the greatest man since Jesus
Christ." In other words, the newspaper editor was recogniz-
ing that Jesus was the greatest of all men. In the case of
Christ, no natural explanation can be given. He can be
ranked neither with the school-trained nor with the self-
trained. He spoke as one who not only knows the truth
but *is* the truth. As Philip Schaff said: "Christ stands . . .
solitary and alone among all the heroes of history, and
presents to us an unsolvable problem, unless we admit Him
to be more than man, even the eternal Son of God."[3]

Thus, all of Christianity is based on a person—Jesus

---

[2] Pascal, *Pensées.*

[3] *The Person of Christ* (London: James Nisbet & Company,
1880), p. 30.

Christ. Christ Himself is the embodiment of the Gospel. He makes the highest claims without the slightest sense of pride, ambition, or vanity, but with the simplicity and authority of self-evident truth. And when Jesus spoke to His own generation, He said: "If ye believe not that I am he, ye shall die in your sins" (Jn. 8:24).

Christ represents Himself as having been "sent from God" and being "not of this world" and having "come from God." He declares Himself to be "the light of the world," "the way, the truth, and the life," and "the resurrection and the life." He promises eternal life to everyone who believes in Him as the Savior. When in view of His approaching death and under a solemn appeal to the living God, He was challenged by a religious leader: "Art thou the Christ, the Son of God?" He calmly and deliberately answered in the affirmative. Furthermore, He referred to His glorious return, thus in the moment of deepest humiliation and in the face of apparent triumph of the powers of darkness proclaiming Himself the divine ruler and judge of mankind (Matt. 26:63, 64).

The God-Man

Where does such overwhelming testimony leave us? It leaves us with the conviction that Jesus was not merely a good man, or a great prophet, but the Son of God, divine as well as human, revealing in His life and by His teaching the mind and heart of God. Indeed, if Jesus were merely a man like other men, although better, then Christianity is simply a superlative philosophy or just another code of ethics. It is actually the deity of Christ that above anything else gives to Christianity its sanction, authority, power, and its true meaning.

Archibald Rutledge has written: "For more than thirty years it was my chief business in life to study and try to teach literature. To anyone earnestly so engaged there naturally comes a certain ability to distinguish the genuine from the spurious, the authentic from the invented. Every time I read the Gospels I am impressed more deeply with the conviction that the narratives concerning Christ do not belong to the realms of fancy, tradition, or folklore. There is about them the ingenuous reality of life itself. These cannot be, as St. Peter expressly tells us they are not, 'cunningly devised fables.' The incidents are such that they could never have been invented; and their effect on the world for two thousand years has been such as no inventions could have produced. These stories possess that patent transparent validity that belongs only to truth."[4]

"In the deity of Jesus Christ," Rutledge affirms, "I have implicit faith, complete and reasoned confidence . . . Christ is God."[5]

This same author asks and answers an important question: "And can we believe that God would give us a way of life based on a fraud? Would God offer us a religion that reason is compelled to refuse? The answer is obvious, and the higher the human intelligence, the more certain it is of its power to recognize truth. The acceptance of every great teaching of Christianity is easy and natural the moment we accept the deity of Christ, and how any honest mind can reject Him as God is beyond me to comprehend."[6]

Ultimately, in one way or another, or at one time or another, we shall be faced with this question: What think ye of Christ? Whose Son is He? If Jesus Christ is not who He claimed to be, He is a deceiver or an egomaniac.

We must answer this question with both belief and action. We must not only believe something about Jesus but we must do something about Him. We must accept Him or reject Him. Jesus made clear who He was, and why He came into the world. He asked His disciples: "Whom do men say that I, the Son of man, am?" They told Him of a variety of designations on the human level. Then Jesus turned to them and asked: "But

[4] Archibald Rutledge, *Christ Is God* (Westwood, N.J.: Fleming H. Revell Co., 1941), pp. 14–15.
[5] Ibid., p. 45.
[6] Ibid., pp. 43–44.

whom say ye that I am?" Whereupon Peter replied with this historic affirmation: "Thou art the Christ, the Son of the living God" (Matt. 16:13–16). This is the apex of faith. This is the pinnacle of belief. This is where the faith of each person must rest if he hopes for salvation. Christ is inescapable! You too must decide "what shall I do with Christ?"

12

God's Foolishness

On the south coast of China on a hill overlooking the harbor of Macao, Portuguese settlers once built a massive cathedral. But a typhoon proved stronger than the work of man's hands, and some centuries ago the building fell in ruins except for the front wall. High on the top of that jutting wall, challenging the elements down through the years, is a great bronze cross. In 1825, Sir John Bowring was shipwrecked near there. Clinging to the wreckage of his ship, he caught sight at long last of that great cross, which showed him where he could find safety. This dramatic rescue moved him to write those words familiar to millions:

> In the cross of Christ I glory,
> Towering o'er the wrecks of time;
> All the light of sacred story
> Gathers round its head sublime.

When the Apostle Paul went to the great intellectual city of Corinth he said: "For I determined not to know any thing among you, save Jesus Christ, and him crucified" (I Cor. 2:2). And when someone asked him what his message was, he answered: "We preach Christ crucified" (I Cor. 1:23).

To the people of Corinth the preaching of the Cross was ridiculous, foolish, and even idiotic. But Paul said: "The foolishness of God is wiser than men; and the weakness of God is stronger than men" (I Cor. 1:25). In that great center, the Cross of Christ was a stumbling block to the children of Israel—and to the Gentiles it was idiocy! The intellectual Corinthians demanded a man-made system of philosophy predicated on the ability of unregenerate man to unravel the divine mysteries. They wanted something their minds could grasp. Yet Paul says that the natural man cannot understand the things of God (I Cor. 2:14). We do not need to understand the chemical elements of a remedy to benefit from it. This should not seem unreasonable. A doctor writes a prescription which we cannot read, for the treatment of a disease we do not understand, and we gladly pay a sum which may seem unreasonable because we rely on authoritative knowledge and have faith that we will be made well. Before the Cross has any meaning at all, the Spirit of God must open the mind. The Scriptures teach that our minds are covered by a veil as a result of our separation from God. To an "outsider" the Cross must appear to be ridiculous and foolish. However, to those of us who have experienced its transforming power, it has become the only remedy for the ills of the individual and the world.

The Gospel of Christ and Him crucified is still foolishness to millions throughout the world. Long ago Paul asked the question: "Where is . . . the philosopher? Where is . . . the scholar? Where is . . . the debater of this present time and age? Has not God shown up the nonsense and the folly of this world's wisdom? For when the world with all its earthly wisdom failed to perceive and recognize and know God by means of its own philosophy, God in His wisdom was pleased through the foolishness of preaching . . . to save those who believed" (I Cor. 1:20, 21, Amplified).

"We preach Christ crucified." The Cross is the focal point in the life and ministry of Jesus Christ. It was no afterthought or emergency measure with God. Christ was "the Lamb slain from the foundation of the world" (Rev. 13:8). The Cross was designed to defeat Satan, who by deception had obtained squatters' rights to the title of the earth.

Many of the great words of Scripture are legal terms. Something was wrong in the universe. A great injustice had been perpetrated, and God was just. All of these are legal terms: justification (Rom. 5:1), reconciliation (Eph. 2:16), redemption (Lk. 2:38), condemnation (Jn. 3:19), advocate (I Jn. 2:1).

When Satan by his wiles separated man from God in the Garden of Eden, he was more than the deceiver of the first couple. In some mysterious manner he exerted a kind of pseudosovereignty over man. But Satan's power was broken at Calvary. "For this purpose the Son of God was manifested, that he might destroy the works of the devil" (I Jn. 3:8). On the Cross, Satan was dealt a delayed deathblow. Although Satan is still the pretender and the usurper, his end and destruction were made certain by the victory of Christ at the Cross. "That through death he might destroy him that had the power of death, that is, the devil" (Heb. 2:14).

If it were possible for one man, Adam, to lead the race to ruin, why should it not be possible for one man to redeem it? The Bible says: "In Adam all die, even so in Christ shall all be made alive" (I Cor. 15:22). Through the Cross, Christ rescued the slaves that Satan held captive—and reconciled them unto Himself. The Bible describes this divine plan in these words: "We speak the wisdom of God in a mystery, even the hidden wisdom, which God ordained before the world unto our glory; which none of the princes of this world knew: for had they known it, they would not have crucified the Lord of glory" (I Cor. 2:7, 8). This was the eternal secret. This was "the mystery, which was kept secret since the world began, but now is made manifest" (Rom. 16:25,26).

Satan was stopped by God and caught in his own trap. He had not figured on God's loving the world so intensely as to let His own Son be subjected to the worst Satan could do; and because the devil miscalculated the greatness of God's love and the wisdom of His plan, Satan was shorn of his authority and power at the Cross. What seemed to be the biggest defeat of history turned into the greatest triumph.

Atonement

When William Tyndale was translating the New Testament into English, he encountered great difficulty in finding a word big enough to convey the meaning of the redeeming work of Christ. Finding no adequate word, Tyndale joined two simple words—"at" and "onement," thus making "atonement" and giving in its etymology a clue to the Bible's teaching of salvation by reconciliation. In Christ's death on the Cross, God and man, who had been severed by sin, were brought together. If man's sins could have been forgiven any other way, God would not have allowed His Son to go to the Cross. If the problems of the world could have been solved any other way, God would not have allowed Jesus to die. In the garden of Gethsemane on the night before Calvary, Jesus prayed: "If it be possible, let this cup pass from me" (Matt. 26:39). In other words, if there is any other way to redeem the human race, Oh God, find it! There was no other way. And then He prayed: "Not as I will, but as thou wilt" (Matt. 26:39).

The orthodox Jewish religion was founded on the sacrificial system. When God entered into the covenant relationship with Israel, in which He was to be their God and they were to be in a special sense His people (Deut. 7:8), that relationship was founded on the law. But the people could not keep the law perfectly. The breaking of the law was sin. The Bible says: "Sin is the transgression of the law" (I Jn. 3:4). When God gave the law, He knew that man was incapable of keeping it. Many persons are confused as to why God gave the law if He knew man could not possibly keep it. The Bible teaches that the law was given as a mirror; I look into the law and see my spiritual condition. I see how far short I come, and this drives me to the Cross of Christ for forgiveness. "Wherefore the law was our schoolmaster to bring us unto Christ, that we might be justified by faith" (Gal. 3:24). The Bible teaches that this is why Christ came—to redeem them that were under the law. Man could not keep the law; he was condemned by the law.

Sin had to be atoned for, so in the beginning God instituted the sacrificial system by which man could be brought into a right relationship with God. This is why John the Baptist said: "Behold the Lamb of God, which

taketh away the sin of the world" (Jn. 1:29). Under
the Jewish law, those who had offended brought sacrifices of lambs and offered them to God. These sacrifices were types and shadows of The Great Sacrifice that
was yet to come.

The sacrifices offered on Hebraic altars pointed to
the Lamb of God Who takes away the sins of the world.
These sacrifices were instituted not because God was
bloodthirsty or unjust in His demands, but that the
attention of men might be directed to the loathsomeness
and awfulness of sin and to the Cross, where God
Himself would provide an eternal sacrifice that would
satisfy forever the demands of His justice. "Neither by
the blood of goats and calves, but by his own blood he
entered in once into the holy place, having obtained
eternal redemption for us" (Heb. 9:12).

In Christ's atonement for sin, He stood in the guilty
sinner's place. If God had forgiven sin by a divine
decree without atonement, which involved the personal
shame, agony, suffering, and death of Christ, then man
could assume that God overlooked, winked at, or was
indifferent to sin. Thus, man would have gone on sinning,
and earth would have become a living hell. But in the
suffering of Jesus we have the participation of God in
the act of atonement. Sin pierced the very heart of God.
God felt every piercing nail and spear thrust. God felt
the burning sun. God felt the mocking derision and the
body blows. Here in the Cross is the suffering love of
God bearing the guilt of man's sin. This love alone is able
to melt the sinner's heart and bring him to repentance
unto salvation. "For he hath made him to be sin for us"
(II Cor. 5:21).

The Cross of Christ

The heart of the Christian Gospel, with its incarnation and atonement, is in the Cross and the resurrection.
Jesus was born to die. Jesus did for man what man
cannot do for himself. He did it through the Cross and
the resurrection. Today we look for man-made philosophical panaceas. Discussions and debates go on in

every center of learning in a search for ultimate wisdom and its resultant happiness. No solution has been found. We still wrestle with the same philosophical problems that concerned Plato and Aristotle. We are searching for a way out of our dilemma, and the universal sign we see is "no exit." But the Cross presents itself in the midst of our dilemma as our only hope. Here we find the justice of God perfectly satisfied—the mercy of God extended to the sinner—the love of God covering every need—the power of God for every emergency— the glory of God for every occasion. Here is power enough to transform human nature. Here is power enough to change the world.

Thousands of people suffer from guilt complexes. Almost everyone senses that somehow they are wrong, like the little boy who said: "I guess I was just born wrong." God said from the Cross: "I love you." He was also saying: "I can forgive you." The most glorious and thrilling word in any language is "forgiveness." God in Christ had a basis for forgiveness. Because Christ died, God can justify the sinner and still be just.

Christ's dying on the Cross was more than the death of a martyr. It was more than His setting a good example by offering His life for His fellowmen. He was the sacrifice that God had appointed and ordained to be the one and only sacrifice for sin. The Scripture says: "The Lord hath laid on him the iniquity of us all . . . it pleased the Lord to bruise him; he hath put him to grief" (Isa. 53:6,10). Because God Himself has set forth Christ to be the covering for human guilt, then God cannot possibly reject the sinner who accepts Jesus Christ as Savior. "Whom God hath set forth to be a propitiation through faith in his blood" (Rom. 3:25). This is what the communion table in the church is all about. Every time we eat the bread we are remembering the body of Christ nailed to the Cross for us, and every time we drink the wine we are remembering the blood that was shed on the Cross as a covering for our sins. A little girl, seeing a cross on the communion table, asked: "Mama, what is that plus sign doing on the table?" The Cross is God's great plus sign of history.

Christ's atonement is sufficient because God said it is. I know that I am a sinner. I know that I have broken God's laws. I know that I have offended God countless times. My heart, mind, and conscience have been troubled. However, when by faith I look at the Cross, there is peace and joy because I know that God was satisfied with the sacrifice of His Son. My sin was committed against God. If God is content with what Christ has done on my behalf and is willing to pardon me, then I have nothing more to worry about. I am redeemed, I am reconciled, I am forgiven, I am assured of heaven—not because of any goodness or good works of my own. It is only because of the love and mercy of God in Christ on the Cross that I have any claim on heaven at all. It was God who permitted Christ to die as my substitute. It was God who accepted His sacrifice when He died.

When Jesus took our place, our sins were laid on Him, and our sins cannot be in two places at the same time. All of my sin was laid on Christ, and I have no sin charged to me for which God will ever hold me accountable. My sin has become Christ's burden. He has taken it away from me. He has become the sin-bearer. All my indebtedness to God was transferred to Christ. He paid all my debts. I will never suffer the shame of judgment or the terrors of hell. "As far as the east is from the west, so far hath he removed our transgressions from us" (Ps. 103:12).

You may say: "But I don't understand all this." How ridiculous! If a man were drowning and I threw him a life belt, would he say: "I will not put this life belt on until I know whether it is made of rubber or cork and whether the material is strong enough to hold me"? A man in danger of drowning—and he talks like this? You who are outside of Christ are incapable of comprehending the mystery of the Cross as long as you are in your unregenerate state. It is not that there is not enough light for you to see the mystery. You have enough light now to drive you to the Cross of Christ for mercy. By faith receive Jesus Christ as your Lord and

Savior, and the Cross will become the most precious thing in the world to you.

The Evidence of Guilt

As we look at the Cross we see several things. *First, here is the clearest evidence of the world's guilt.* At the Cross of Christ, sin reached its climax. Its most terrible display took place at Calvary. It was never blacker or more hideous. We see the human heart laid bare and its corruption fully exposed. Some people have said that man has improved since that day, that if Christ came back today, He would not be crucified but would be given a glorious reception. Christ does come to us every day in the form of Bibles that we do not read, in the form of churches that we do not attend, in the form of human need that we pass by. I am convinced that if Christ came back today, He would be crucified more quickly than He was two thousand years ago. Sin never improves any more than a cancerous condition can improve. Human nature has not changed. As we stand and gaze at the Cross, we see clear evidence that man is inherently wrong and we hear the inescapable verdict of God Himself: "All have sinned, and come short of the glory of God" (Rom. 3:23).

Proof That God Hates Sin

Second, in the Cross we find the strongest proof of God's hatred of sin. God has said repeatedly that the soul that sins shall die. To gain a clear understanding of God's attitude toward sin, we have only to consider the purpose of Christ's death. The Scripture says: "Without the shedding of blood there is no forgiveness of sins" (Heb. 9:22, RSV). Here is a positive statement that there can be no forgiveness of sin unless our debt has been paid. God will not tolerate sin. Moral law condemns and demands payment for sin. God as the moral judge of the universe cannot compromise and remain just. His holiness and His justice demand the penalty for a broken law.

The tendency today is to feel that such a position on God's part is too severe. Thus we find ourselves manufacturing another gospel: (Gal. 1:8). There are many today who ascribe sin to psychological causes. Many say that they are not responsible for what they do. But God says that we are responsible. When we look at the Cross, we see how drastically God deals with sin. The Scripture says: "He that spared not his own Son, but delivered him up for us all, how shall he not with him also freely give us all things?" (Rom. 8:32). "For our sake he made him to be sin who knew no sin" (II Cor. 5:21, RSV). If God had to send His only Son to the Cross in order to pay the penalty for sin, then sin must be black indeed in the sight of God.

The Glory of God's Love

Third, as we stand at the Cross we see a glorious exhibition of God's love. "For God so loved the world, that he gave his only begotten Son, that whosoever believeth in him should not perish, but have everlasting life" (Jn. 3:16). Paul wrote to the Christians in Rome: "While we were powerless to help ourselves . . . Christ died for sinful men. In human experience it is a rare thing for one man to give his life for another, even if the latter be a good man, though there have been a few who have had the courage to do it. Yet the proof of God's amazing love is this: that it was while we were sinners that Christ died for us" (Rom. 5:6-8, Phillips).

A beautiful young society leader came to visit my wife and me. She had been converted to Christ in one of our Crusades, and she was absolutely radiant in her transformation. Already, she had learned scores of Scripture verses by heart and was so full of Christ that we sat for two hours listening to her give her moving testimony. Over and over she said: "I cannot understand how God could forgive me. I have been such a wicked sinner. I just cannot understand the love of God."

The Basis of Brotherhood

Fourth, as we stand at the Cross, we see in it a basis of true world brotherhood. There is a great deal of talk today about the universal Fatherhood of God and the universal brotherhood of man. The majority of appeals made in behalf of peace are based on the idea of brotherhood. There is a sense in which God is the Father of us all by creation. But the world seems to be blinded to the fact that for men to know God spiritually as Father they must take Christ in personal salvation. Only thus are we brought into the family of God. His spiritual Fatherhood belongs only to those who trust in Christ.

The Bible says that God sees two classes of men. He sees the saved and the lost, those who are going to heaven and those who are going to hell. Jesus made this plain when He said: "Enter by the narrow gate; for the gate is wide and the way is easy, that leads to destruction, and those who enter by it are many. For the gate is narrow and the way is hard, that leads to life, and those who find it are few" (Matt. 7:13, 14, RSV).

However, the Bible teaches that there is a glorious brotherhood and Fatherhood through the Cross. "For he is our peace, who hath made both one, and hath broken down the middle wall of partition between us; having abolished in his flesh the enmity, even the law of commandments contained in ordinances; for to make in himself of twain one new man, so making peace" (Eph. 2:14, 15). Outside the work of the Cross, there is bitterness, intolerance, sedition, ill will, prejudice, lust, greed, and hatred. Within the efficacy of the Cross, there is love and fellowship, new life and new brotherhood. The only human hope for peace lies at the Cross of Christ, where all men, whatever their nationality or race, can become a new brotherhood.

Recently a university professor said: "There are two things that will never be solved, the problems of race and war." I say that these and all other problems can be solved, but only at the Cross. The Cross of Christ is not only the basis of our peace and hope; but it is also the means of our eternal salvation. The object of the Cross is not only a full and free pardon; it is also a changed life, lived in fellowship with God. No wonder Paul said two thousand years ago: "We preach Christ crucified." This is the message for the world today. This is the message of hope and peace and brotherhood. This is what the world calls foolishness but what God has been pleased to call wisdom.

13

The Day Death Died

When my wife and I were students in college, we used to take long walks into the country. Nearby was an old graveyard where we used to go to read the epitaphs on the tombstones. Ever since then, I have liked to go to old cemeteries in various parts of the world. When we wander through a graveyard and look at the tombstones or go into a church and examine the old monuments, we see one heading on most of them: "Here lies." Then follows the name, with the date of death and perhaps some praise of the good qualities of the deceased. But how different is the epitaph on the tomb of Jesus! It is neither written in gold nor cut in stone. It is spoken by the mouth of an angel and is the exact reverse of what is put on all other tombstones: "He is not here: for he is risen, as he said" (Matt. 28:6).

The most important events in human history were the death and the resurrection of Jesus Christ. The Apostle Paul said: "If Christ has not been raised, then our preaching is in vain and your faith is in vain . . . If Christ has not been raised, your faith is futile and you are still in your sins" (I Cor. 15:14, 17, RSV).

In reading about the early church, we find that the central theme of the early Christians' witness to the world was the fact that Jesus Christ, who was crucified, had been raised from the dead. We usually hear a sermon on the resurrection every Easter, and that is about all. However, in the preaching of the early Apostles, the Cross and the resurrection were their constant themes. The Cross and resurrection were linked together. Without the resurrection, the Cross is meaningless. Apart from the resurrection, the Cross was a tragedy and a defeat. If Christ's bones lie decayed in a grave, then there is no Good News, the darkness of the world is indeed black, and life has no meaning. The New Testament becomes a myth. Christianity is a fable. And millions living and dead are victims of a gigantic hoax.

At the end of his great book, *Fathers and Sons,* Ivan Turgenev describes a village graveyard in one of the remote corners of Russia. Among the many neglected graves was one untouched by man, untrampled by beast. Only the birds rested upon it and sang at daybreak. Often from the nearby village two feeble old people, husband and wife, moving with heavy steps and supporting one another, came to visit this grave. Kneeling down at the railing and gazing intently at the stone under which their son was lying, they yearned and wept. After a brief word, they wiped the dust away from the stone, set straight a branch of a fir tree, and then began to pray. In this spot they seemed to be nearer their son and their memories of him. And then Turgenev asks: "Can it be that their prayers, their tears, are fruitless? Can it be that love, sacred, devoted love, is not all powerful? Oh no, however passionate, sinning and rebellious the heart hidden in the tomb, the flowers growing over it peep serenely at us with their innocent eyes. They tell us not of eternal peace alone, of that great peace of indifferent nature; they tell us, too, of eternal reconciliation and of life without end."

Thus Turgenev was offering hope of an eternal reconciliation. But upon what is that hope based? It is based upon the resurrection of Jesus Christ.

Shall Man Live Again?

The great question of the ages has been: "If a man die, shall he live again?" We know that the first part of that sentence is fulfilled every day. There is no "if" about it. "It is appointed unto men once to die" (Heb. 9:27). The question is "Shall man live again?"

There are those who say that all there is to man is just bone, flesh, and blood. They say that when you are dead, when you die, nothing happens; you don't go anywhere. It is dust to dust and ashes to ashes.

Ask the scientist and he cannot give an answer. I have asked a number of scientists questions concerning life after death, and most of them say: "We just do not know." Science deals in formulas and test tubes, but there is a spiritual world that science knows nothing about.

Because many do not believe in life after death, their writings are filled with tragedy and pessimism. The writings of William Faulkner, James Joyce, Ernest Hemingway, Eugene O'Neill, and many others are filled with pessimism, darkness, and tragedy.

How different from Jesus Christ who said: "I am the resurrection, and the life: he that believeth in me, though he were dead, yet shall he live: and whosoever liveth and believeth in me shall never die" (Jn. 11:25, 26). Again he said: "Because I live, ye shall live also" (Jn. 14:19). And again: "Ye believe in God, believe also in me" (Jn. 14:1). Our hope of immortality is based on Christ alone—not on any desires, longings, arguments, or any instincts of immortality. Yet the hope of immortality that is revealed in Christ agrees with all those great desires and instincts. "The heart," Pascal said, "has its reasons which reason does not know."[1] In the case of the resurrection of Christ, we ·have the witness not only of the heart but of reason as well.

The Bible deals with the resurrection of Jesus as an event that could be examined by the physical senses. It involved the eyes, for the disciples saw the numerous appearances of Jesus under every conceivable condition. On one occasion He appeared to a single disciple, while at another time to more than five hundred. Some saw Jesus separately, some together. Some for a moment, and some for a long time. Some at a distance, and some close by. Some once, and some several times. The resurrection involved the ears, for the disciples heard Jesus in conversation. It involved the touch, for the disciples

---

[1] Pascal, *Pensées.*

were told to handle Jesus and thus to verify His physical reality. They not only saw Him, but they touched Him, walked with Him, conversed with Him, ate with Him, and scrutinized Him. This took the resurrection appearances of Jesus out of the realm of hallucination and put them into the realm of demonstrable physical facts.

There is a basis of historical fact for our belief in the bodily resurrection of Christ. It rests on more evidence than any event that took place in that time.

Historical Evidences of Christ's Resurrection

1. THE ACTUAL DEATH OF JESUS

There are those who say that Jesus did not actually die, but that He only fainted. A resurrection presupposes a death. In order to be raised from the dead, Jesus had to die. This is a self-evident fact deduced from the crucifixion. The soldiers were certain that Jesus was dead and that they did not need to induce death by shock by breaking His legs, as in the cases of the two thieves. It was the enemies, not the friends of Jesus, who attested his death, and they made certain when they thrust a spear into His heart.

2. THE PHYSICAL BURIAL OF JESUS

The body of Jesus was wrapped in fine linen with spices, according to the local custom. An actual tomb was involved, which required the placing of a body. Moreover, a stone was rolled against the face of the tomb, a seal was placed upon it, and a Roman guard set before it. This burial of the body of Jesus eliminates the possibility of burying a spirit. Spirits are immaterial and cannot be buried. The body of Jesus was physical and material.

It was not only buried so that it occupied space in a tomb, but it was buried for three days. This could not have been true of a spirit, for spirits occupy neither time nor space.

3. THE EMPTY TOMB

When the disciples saw the tomb in which they had previously buried the body of Jesus, it was empty. The burial garments were in such shape and place as to indicate their abandonment by the orderly departure of the body of Jesus. When Jesus later appeared to His disciples, it was in a body, for He said: "A spirit hath not flesh and bones, as ye see me have" (Lk. 24:39). His resurrection body occupied space and performed the functions of movement, appearance, and the eating of food. He talked and heard. He occupied a room but did not need a door for access. It was the same body, in its glorified resurrection form, that Jesus took from the tomb, leaving it empty and without occupant.

4. THE BODILY RESURRECTION

There were thirteen different appearances of Jesus under every conceivable condition and circumstance. Unlike hallucinations, which can continue to occur, the appearances of Jesus ceased, for they ended with His ascension.

Any notion that seeks to disprove the bodily resurrection of Jesus is confronted with these appearances of Jesus in His own body. It was a body both similar and dissimilar to that which was nailed to the tree. It was so similar that Mary mistook Him for the caretaker of the garden. It was so similar that it could receive food, engage in conversation, and occupy a room.

The dissimilarity was in its properties. It combined both material and immaterial properties. It could pass through closed doors or vanish. When viewed scientifically, this would not seem to be incredible. "No material substance or door or anything else is solid. There are always spaces between the molecules so that for one such body to pass through another is no more difficult to imagine than for one regiment to march through another on parade; and if a regiment contained anything like as many men as there are molecules in a door, it would probably look just as solid. Moreover

Christ's risen body, though possessing some material properties, is represented to have been spiritual as well; and the nearest approach to a spiritual substance of which we have any scientific knowledge is ether, and this also seems to combine material and immaterial properties, being in some respects more like a solid than a gas. Yet it can pass through all material substances, and this certainly prevents us from saying that it is incredible that Christ's spiritual body should pass through closed doors. Indeed for all we know, it may be one of the properties of spiritual beings that they can pass through material substances (just as X-rays can) and be generally invisible, yet be able if they wish to assume some of the properties of matter, such as becoming visible or audible. In fact, unless they were able to do this, it is hard to see how they could manifest themselves at all. And a slight alteration in the waves of light coming from a body would make it visible to the human eye, and it is out of the question to say that God, the Omnipotent One, could not produce such a change in a spiritual body. While for such a body to become tangible or to take food is not really more wonderful than for it to become visible or audible, since when once we pass the boundary between the natural and the supernatural everything is mysterious."[2]

It was in the spirit of this evidence and truth that Paul said to King Agrippa: "Why should it be thought a thing incredible with you, that God should raise the dead?" (Acts 26:8).

With a frequency that is amazing, the Bible affirms the fact of the bodily resurrection of Christ. Perhaps the most direct of all its statements is Luke's account in the book of Acts, where he reports: "To whom also he showed himself alive after his passion by many infallible proofs, being seen of them forty days" (Acts 1:3). What are we going to do with these "many infallible proofs?" Someone asked my colleague George Beverly Shea how much he knew about God. He said: "I don't

---

[2] Fathers Doyle, Chetwood, and Herzog, *The Truth of Christianity Series*, 4 vols. (New York: Benziger Brothers, Inc.), p. 245.

know much, but what I do know has changed my life." We may not be able to take all of this evidence into a scientific laboratory and prove it; but if we accept any fact of history, we must accept the fact that Jesus Christ rose from the dead.

The resurrection of Christ was not simply a postscript to the earthly life of Jesus, but it is one of a series of redemptive events that are links in a chain from eternity to eternity. These include the incarnation, the crucifixion, the resurrection, the ascension, and the return. Any missing link would destroy the chain and thus make redemption impossible.

For personal Christianity, the resurrection is all-important. There is a vital interrelation between the very existence of Christianity itself and the individual believer in the message of the Gospel. The Swiss theologian, Karl Barth, said: "Do you want to believe in the living Christ? We may believe in him only if we believe in his corporeal resurrection. This is the content of the New Testament. We are always free to reject it, but not to modify it, nor to pretend that the New Testament tells something else. We may accept or refuse the message, but we may not change it."[3]

The Resurrection Essential

1. *Christianity as a system of truth* collapses if the resurrection is rejected. That Jesus rose from the dead is one of the foundation stones of our faith. As Paul said: "If Christ be not risen, then is our preaching vain, and your faith is also vain" (I Cor. 15:14).

2. *The Gospel message*—that is, the good news of salvation—is related to a belief in the resurrection. Along with the crucifixion, it was the central theme of the apostolic preachers at the beginning of the Christian era. They proclaimed the resurrection as central in the Gospel. This is what Paul said: "Moreover, brethren, I declare unto you the gospel which I preached unto you, which also ye have received, and wherein ye stand; by

---

3 *Time*, April 20, 1962, p. 59.

which also ye are saved, if ye keep in memory what I preached unto you, unless ye have believed in vain. For I delivered unto you first of all that which I also received, how that Christ died for our sins according to the Scriptures; and that he was buried, and that he rose again the third day according to the Scriptures" (I Cor. 15:1-4).

Charles Reynolds Brown tells of a conversation between Auguste Comte, the French philosopher, and Thomas Carlyle, the Scottish essayist. Comte declared his intention of starting a new religion that would supplant entirely the religion of Christ. It was to have no mysteries, was to be as plain as the multiplication table, and its name was to be positivism. "Very good, Mr. Comte," Carlyle replied, "very good. All you will need to do will be to speak as never a man spake, and live as never a man lived, and be crucified, and rise again the third day, and get the world to believe that you are still alive. Then your religion will have a chance to get on."

3. *A personal salvation experience* is related to a belief in the resurrection. When Paul gave the formula of saving faith, it was centered in a belief in the resurrection: "If thou shalt confess with thy mouth the Lord Jesus, and shalt believe in thine heart that God hath raised him from the dead, thou shalt be saved. For with the heart man believeth unto righteousness; and with the mouth confession is made unto salvation" (Rom. 10:9,10). Whenever the argument arises that the resurrection of Jesus did not involve the reanimation of His Body, those who hold this view argue that the resurrection is resurrection from death, never from the grave. They say that Jesus immediately rose out of death into spiritual life with God. This means a spiritual but not physical resurrection. This is what many modern preachers proclaim on Easter morning when they talk about, but do not explain, the resurrection of Jesus. One minister told me recently that even when he said the Apostles' Creed he crossed his fingers. He said: "I cannot believe in the resurrection of Jesus Christ."

The New Testament Scriptures speak unanimously of eyewitnesses of the resurrected Christ. They say:

"We saw his glory"

"This Jesus hath God raised up, whereof we all are witnesses"

"You seek Jesus of Nazareth, which was crucified; he is risen"

"You will see him"

"He appeared"

"I have seen Jesus the Lord"

Within the short span of three days, both events, the death and resurrection, took place bodily and not symbolically—tangibly, not spiritually—watched by men of flesh and blood, not fabricated by hallucination. "Had the New Testament writers known of the devices of the twentieth century, they would perhaps have insisted upon the confirmation afforded by a camera, a recording machine, or a newspaper report."[4]

Jesus could have returned to heaven without a bodily resurrection. Before His incarnation, He had existed in heaven without a body and had been the source of all life. But such a return would not have been complete triumph over death. Satan would have won a partial victory.

When properly understood, death is not merely the cessation of existence. It affects the personality and its relation to the body. The body bears the sentence of death as well as the personality. The body has to be retrieved from its lost estate as well as the soul. Only by the resurrection of the body could the conquest of death be made complete. This not only involved the body of Jesus, but it will also involve the body of all those who believe. Thus we are saved ultimately from physical death, spiritual death, and eternal death. As the judgment of death was total, so salvation from its penalty is total, involving the physical, spiritual, and eternal.

This is Paul's statement: "We shall all be changed, in

---

[4]Marcus Barth and Verne H. Flesher, *Acquittal by Resurrection* (New York: Holt, Rinehart and Winston, 1963), p. 13.

a moment, in the twinkling of an eye, at the last trump: for the trumpet shall sound, and the dead shall be raised incorruptible . . . Then shall be brought to pass the saying that is written, Death is swallowed up in victory. O death, where is thy sting? O grave, where is thy victory?" (I Cor. 15:51, 52, 54, 55).

The resurrection was the confirmation of the nature and ministry of Jesus, who was "declared to be the Son of God with power, according to the Spirit of holiness, by the resurrection from the dead" (Rom. 1:4). The resurrection was also the pledge and promise of our own resurrection. "For if we believe that Jesus died and rose again, even so them also which sleep in Jesus will God bring with him" (I Thess. 4:14). "But now is Christ risen from the dead, and become the firstfruits of them that slept" (I Cor. 15:20).

Furthermore, Jesus staked the validity of all His claims and the reality of all His works upon His resurrection. Everything hinged upon His rising from the dead. By this He would be judged true or false.

What Does the Resurrection Mean to Us?

1. *It means the presence of the living Christ.* Christ is the living companion of every person who puts his trust in Him. He said: "Lo, I am with you alway, even unto the end of the world" (Matt. 28:20). He is the guarantee that life has a new meaning. After the crucifixion, the disappointed disciples despaired and said: "We had hoped that he was the one to redeem Israel" (Lk. 24:21, RSV). There was anguish, despair, and tragedy in their midst. Life had lost its meaning and purpose. But when the resurrection became apparent, life took on a new meaning. It had purpose and reason.

David Livingstone once addressed a group of students at Glasgow University. When he rose to speak, he bore on his body the marks of his African struggles. Severe illnesses on nearly thirty occasions had left him gaunt and haggard. His left arm, crushed by a lion, hung limp at his side. After describing his trials and tribulations, he said: "Would you like me to tell you what supported me through all the years of exile among people whose language I could not understand and whose attitude toward me was always uncertain and often hostile? It was this: 'Lo, I am with you alway, even unto the end of the world.' On these words I staked everything, and they never failed."

2. *The prayers of the living Christ.* The Scripture says: "It is Christ that died, yea rather, that is risen again, who is even at the right hand of God, who also maketh intercession for us" (Rom. 8:34). In other words, there is a Man at the right hand of God the Father. He is living in a body that still has the nail prints in His hands. He is interceding for us with God the Father as our great High Priest.

3. *The power of the living Christ.* The resurrection made it possible for Christ to be identified with all Christians in all ages and to give them power to serve Him. "Verily, verily, I say unto you, He that believeth on me, the works that I do shall he do also; and greater works than these shall he do; because I go unto my Father" (Jn. 14:12). Paul even prayed: "That I may know him, and the power of his resurrection" (Phil. 3:10). His resurrection presence gives us strength and power for each day's task.

4. *The pattern of our new bodies.* The resurrected body of Jesus Christ is the pattern of what our bodies will be when we too are raised from the dead. "For our conversation is in heaven; from whence also we look for the Saviour, the Lord Jesus Christ: who shall change our vile body, that it may be fashioned like unto his glorious body, according to the working whereby he is able even to subdue all things unto himself" (Phil. 3:20, 21).

5. *The promise of a returning Redeemer.* The entire plan for the future has its key in the resurrection. Unless Christ is raised from the dead, there can be no kingdom and no returning King. When the disciples stood at the place of the ascension, they were given angelic assurance that the Christ of resurrection would be the Christ of returning glory. "Ye men of Galilee,

why stand ye gazing up into heaven? this same Jesus, which is taken up from you into heaven, shall so come in like manner as ye have seen him go into heaven" (Acts 1:11). Thus the resurrection is an event that was both preparatory for and confirmative of a future event, even His second coming.[5]

Yes, our leader Jesus Christ is alive.

When I was in Russia, I heard a story about a Russian village. After the Bolshevik revolution, the local Communist leader had been sent to tell the people the virtues of Communism and to take their minds away from religion, which Karl Marx called "the opium of the people." After the Communist had harangued them for a long time, he said to the local Christian pastor rather contemptuously: "I will give you five minutes to reply." The pastor replied: "I do not need five minutes, only five seconds." He rose to the platform and gave the Easter greeting: "The Lord is risen!" As one man, the villagers thundered back: "He is risen indeed!"

---

[5] Ibid.

14

The Possibility of the New Man

Aldous Huxley, in his *Brave New World,* devised a drug called "soma," which was intended to take all the rough edges from life. There is no doubt that if mankind is to be saved, something radical needs to be done quickly. Man stands on the brink of hell. The forces building up in our world are so overwhelming that man everywhere is beginning to cry out in desperation: "What must I do to be saved?"

Everything in our world seems to improve but man. In his essential moral nature, which governs his relationship to his fellow man, he steals, murders, lies, cheats, and grabs. Since the beginning of time, he has remained essentially unchanged. The newspaper accounts of murder, rape, and brutality indicate that somewhere we have failed. After years of psychological study, Carl Jung said: "All the old primitive sins are not dead but are crouching in the dark corners of our modern hearts . . . still there, and still ghastly as ever."

Man is being forced to accept the reality of sin and the necessity of a new birth. Walter Lippmann said: "We ourselves were so pure that at long last a generation had arisen, keen and eager, to put this disorderly earth to right . . . and fit to do it . . . we meant so well, we tried so hard, and look what we have made of it. We can only muddle into muddle. What is required is a new kind of man." The great Danish philosopher Kierkegaard wrote a book entitled *The Sickness unto Death* in which he said: "Man is born and lives in sin. He cannot do anything for himself but can only do harm to himself."

We are beginning to recognize the inability of man, over the centuries of futile religious, cultural, moral, and educational efforts, to change his own heart. Man has labored ineffectually to achieve his moral goals and change himself by the improvement of his environment. Now we are disillusioned and know that somehow the change must come from within.

Man's Attempts to Change Himself

At present, man is experimenting in what are called the behavioral sciences, including anthropology, psychology, and sociology, in order to discover the laws of human behavior. The trouble with these experiments is that they ignore the fact of human sin. According to the new sciences, sin is largely imaginary. Man is the product of his environment. He is the happy or unhappy product of a combination of genes and chromosomes. In this pseudoscientific sentimentality, a juvenile delinquent is merely underprivileged and a robber is simply maladjusted. In this philosophy, we abandon the idea of sin and individual responsibility and blame everything but the offender. Therefore we have nothing to cure but man's environment in terms of bad housing, slums, poverty, unemployment, and racial discrimination, while the prime suspect, the individual, remains untouched and unchanged. Man himself and his behavior, according to this new science, are considered to be the result of natural selection.

Then there is man's attempt to change himself by chemistry. Scientists at present are deeply involved in the control of behavior by pharmacological agents. We are on the verge of a vast development of drugs to control man's behavior. At first, these drugs will be used only in mental illness, but there always lurks the possibility that world dictators may use them to control entire segments of society. These are the drugs "that shape men's minds," for "with new devices scientists are finding out how to manipulate your emotions, your thoughts, and your behavior." These drugs "change minds, alter sensations, perceptions, moods, desires, ways of thinking, and acting."[1]

Professor B. F. Skinner of Harvard University said: "We are entering the age of the chemical control of human behavior. The motivational and emotional conditions of normal daily life probably will be maintained in any desired state through the use of drugs." At best, however, such drugs will provide only temporary changes either for better or worse, depending upon the nature of the administrator, with probable permanent damage to the brain.

The New Birth

Jesus Christ demanded: "Ye must be born again" (Jn. 3:7). He would never have given such a challenge, had it not been a possibility. Yes, man can be changed, radically and permanently. Here only is the possibility of a completely new man.

It is interesting that Jesus made this statement concerning being born again to Nicodemus, an upright and devout religious leader, who must have been stunned by it. If Christ had said this to Zacchaeus, who had cheated his way to the top of his own financial world—or to. the woman at the well, who had had several husbands—or to the thief on the cross—or to the woman taken in adultery, it would have been easier to understand. We know that those persons needed changing. But Jesus said this to one of the great religious leaders of His time. Nicodemus fasted two days a week, spent two hours daily in prayer at the temple, tithed all his income, taught as a professor of theology at the seminary. Most churches would have been glad to have him; but Jesus said: "It is not enough. You must be born again." This implies that all men need the new birth, and it also implies that all men can be born again.

Dr. Wilbur M. Smith in a recent volume of *Peloubet's Select Notes* has given the following specific

---

[1]Gordon Wolstenholme, ed., *Man and His Future*, p. 275.

analysis of some aspects of the new birth: "What do we mean by a man being born anew, or born again? To begin with, it means something tremendously radical. What we are by nature we are because of what we were when born. At birth our sex is settled, the very frame of our body is already determined. No doubt our very temperament, our capacities, our habits, our inclinations, are all given to us at birth, at least fundamentally; indeed, our very appearance. To be born again at least implies an absolutely new beginning, not a reformation of life, not a turning over of a new leaf, not the addition of some one new attribute or aspect or capacity, but something so radical that by it we are going to be something altogether different from what we have been. Of course, anyone knows that we cannot be born the second time physically. Therefore the reference here is spiritual, a rebirth not of body, but of soul, and mind, and character. Again, we should notice . . . the universal inclusiveness and absolute necessity for such a miracle as this, if one is to be a member of the kingdom of God. No one is excepted, and no one can substitute something else for this tremendous reality."

To its own shame and to the detriment of society, the modern church has to a large extent abandoned this message of the new birth. It preaches social change, disarmament, and legislation; but it does not major in the one thing that will solve the problems of our world —changed men. Man's basic problem is spiritual, not social. Man needs a complete change from within.

The Bible refers many times to this change about which Jesus talked. The prophet Ezekiel said: "A new heart also will I give you, and a new spirit will I put within you" (Ezek. 36:26). In the book of Acts, Peter called it repenting and being converted; Paul speaks of it in Romans as being "alive from the dead" (Rom. 6:13). In Colossians, Paul calls it "[a putting off of] the old man with his deeds; and [putting] on the new man, which is renewed in knowledge after the image of him that created him" (Col. 3:9, 10). In Titus, he calls it "the washing of regeneration, and renewing of the Holy Ghost" (Tit. 3:5). Peter said it was being "partakers of the divine nature" (II Pet. 1:4). John termed it passing "from death unto life" (Jn. 5:24). In the Church of England catechism, it is called "a death unto sin and a new birth unto righteousness."

Thus the Bible teaches that man can undergo a radical spiritual and moral change that is brought about by God Himself. The word that Jesus used, and which is translated "again," actually means "from above." The context of the third chapter of John teaches that the new birth is something that God does for man when man is willing to yield to God. As we have already seen, the Bible teaches that man is dead in trespasses and sins, and his great need is LIFE. Man does not have within himself the seed of the new life; this must come from God Himself.

One day a caterpillar climbs up into a tree where nature throws a fiber robe about him. He goes to sleep and in a few weeks he emerges a beautiful butterfly. So man—distressed, discouraged, unhappy, hounded by conscience, driven by passion, ruled by selfishness, belligerent, quarrelsome, confused, depressed, miserable, taking alcohol and barbiturates, looking for escapisms—can come to Christ by faith and emerge a new man. This sounds incredible, even impossible, and yet it is precisely what the Bible teaches.

More Than Reformation

This new birth is far more than reformation. Many persons make New Year's resolutions only to break them because they do not have the capacity to keep them. Man is ever reforming, but reformation at best is only temporary. Man's nature must be transformed.

A group of barbers at their annual convention decided to exhibit the value of their tonsorial art. They found a derelict on skid row, gave him a haircut, shave, and a bath; and they dressed him in new clothes of the finest tailoring. They had demonstrated to their satisfaction the worth of tonsorial excellence, but three days later the man was in the gutter again. He had been outwardly transformed into a respectable-looking man, but the impulses and drives of his inner being had not been changed. He had been powdered and perfumed, but not changed.

You can scrub a pig, sprinkle Chanel No. 5 on him, put a ribbon around his neck, and take him into your living room. But when you turn him loose, he will jump into the first mud puddle he sees because his nature has never been changed. He is still a pig.

Through the new birth, the Bible teaches that man enters a new world. There is a new dimension of living. The change that comes over a man is expressed in the Bible by various contrasts: lust and holiness, darkness and light, death and resurrection, a stranger to the Kingdom of God and now a citizen. The man who has experienced the new birth is called a member of God's household. The Bible teaches that his will is changed, his objectives for living are changed, his disposition is changed, his affections are changed, and he now has purpose and meaning in his life. In the new birth, a new life has been born in his soul. He receives a new nature and a new heart. He becomes a new creation.

Nicodemus was puzzled by these statements of Christ, and he asked: "Can I enter into my mother's womb and be born the second time?" This was a natural response any one of us would have made. So much of what Nicodemus believed had been swept away. He was finding out that religion was not sufficient. The Law of Moses could not save him, because he was not really fulfilling its requirements. He had to be born from above. He was told that no one could enter the Kingdom of Heaven without having eternal life, for nothing but "God-life" can exist there. He who has that life will be admitted. The great question is: Do I possess eternal life? If not, how do I get it? This is the most important question a man can ask or have answered.

The Bible tells of many men who have been changed by an encounter with Jesus Christ. There is the demoniac whose chains could not hold against the power of his seizures, but when he met Jesus he was changed, and later was found in his home "clothed and in his right mind." No longer was he the prey of hallucinations.

No longer was he in the grip of Satanic power. No longer had he the fears that had constantly beset him. No longer was he a menace to the community. He had become a changed man in character, dress, conduct, and even in environment (Lk. 8).

There is Zacchaeus, who defrauded the people as a tax-gatherer. When he met Jesus, all was changed. He proceeded to make restitution. "The half of my goods I give to the poor; and if I have taken any thing from any man by false accusation, I restore him fourfold" (Lk. 19:8).

Most of these encounters with Christ resulted in an instantaneous transformation. On the day of Pentecost there were three thousand who were born again that very day. In the morning they were lost, confused, and sinful. Before the day had ended, they had been born into the Kingdom of God. Each one had passed out of death into life (Acts 2:41).

A young man named Saul was on the road to Damascus to persecute Christians when he met Christ under the hot Syrian sun. He was never to be the same again. Over and over, he referred back to that encounter. He was able to look back and speak about it years later, remembering the very day and the very moment when he met Christ (Acts 9, 22, 26).

The Philippian jailer had a similar experience. When he was gripped by fear, he cried out: "What must I do to be saved?" The Apostle Paul told him: "Believe on the Lord Jesus Christ and thou shalt be saved." Many modern psychiatrists might say that he was in no emotional state to make a permanent decision. Paul did not look at it that way, and he baptized the jailer that very night. The jailer then began to wash their wounds as a token of the new life he had received from God (Acts 16).

Any person who is willing to trust Jesus Christ as his personal Savior can receive the new birth now. The early Methodist preachers were called the "now preachers" because they offered salvation on the spot. It is not something to be received at death or after death; it is to be received now. "Now is the accepted time; behold, now is the day of salvation" (II Cor. 6:2). God offers eternal life to anyone who will receive it.

Suppose I offer a gift to you. There is a moment when you do not have it, and the next moment you do have it. Eternal life is a gift from God. There is a time when you do not possess it, and there is a time when you do possess it. There must be a moment when you accept it.

Joan Winmill, a young actress on the London stage, had everything and yet nothing. She was like thousands of professional people today who have talent, money, and success—but a life of emptiness. She had reached the place of considering suicide when out of curiosity she came to an evangelistic Crusade in Harringay Arena. When the invitation was given to receive Christ, hardly knowing what she was doing, she responded and received new life. She became a completely new woman, and today she is one of the most radiant Christians I have ever known. She has purpose and meaning in her life.

Jim Vaus was Mickey Cohen's wiretapper and a leader in the underworld on the West Coast. Somehow he wandered into a tent where an evangelistic meeting was being held in Los Angeles. He responded to the appeal to give himself to Christ, Who so completely changed Jim Vaus that he has become one of the great religious and social workers of our time.

I could recount countless illustrations of men and women who have encountered Jesus Christ. They have become new creations. Their whole lives have been transformed. They have entered a new dimension of life. They have been born from above. God's nature has been imparted to them. Where once they were filled with lust, greed, and selfishness, they now seek to glorify God by helping their neighbors.

Yes, man can regain paradise. He lost it in the Garden of Eden, but he can find it again through Jesus Christ. If enough men and women had this new life, it could change the world in which we live! This is the only hope, the only remedy. There is no other. Man must undergo a complete renovation from above.

15

How to Become a New Man

Some time ago, during a question-and-answer session at Harvard Divinity School, a student stood up and asked me: "Can you tell me in plain and clear language what I must do to be saved?"

Over and over again, I am asked that question at colleges and universities where I often lecture. Can the alcoholic, the thief, the murderer, the sex pervert be changed radically and made a new man? At a West Coast university, a professor of science came to see me in my room at the Student Union, and he said: "You are going to be amazed at the ultimate question I am here to ask you." Then he told me a long story of his own inward struggle in moral, spiritual, and intellectual issues. "More and more," he said, "I have come to realize that my problem with Christianity is really not intellectual at all. It is moral. I have not been willing to meet the moral requirements of Christianity." And he added: "Here is my question: What can I do to receive Jesus Christ?"

When the governor of one of our states entertained us in his home, he asked to talk to me privately. We went into a back room, where he locked the door. I could see that he was struggling with his emotions, but finally he said to me: "I am at the end of my rope. I need God. Can you tell me how to find God?"

On another occasion when I visited a group of men on death row in a prison, a strong and intelligent-looking man listened to what I had to say. Then I asked the men if they would be willing to kneel down while I prayed. Just before we knelt there, the man said: "Can you explain once again what I must do to be forgiven of my sins? I want to know that I am going to heaven."

These are precisely the same questions asked of Jesus Christ nearly two thousand years ago. These are the same questions asked of the Apostles as they proclaimed the Gospel throughout the Roman Empire. The questions indicate that man's inward spiritual longings have changed very little.

The rich young ruler came running to kneel before Christ, and asked Him: "Good Master, what shall I do that I may inherit eternal life?" (Mk. 10:17). After Peter preached his great sermon at Pentecost, the Bible says that the people were "pricked in their heart, and said unto Peter . . . 'What shall we do?'" (Acts 2:37). The African nobleman riding in his chariot across the desert talked with Philip the evangelist. Suddenly the nobleman stopped his chariot and said: "What doth hinder me?" (Acts 8:36). At midnight the Philippian jailer asked Paul and Silas: "Sirs, what must I do to be saved?" (Acts 16:30).

Twentieth-century man asks the same question that man has always asked. It is old, but it is ever new. It is just as relevant today as in the past.

Just what must one do to be reconciled to God? What does the Bible mean by such words as conversion, repentance, and faith? These are all salvation words, but so little understood.

Jesus made everything so simple and we have made it so complicated. He spoke to the people in short sentences and everyday words, illustrating His messages with never-to-be-forgotten stories. He presented the message of God in such simplicity that many could not understand what He said.

In the book of Acts the Philippian jailer asked the Apostle Paul: "What must I do to be saved?" Paul gave him a very simple answer: "Believe on the Lord Jesus Christ, and thou shalt be saved" (Acts 16:30, 31). This is so simple that millions stumble over it. The one and only way by which you can be converted is your choosing to believe on the Lord Jesus as your own personal Lord and Savior. You don't have to straighten out your life first. You don't have to make things right at home or in your business first. You don't have to try to give up some habit that is keeping you from God. You have tried all that and failed many times. In our Crusades when I give the invitation to receive Christ, we sing the hymn entitled "Just As I Am," and you come to Christ just as you are. The blind man came as he was. The leper came as he was. Mary Magdalene with seven devils came as she was. The thief on the cross came as he was. You can come to Christ just as you are.

Conversion

The word "conversion" means simply "turning." From the beginning of the Bible to the end, God pleads with man to turn to Him (Prov. 1:23; Isa. 31:6; 59:20; Ezek. 14:6; 18:32; 33:9; Joel 2:12; Matt. 18:3; Acts 3:19). However, it is impossible for man to turn to God or to repent, or even to believe, without God's help! All you can do is call upon God to "turn" you. Many times in the Bible it is recorded that men did that very thing (Ps. 85:4; Song of Sol. 1:4; Jer. 31:18; Lam. 5:21). When a man calls upon God, he is given true repentance and faith. That is why the Apostle Paul could say: "Whosoever shall call upon the name of the Lord shall be saved" (Rom. 10:13). The Bible never asks man to justify himself, to regenerate himself, to convert himself, or to save himself. God alone can do these things.

There are at least *two elements in conversion— repentance* and *faith.* Jesus said: "Except ye repent, ye shall . . . perish" (Lk. 13:3). Repentance carries with it a recognition of sin involving personal guilt and defilement before God. It does not mean a cringing self-contempt. It is a simple recognition of what we are. We see ourselves as God sees us, and we say "God be merciful to me a sinner" (Lk. 18:13). Job said: "I have heard of thee by the hearing of the ear; but now mine eye seeth thee. Wherefore I abhor myself, and repent in dust and ashes" (Job 42:5, 6).

Repentance

Repentance means also a change of feeling. This means a genuine sorrow for sin committed against God (Ps. 51). As Paul said in II Corinthians 7:9, 10: "Now I rejoice, not that ye were made sorry, but that ye sorrowed to repentance . . . for godly sorrow worketh repentance to salvation."

Repentance means also a change of purpose, and carries with it the idea of an inward turning from sin by the exercise of the will. However, all you have to do is to be willing. God will help you.

In the Middle Ages, the master of an estate in England lay dying. He called to him a servant, whom he knew to be a devout Christian, and said: "Jim, I am dying. I am not sure that I am going to Heaven. Can you tell me what I must do?"

The wise old servant knew the pride of his master, and he said: "Sir, if you want to be saved, you will have to go to the pigpen, get on your knees in the mud, and say, 'God be merciful to me a sinner.'"

The master said: "I could not possibly do that. What would the neighbors and servants think?"

A week passed and he called his servant back and said: "Jim, what did you say I had to do to be saved?" The old servant replied: "Sir, you will have to go to the pigpen." The master said: "I have been thinking it over, Jim, and I am ready to go."

The servant then said: "Master, you don't really have to go to the pigpen. You just have to be willing."

We have to be willing. Many persons have strange ideas about repentance. Some think of the old mourners' bench, and it might not be such a bad idea to get back to the mourners' bench. A Beverly Hills, California, psychologist said recently: "What many people need is an experience at an old Methodist mourners' bench." Repentance can be one of the most glorious experiences you will ever have.

Repentance is the launching pad where the soul is sent on its eternal orbit with God at the center of the arc. When our hearts are bowed as low as they can get, and we truly acknowledge and forsake our sins, then God takes over and like the second stage of a rocket, He lifts us toward His Kingdom. The way up is down. Man got into difficulty when he lifted his will against God's. He gets out of trouble when he bows to the divine superiority, when he repents and says humbly: "God be merciful to me a sinner." Man's extremity then becomes God's opportunity.

The psychiatrist realizes that there are curative powers in confession. "Relax and tell me all about yourself," he says to his patient. The psychology of this method is to have the patient tell so much about himself that he finally unravels the strands that bind him. There is, no doubt, much value in gettings things off your chest, in revealing your innermost thoughts to some neutral person. But Biblical repentance goes much deeper than this. Granted that the psychiatrists' technique can discover the psychological difficulty within the personality, but where do they go from there? It is not enough to locate the flaw in the subconscious. Sin is a disease of the soul, and Christ is the only Physician who can provide the cure. There are difficulties, burdens, and guilts beyond the ability of the psychiatrist or any other physician. Repentance becomes the key, and forgiveness the gateway to the Kingdom of God.

Faith

The second element in conversion is *faith*. In order to be converted, you must make a choice. The Scripture says: "He that believeth on him is not condemned: but he that believeth not is condemned already, because he hath not believed in the name of the only begotten Son of God" (Jn. 3:18). Now, who is it that is not condemned? It is he that believes. And who is condemned already? It is he that does not believe. Then what must you do in order to be "not condemned"? The answer is simple. You must believe.

Now, of course, we must understand what this word "believe" implies. It means "commit" and "surrender."

teaches that without faith it is impossible to ...od. The Bible says: "He that cometh to God ...elieve that he is, and that he is a rewarder of the.. that diligently seek him" (Heb. 11:6). Believing is your response to God's offer of mercy, love, and forgiveness. God took the initiative. Salvation is all of God. When Christ bowed His head on the Cross and said, "It is finished," He meant just that (Jn. 19:30). God's plan for our reconciliation and redemption was completed in His Son. However, man must respond by receiving and trusting.

Faith is described in the Bible as "the substance of things hoped for, the evidence of things not seen" (Heb. 11:1). Faith is not just hanging on. It is laying hold of Christ, for Christ is the object of our faith. It is not simply a subjective feeling, but an objective act.

The two words "belief" and "faith" are translated from the same Greek word in the New Testament, and it is a word that is never used in the New Testament in the plural. Christian faith does not mean believing in a number of things; it means a single, individual disposition of mind and heart toward Jesus Christ.

The most obvious thing about saving faith is that *it believes something*. It does not believe everything or just anything. It is belief in a person, and that person is Christ. Neither is faith antagonistic to reason or knowledge. Faith is not anti-intellectual. It is an act of man that reaches beyond the limits of our five senses. It is the recognition that God is greater than man. It is the recognition that God has provided a way of reconciliation that we could not provide through self-effort.

The psychiatrist tells us that before he can be of any help to his patient, the patient must come to him sincerely, asking for help and yielding to his guidance. The patient cannot be coerced or forced. Spiritually, this is just as true with faith.

Commitment

Faith is also commitment. Leighton Ford has said: "Belief is not faith without evidence but commitment without reservation." Belief involves the intellect. Desire involves the emotions. Commitment involves the will. Thus the whole man is involved in an act of proper faith. Faith is actually what we know, how we feel, and what we do about Jesus Christ. Thus faith becomes action, and the action is faith as commitment.

Dr. Ernest White points out that the first movement to be discerned in the process of conversion is conviction. This is done by the Holy Spirit. This will probably involve a period of conflict, the type of conflict to depend largely upon the environment and temperament of the individual. Not all pass through the same kind of experience in the process of conversion. Some persons, with what the psychologists describe as a pronounced superego or hypersensitive conscience, suffer extended periods of self-accusation and self-condemnation.

John Bunyan was such an individual, who passed through many weeks during which he heard condemning voices. In this period of fear and depression, he had an intense longing to be accepted of Christ and to find peace and forgiveness. St. Augustine had a similar experience during his long period of conviction of sin.

On the other hand, there are those who have a much quieter conversion when they accept some statement of Scripture, or receive and apply to themselves some sermon without any great stress or conflict. Conversion is no less real to these quiet people than to the more volatile ones.

In the sixteenth chapter of Acts, there is the account of the conversion of two persons. One was Lydia, a businesswoman of the city of Thyatira. She was a worshiper of God and went for prayer to the riverside, where she heard Paul preach. She opened her heart, believed, and was converted without struggle or conflict. The other was the Philippian jailer whom we have already mentioned. He was thrown into panic when an earthquake put some of his prisoners into a position to escape. He saw that the prison doors were open, drew out his sword to kill himself, and then heard the Apostle Paul's reassuring words. The jailer called for a light and sprang in trembling, to fall down before Paul and Silas.

He asked: "Sirs, what must I do to be saved?" He heard from Paul the Gospel, with the instruction to believe and he rejoiced, believing in God. Here were drama, excitement, and crisis.

Emotion

With some persons, there may be in conversion an emotional crisis, the symptoms of which are similar to those of mental conflict. There may be deep feeling and outbursts of tears and anxiety. There may be none of these things. There are those who experience little, if any, emotion. They accept salvation without any particular crisis of mind or emotion. They cannot, in fact, specify any definite time when they first entered into their knowledge of Christ. My wife is one of the finest Christians I have ever known, but she cannot pinpoint the moment of her conversion. Yet she is sure of her conversion because she knows Christ personally in the reality of daily life and service, and she has the joy of the Lord.

When Jesus described the new birth to intellectual, dignified Nicodemus, He said: "The wind bloweth where it listeth, and thou hearest the sound thereof, but canst not tell whence it cometh, and whither it goeth: so is every one that is born of the Spirit" (Jn. 3:8). Jesus said it was like the movement of the wind, which sometimes is as imperceptible as a zephyr and at other times as revolutionary as a cyclone. Conversion is like that, too—sometimes quiet and tender, sometimes uprooting and rearranging the life under great emotional manifestation.

An Act of the Will

There is also volitional resolution. The will is necessarily involved in conversion. People can pass through mental conflicts and emotional crises without being converted. Not until they exercise the prerogative of a free moral agent and will to be converted are they actually converted. This act of will is an act of acceptance and commitment. They willingly accept God's mercy and receive God's Son and then commit themselves to do God's will. In every true conversion the will of man comes into line with the will of God. Almost the last word of the Bible is this invitation: "And whosoever will, let him take the water of life freely" (Rev. 22:17). It is up to you. You must will to be saved. It is God's will, but it must become your will, too.

Every week I receive scores of letters from those who say they have doubts and uncertainties concerning the Christian life. They wonder if they are Christians. They are not sure they have been converted. They think perhaps they have, but they have little of the joy of the Christian faith. Particularly is this true of those who did not have a crisis experience at the time of their conversion. At the turn of the century, Professor Edwin Starbuck, a leader in the field of psychology, observed that Christian workers generally were recruited from the ranks of those who had had a vital, dramatic conversion. In other words, they had a clear concept of what it means to be converted. They had experienced it.

Much of the philosophy of modern religious education has been based on the idea that a person can become a Christian by a process of education. Therefore, we have herded into the church tens of thousands of people who have never had a personal encounter with Jesus Christ. Great numbers of so-called Christians have missed this "encounter experience" with Christ, having had in its place only religious training.

Rarely do we conduct a Crusade without having some seminary students or even pastors make a profession of conversion. In one recent Crusade sixteen clergymen came forward to receive Jesus Christ as Savior. Many of these men had been trained theologically, but some of them had never had a genuine encounter with the person of Christ. To one of the most religious men of His day, Jesus said: "Ye must be born again" (Jn. 3:7). Nicodemus could not substitute his profound knowledge of religion for spiritual rebirth, and neither can we.

I have read a book on water skiing, and it did not take long for me to learn that I could never learn to water ski by reading a book—I would have to experience it. I have read a number of books on golf, but none of them seems to improve my game. I must get out on the golf course and play. You may study theology and religion, but there comes a time when you must experience Christ for yourself.

The ugly larva in its cocoon spends months in almost unnoticeable growth and change; but no matter how great that growth may be, there comes a moment when it passes through a crisis and emerges a butterfly. The weeks of silent growth are important, but they cannot take the place of that experience when the old and the ugly are left behind, and the new and the beautiful come into being.

It is true that there are multitudes of Christians whose lives and faith testify that consciously or unconsciously they have been converted to Christ. They may not know the exact hour. It is my opinion, however, that this may be the exception rather than the rule. Whether they can remember the time or not, there was a moment when they crossed over the line from death to life. You cannot tell the exact moment when night becomes day, but you know when it is daylight.

Dr. Donald Grey Barnhouse once said: "It is not presumption for me to say that I am just as sure that I shall be in Heaven as I am sure Jesus Christ will be there. If any percentage of my doings had a part in it, then it would be presumption; but when I say that my doings, the 2 percent or the 50 percent or the 80 percent . . . are all set aside, and God's 100 percent of righteousness is my salvation, then surely boasting is excluded." As Paul wrote: "Where is boasting then? It is excluded. By what law? of works? Nay; but by the law of faith" (Rom. 3:27).

Assurance

There are three ways that I may know that I have eternal life: objectively, because God's Word says it;

subjectively, because of the witness of the Spirit within; and experimentally, because little by little as time goes on I can see the experimental working of God in my life. It is a slower process than I would like, but it is a process. Therefore I can say: "I know."

How to Receive Christ

The question that comes to many minds is this: Just what must I do actually to receive Christ? I wish it were possible for me to wrap it up in a neat little formula and hand it to you, but that is impossible. As I have already suggested, each person's experience is different from all others. Just as there are no two snowflakes alike, there are no two experiences with Christ exactly the same. However, there are certain guidelines in the Bible that will help to guide you to accept Jesus Christ as your Savior. Therefore, let me summarize what you must do.

First, you must recognize that God loved you so much that He gave His Son to die on the Cross. "For God so loved the world, that he gave his only begotten Son, that whosoever believeth in him should not perish, but have everlasting life" (Jn. 3:16). "The Son of God . . . loved me, and gave himself for me" (Gal. 2:20).

Second, you must repent of your sins. Jesus said: "Except ye repent, ye shall . . . perish" (Lk. 13:3). He said: "Repent . . . and believe" (Mk. 1:15). As John Stott, pastor of All Souls Church in London, wrote: "The faith which receives Christ must be accompanied by the repentance which rejects sin." Repentance does not mean simply that you are to be sorry for the past. To be sorry is not enough; you must repent. This means that you must turn your back on your sins.

Third, you must receive Jesus Christ as Savior and Lord. "But as many as received him, to them gave he power to become the sons of God, even to them that believe on his name" (Jn. 1:12). This means that you accept God's offer of love, mercy, and forgiveness. This means that you accept Jesus Christ as your only Lord and your only Savior. This means that you cease struggling and trying to save yourself. You trust Him completely, without reservation, as your Lord and Savior.

Fourth, you must confess Christ publicly. Jesus said: "Whosoever therefore shall confess me before men, him will I confess also before my Father which is in heaven" (Matt. 10:32). This confession carries with it the idea of a life so lived in front of your fellowmen that they will see a difference. It means also that you acknowledge with your mouth the Lord Jesus. "If thou shalt confess with thy mouth the Lord Jesus, and shalt believe in thine heart that God hath raised him from the dead, thou shalt be saved" (Rom. 10:9). It is extremely important that when you receive Christ you tell someone else about it just as soon as possible. This gives you strength and courage to witness.

It is important that you make your decision and your commitment to Christ now. "Now is the accepted time . . . now is the day of salvation" (II Cor. 6:2). If you are willing to repent of your sins and to receive Jesus Christ as your Savior, you can do it now. At this moment you can either bow your head or get on your knees and say this little prayer that I have used with thousands of persons on every continent:

O God, I acknowledge that I have sinned against Thee. I am sorry for my sins. I am willing to turn from my sins. I openly receive and acknowledge Jesus Christ as my Savior. I confess Him as Lord. From this moment on I want to live for Him and serve Him. In Jesus' name, Amen.

If you are willing to make this decision, if you have to the best of your knowledge received Jesus Christ, God's Son, as your own Savior, then according to the preceding statements of Scripture, you have become a child of God in whom Jesus Christ dwells. Altogether too many people make the mistake of measuring the certainty of their salvation by their feelings. Don't make this serious mistake. Believe God. Take Him at His word.

16

The Dynamics of the New Man

In the third century, Cyprian, the Bishop of Carthage, wrote to his friend Donatus: "It is a bad world, Donatus, an incredibly bad world. But I have discovered in the midst of it a quiet and holy people who have learned a great secret. They have found a joy which is a thousand times better than any of the pleasures of our sinful life. They are despised and persecuted, but they care not. They are masters of their souls. They have overcome the world. These people, Donatus, are Christians . . . and I am one of them."

If you have repented of your sins and have received Christ as Savior, then you, too, are one of them.

Forgiven and Justified

The moment you were converted to Christ, several dramatic things happened, whether you were aware of them or not. *First, your sin was forgiven.* "In whom we have redemption through his blood, even the forgiveness of sins" (Col. 1:14). "Your sins are forgiven you for his name's sake" (I Jn. 2:12). Through the New Testament we are told that the one who receives Christ as Savior also receives immediately, as a gift from God, the forgiveness of sin. The Bible says: "As far as the east is from the west, so far hath he removed our transgressions from us" (Ps. 103:12). The only reason our sins can be forgiven is, of course, because Jesus Christ paid the full penalty for our sins on the Cross. He was "delivered for our offenses" (Rom. 4:25).

149

However, God's forgiveness goes much farther than the forgiveness of sin. God not only forgives, He justifies. This means that man is actually without guilt in God's sight. As someone has said: "I am justified, and it is just-as-if-I'd-never-sinned." My secretary often uses an erasable bond, a chemically treated paper from which errors can be erased without blemish. God treats our hearts with the chemistry of His grace and erases the errors so that we are without spot and without blemish in His sight.

Every person who puts his trust in Jesus Christ stands guiltless before God. He is cleared of every charge. It is not a matter of feeling; it is a fact. You can apply Galatians 2:16 to yourself: "Knowing that a man is not justified by the works of the law, but by the faith of Jesus Christ." Justification and forgiveness are God's free gifts. They involve absolutely no merit on man's part; all is of God. They are His unmerited favor. Forgiveness and justification are transmitted to us through faith.

In these days of guilt complexes, perhaps the most glorious word in the English language is "forgiveness."

A man serving a life sentence for murder escaped from the Oklahoma State Penitentiary. The warden offered the fugitive 1,500 dollars to present himself at the gate of the prison, but there was a catch to the offer. The reward was to be earned and saved by the escaped prisoner through his working in the prison. "If he comes, we will see that he does not get out again," said the warden. "Justice must prevail."

How different is the offer God makes to all fugitives from divine justice. There is no catch to His offer. "Let the wicked forsake his way . . . and let him return unto the Lord . . . for he will abundantly pardon" (Isa. 55:7). Civil justice seeks to catch the criminal. Divine justice is intent on setting him free. Justice has been satisfied by the death of Christ. All who present themselves to God in faith and repentance will be received not as fugitives, but as sons of God "justified from all things" (Acts 13:39).

Adopted

Second, the new man is adopted. "To redeem them that were under the law, that we might receive the adoption of sons" (Gal. 4:5). The moment we receive Christ as Savior, we receive the divine nature of the sons of God. We are now placed in the position of a joint heir with Jesus Christ. "Having predestinated us unto the adoption of children" (Eph. 1:5). We have now all the rights of a son. All things in the Kingdom are now ours to enjoy.

My friends, Roy Rogers and Dale Evans, have adopted several children. Once I asked them if they gave the same rights and privileges to their adopted children as they gave to their real children. They were shocked by my question and said: "Of course, we do. They are ours as much as the ones who were born to us. They have all the rights and privileges of our own flesh and blood." We, too, have been adopted into the family of God, with all the rights and privileges of sonship.

The Holy Spirit

Third, the new man is indwelt by the Spirit of God. Before He ascended into Heaven, Jesus Christ said: "And I will pray the Father, and he shall give you another Comforter, that he may abide with you for ever; even the Spirit of truth . . . ye know him; for he dwelleth with you, and shall be in you" (Jn. 14:16, 17). During His lifetime on earth, Christ's presence could be experienced only by a small group of men at any given time. Now Christ dwells through the Spirit in the hearts of all those who have received Him as Savior. The Apostle Paul wrote to the Romans: "But ye are not in the flesh, but in the Spirit, if so be that the Spirit of God dwell in you" (Rom. 8:9). Later he wrote to the Corinthians: "Know ye not that ye are the temple of God, and that the Spirit of God dwelleth in you?" (I Cor. 3:16).

The Holy Spirit is given to every believer—not for a limited time but forever. Were He to leave us for one moment, we would be in deep trouble.

With some disdain and contempt, a lady said to a clergyman to whom she had listened: "You are not abreast of the spirit of the age." The minister replied: "You are quite right, I am not abreast of the spirit of the age. But I do have within me the Holy Spirit of this age."

Walter Knight tells the story about a little boy who had recently received Christ. "Daddy, how can I believe in the Holy Spirit when I have never seen Him?" asked Jim. "I'll show you how," said his father, who was an electrician. Later, Jim went with his father to the power plant where he was shown the generators. "This is where the power comes from to heat our stove and to give us light. We cannot see the power, but it is in that machine and in the power lines," said the father.

"I believe in electricity," said Jim.

"Of course, you do," said his father, "but you don't believe in it because you see it. You believe in it because you see what it can do. Likewise you can believe in the Holy Spirit because you see what He does in people's lives when they are surrendered to Christ and possess His power."

Thus, by faith you accept the fact that you are indwelt by the Spirit of God. He is there to give you special power to work for Christ. He is there to give you strength in the moment of temptation. He is there to produce the supernatural fruit of the Spirit, such as "love, joy, peace, long-suffering, gentleness, goodness, faith, meekness, temperance" (Gal. 5:22, 23). He is there to guide you over all the difficult terrain you must cross as a Christian.

Sometimes when I go to Europe to preach I like to go by sea, and I enjoy the five days on the ship. On one of my voyages, Captain Anderson of the *United States* took me down to see the ship's gyroscope. He said: "When the sea is rough, the gyroscope helps to keep the ship on an even keel. Though the waves may reach tremendous proportions, the gyroscope helps to stabilize the vessel and maintain a high degree of equilibrium." As I listened, I thought how like the gyroscope is the Holy Spirit. Let the storms of life break over our heads. Let the enemy Satan come in like a flood. Let the waves of sorrow, suffering, temptation, and testing be unleashed upon us. Our souls will be kept on an even keel and in perfect peace when the Holy Spirit dwells in our hearts.

Strength to Resist Temptation

Fourth, the new man has the possibility of victory over temptation and sin. "There hath no temptation taken you but such as is common to man: but God is faithful, who will not suffer you to be tempted above that ye are able; but will with the temptation also make a way to escape, that ye may be able to bear it" (I Cor. 10:13).

The Bible teaches that the new man is to "abhor that which is evil" (Rom. 12:9) and to "put off concerning the former conversation the old man, which is corrupt according to the deceitful lusts" (Eph. 4:22). We are told also to "make not provision for the flesh, to fulfil the lusts thereof" (Rom. 13:14).

However, the great problem is: How do we do it? Where do we get such capacity and such strength?

This new capacity and this new strength come from the Holy Spirit, who lives within every true believer. It is not the result of our own struggling against temptation. It is the life of God within us. He lives in our hearts to help us to resist sin. It is our job to believe and to yield to Him. The Christian life from this point on is to be lived through the activity of faith. Faith is the shield of our defense against Satan (Eph. 6:16) and this faith enables us to overcome the evil world around us (I Jn. 5:4).

The Bible teaches us that as Christians we can become "more than conquerors" (Rom. 8:37). The strength for our conquering and our victory is drawn continually from Christ. The Bible does not teach that sin is completely eradicated from the Christian in this life, but it does teach that sin shall no longer reign over you. The strength and power of sin have been broken. The Christian now has resources available to live above and beyond this world. The Bible teaches that whosoever is born of God does not practice sin (I Jn. 3:6-9). It is like the little girl who said that when the devil came knocking with a temptation, she just sent Jesus to the door.

Thus in Jesus Christ, the new man is actually a new man. What does it mean to be a new creature or a new person? Let it be said at once that the new man is not the old man improved or made over. He is not even the old man reformed or remodeled, for God does not make the new out of the old nor put new wine in old bottles. The new man is Christ formed in us. In the creation, we were created in the image of God. In the new creation, we are re-created in the image of Christ. Paul said: "For whom he did foreknow, he also did predestinate to be conformed to the image of his Son" (Rom. 8:29). This new man is not the product of psychological change. According to psychiatrist Ernest White, Christian conversion "has permanent results in the depths of the personality and sets a man forward on the path of sanctity. Psychological treatment can bring about a rearrangement of the mental and emotional pattern, but it does not introduce a new power into the life."

The new man is actually Christ in the heart, and Christ in the heart means that He is in the center of our being. The Biblical use of the word "heart" symbolizes the whole realm of the affections. Into this area Christ comes to transform our affections, with the result that the things for which we formerly had affection pass away, and the things for which we now have affection are new and of God. If Christ dwells in the heart, it means that He dwells also in the mind with its varied functions of thinking and self-determination. In the process of change into a new creature when Christ indwells the heart, the human personality is neither absorbed nor destroyed. Instead it is enriched and empowered by this union with Christ.

The New Man Not Perfect

There is one problem that Christians face immediately upon conversion. Some people get the idea that they become perfect right away, and then they find themselves tempted, in conflict, and even on occasion yielding to temptation. Many of them become filled with confusion, frustration, and discouragement. They say the Christian life is not what they thought it was going to be. The Bible does teach that we can become mature, but that does not mean that we are ever flawless. Ernest F. Kevan says: "The perfect Christian is the one who, having a sense of his own failure to attain, is minded to press toward the mark" (Phil. 3:14).[1]

The Bible teaches: "For the flesh lusteth against the Spirit, and the Spirit against the flesh: and these are contrary the one to the other; so that ye cannot do the things that ye would" (Gal. 5:17). It teaches that there is a spiritual conflict in the heart of every true believer. It is true that the Christian possesses a new nature, but the old nature is still there. It is now up to us, day by day, to yield to the reign and control of the new nature, which is dominated by Christ. Because we are a new creation for whom all old things have passed away and all things have become new, we no longer practice sin.

We may fall into sin, but we hate it. The new nature commits no sin; but when the Christian sins, it is because the old nature has been yielded to for a moment. And when the Christian sins he is miserable until the sin is confessed and fellowship with God is restored. This is the difference between the believer and the unbeliever. The unbeliever makes sin a practice, and the believer does not make a practice of sin. He abhors it, and rather than live in the former lawlessness, he seeks to abide by the commands of God. Thus Paul says: "Who walk not after the flesh, but after the Spirit" (Rom. 8:4). It means that we are to be submissive to the new nature, to the Holy Spirit who indwells us.

[1] Ernest F. Kevan, *Salvation* (Grand Rapids, Mich.: Baker Book House, 1963).

"Neither yield ye your members as instruments of unrighteousness unto sin: but yield yourselves unto God,
as those that are alive from the dead, and your members as instruments of righteousness unto God" (Rom.
6:13).

New Standards

We are to feed the new nature on the Word of God
constantly, and we are to starve the old nature, which
craves the world and the flesh. We are told to "make
not provision for the flesh" (Rom. 13:14). We are told
to "present your bodies a living sacrifice, holy, acceptable unto God" (Rom. 12:1).

From now on our choices are made from a new
perspective and a new dimension. When we are living
up to the full privileges and powers of our new life in
Christ, sin loses its control over these choices and dis-
positions. The Christian is under the domination of
Christ and consequently lives according to new standards, with a new power.

In London, England, an alcoholic was placed under
the care of a psychiatrist who soon gave up because the
alcoholic was getting no better. During our meetings at
the Harringay Arena, the alcoholic was invited to
attend. He listened in wonderment to the Gospel messages. "Maybe there is some hope for me," he thought.
One night when the invitation was given, he went forward with several others. He was converted, and a new
power came into his life. That night before he went to
sleep, he reached as usual for the nearby bottle of
liquor; but something—or rather, Someone—restrained
his hand. Getting out of bed, he took the bottle and
emptied it down the drain. When he awakened in the
morning, through habit he reached again for his usual
morning bracer. It was not there, but there was no
sense of disappointment.

The man called his psychiatrist and said. "You have
lost a patient. Christ has saved me from drink. I am
now a new man." The psychiatrist said: "That sounds

fine. Maybe I can find help where you found it. I am not an alcoholic, but I have my own needs and problems." The psychiatrist began, too, to attend the meetings and he, too, accepted Christ as his Savior.

One year later, in the lobby of a fashionable London hotel both the psychiatrist and the former alcoholic testified to the saving power of Jesus Christ. Christ had kept them both.

To be a new creature in Christ does not mean that there has been a change in the personality elements of the person. It means that a new principle of life has been introduced at the center of his being, the heart, directing the will to new motives and new conduct and new ideals.

It often happens, as Dr. White says, that after conversion a man's tastes alter completely, not from any conscious effort of the will or of choice, but because of the change that has occurred at the deeper level. The Christian no longer wants to do some of the things he wanted to do before, and he develops an urge to do things that previously he would have shunned. Sometimes this change comes in a sudden cyclonic way, as when an alcoholic gives up his drinking or when a gossip gives up gossiping. In other cases, it is a gradual change permeating the whole life and outlook, transforming the individual more and more into the likeness of Christ.

New Orientation

The reason we as new creatures experience the passing away of old things and the beginning of new things is five-fold. *First, the new man has a new orientation.* Before conversion, he was oriented to the world and its materialistic, secular pursuits. Now he is oriented to Jesus Christ with the higher ideals of the Christian life.

New Motivation

Second, the new man has a new motivation. Before conversion, the motives for life were centered around his wills and appetites. He wanted what *he* wanted to do, to get, and to be. It was sometimes good and sometimes bad, but it was usually away from God. Now his motivation is God's will. This is the highest possible motive of life, and as long as we are inspired and activated by this motivation, we act in the character of the new creatures we are.

New Direction

Third, the new man has a new direction. Before conversion the direction of life was away from God. It was easy for him to do wrong. It was natural for him to sin. Now his life takes on a new direction. "We all had our conversation in times past in the lusts of our flesh . . . and were by nature the children of wrath, even as others. But God, who is rich in mercy . . . hath quickened us together with Christ" (Eph. 2:3-5).

We now move in the direction of God's will. New and different emotions flood our hearts. We find sinful practices unattractive and even abhorrent. We move in the direction of righteousness and godliness. We think God's thoughts after Him. We move with the mind of Christ, and we are free from the enslavements of the natural mind. We are free from envy and resentments, and become more gracious and kind, as He was.

New Growth

Fourth, the new man will experience a new growth spiritually and morally. One can imitate the Christian life by religious effort, but one can always detect an artificial flower. There is a difference between a spiritually natural growth of Christian principle and a moral copy of it. One is growth; the other is accretion. Jesus said: "Consider the lilies how they grow" (Lk. 12:27). How do they grow? They grow organically and spontaneously, automatically, without trying or struggling or fretting, just as we grow physically without conscious effort.

One of my sons said once: "I am going to be big like Daddy," and he stretched himself up. But his effort did not make him a fraction of an inch taller.

The moment you receive Christ you start out as a spiritual baby. "As newborn babes, desire the sincere milk of the word, that ye may grow thereby" (I Pet. 2:2). A child may be born into a wealthy home and thus become the possessor of rich parents, brothers and sisters, houses and lands; but at the time of his birth, the main point is not that he be informed of all these wonderful things. There are other important matters that must be taken care of first. He must be fed because he is hungry and needs to grow. He must be protected because he has been born into a world of many enemies. In the hospital room, he is handled with sterilized gloves and kept from outsiders, so that he will not fall victim to any of the myriads of germs waiting to attack.

A European friend was converted to Christ when he read *Peace with God.* There he learned that the believer is a new creation, that old things have passed away and all things have become new (II Cor. 5:17). He said: "If this be so, I shall make no effort to reform or to do good, lest it appear that I am changing myself. I shall test this promise of God to see what change He makes in me as the result of my believing." He decided only to nourish the "new man" by reading his Bible, by praying, and by going to church. The transformation in him came, not by his personal efforts, but by the power of the indwelling Holy Spirit.

You have become a child of God. You have been born into His family as a baby. This is a strategic moment in your life, and there are two or three things that will help to strengthen you for the battle ahead and to keep you safe from the wiles of Satan, the enemy of your soul.

1. It is important that you build up your soul by *reading the Scriptures.* If you do not have a Bible, get one as quickly as possible and begin reading the New Testament. "Wherewithal shall a young man cleanse his way? by taking heed thereto according to thy word"

(Ps. 119:9). "Thy word have I hid in mine heart, that I might not sin against thee" (Ps. 119:11). So I challenge you to read and to memorize portions of the Word of God.

Satan will do everything in his power to keep you from reading the Bible and to defeat you in your new-found Christian life. In the past you may not have been attacked viciously by Satan, but now he has seen you take the step that angers him more than any other. You have renounced him and joined the ranks of those who believe in the Son of God. You are no longer Satan's property; you belong to the One who has bought and paid for you with a price—the price of His blood on the Cross. You may be sure that Satan will attempt to trouble you. His attacks assume many forms, and you can overcome them only as you use the defenses that God has provided. "Take . . . the sword of the Spirit, which is the word of God" (Eph. 6:17). The Word of God is an offensive sword; defensive armor will ward off the darts of the enemy (Rom. 10:17; Eph. 6:10-17).

Therefore, it is vitally important for you to study the Scriptures. When Christ in the wilderness was tempted three times by the devil, He met each temptation with Scripture, saying: "It is written" (Matt. 4). If Jesus Christ found it necessary to thwart Satan's attacks by quoting the Scriptures, how much more you need this mighty weapon.

2. It is important that you *learn to pray.* Jesus said: "Men ought always to pray" (Lk. 18:1). Again He said: "Hitherto have ye asked nothing in my name: ask, and ye shall receive, that your joy may be full" (Jn. 16:24). The Apostle Paul went so far as to say: "Pray without ceasing" (I Thess. 5:17). Since you have made your decision for Christ, you may now address God as Father. In the beginning you will not be able to pray very fluently, yet it is important that you begin immediately. The first prayer you pray may be something like this: "O Father, thank you for saving my soul. I love You. In Christ's name, Amen." It may be just that simple, but you will find that soon you will be praying about everything. Soon your prayers will be constantly

in your subconscious. This is when you begin to "pray without ceasing."

George Washington Carver used to rise every morning at four o'clock to pray. Commenting on the blessings of those early morning hours, he said: "At no other time have I so sharp an understanding of what God means to do with me, as those hours when other folks are still asleep. Then I hear God best and learn His plan."

3. It is important for you to have *fellowship with other Christians*. God does not intend for you to live the Christian life alone. You need to be in the fellowship of a church. "Not forsaking the assembling of ourselves together" (Heb. 10:25). If you separate a live coal from the others, it will soon die out. However, if you put a live coal in with other live coals, it will be a glow that will last for hours. There may be a Bible class or prayer group in your community that you know nothing about. You can soon find your way into Christian fellowship that will give you new friendships and will strengthen your faith.

You are now a member of a worldwide brotherhood that spans every national, racial, and linguistic barrier. I have walked down jungle trails in Africa where I met fellow Christians; and immediately we were brothers even though we were separated by language, race, and culture. One of the great joys of my life has been to travel around the world and meet thousands of Christians in every country. Once when I was in Russia I attended the Moscow circus. Russia is one place where I would not be recognized by anyone—or so I thought. As we sat watching the circus, a very distinguished gentleman came up and sat beside me for a moment. He said: "Aren't you Billy Graham, the American evangelist?" With a look of surprise on my face, I told him I was. Then he said: "I am a Hungarian government official visiting Moscow on business. I wanted you to know that I am a believer in our Lord Jesus Christ." That was all. You can imagine the joy that leaped in my heart to find a brother in Christ in Moscow! I have found that God has His own people every-

where. As there were saints in Caesar's household, so
there are saints in the palaces of kings and dictators.

New Social Concern

*Fifth, the new man should have a new social con-
cern.* This will affect your family relationships, your
business relationships, your attitude toward your work,
and your attitude toward your neighbor.

The whole difference between the Christian and the
moralist lies right here. The Christian works from the
center, the moralist from the circumference. One is an
organism in the center of which is a living germ planted
by the living God. The other is crystal, very beautiful it
may be, but only a crystal. It lacks the vital principle of
growth.

You will understand that God is interested in the
great social issues of our day, such as immorality, desti-
tution, racial problems, and crime. The Apostle James
said: "Faith without works is dead" (Jas. 2:20). Our
good works testify that we have received Christ. We are
to visit the sick, to visit the prisoners, to give friendship
to the lonely, and to try to get those who are estranged
back together again. We will try to point wasted lives to
new values. We will go out of our way to show kindness, courtesy, and love to persons of another race. We
will be willing to suffer, to be persecuted, to take abuse
and ridicule from a hostile world, which does not understand our motives.

It is an exhilarating experience to live the new life
with Christ within me enabling me to live it. As a man
was riding along in his Ford, suddenly something went
wrong. He got out and looked at the engine, but he
could find nothing wrong. As he stood there, another
car came in sight, and he waved it down to ask for
help. Out stepped a tall, friendly man who asked:
"Well, what's the trouble?" "I cannot get this Ford to
move," was the reply. The stranger made a few adjust-
ments under the hood and then said: "Now start the car."
When the motor started, its grateful owner introduced

himself and said: "What is your name, sir?" "My name," answered the stranger, "is Henry Ford."

The one who made the Ford knew how to make it run. God made you and me, and He alone knows how to run your life and mine. We could make a complete wreck of our lives without Christ. When He is at the controls, all goes well. Without Him we can do nothing.

17

Social Involvement of the New Man

Even a casual study of the life of Jesus reveals that He was interested in man's response to the social problems he faces. Since Jesus Christ walked the earth, the thinking of the world concerning social matters has changed radically. Because of Him, the world has witnessed a new reverence for human life and learned something of the dignity and worth of man. Three out of every five men whom Paul passed on the streets of Rome were slaves. It was Christ's assertion that every individual has immeasurable value in the sight of God, and it was this message that helped eventually to free the slaves. He said: "Of how much more value is a man than a sheep?" (Matt. 12:12, RSV). It was Jesus who taught us that every man is a potential child of God. When He lived on earth, no one was His special pet whether on account of riches or of poverty. Rank and social distinction meant nothing to Him. It was for man, as man, that Christ cared. In taking our human nature upon Himself, He showed us what we might become, what God intended us to be.

Because of Jesus, woman has been lifted to her present position. In much of ancient literature, woman was regarded as little more than an animal. Here is an extract from the Laws of Manu: "Day and night must women be kept in dependence by the male members of the family. They are never fit for independence. They are as impure as falsehood itself." The coming of Jesus altered all that. He elevated womanhood forever when He was born of Mary. Mary's song, "The Magnificat," is the charter of woman's liberty. Some of His most faithful followers were women, and He included them among His closest friends, such as Mary Magdalene, Mary, and Martha.

The coming of Jesus Christ has changed the conduct of much of the world. Christians have given their lives to help their neighbors, to relieve poverty, to care for the sick. Many hospitals, orphanages, institutions for the poor, and asylums have their origin in love for Him. The social conscience of man was deepened by Jesus' coming. The history of the Christian church through the centuries, with its triumphs and its failures alike, points to the fact that Christ has sensitized the life of the world. He has pointed man in a new direction.

Why then is the world in such a desperate plight? The answer is because it will not come to Jesus Christ that it may have life. The world has rejected Him. To be sure, part of its conscience is still with Jesus, but not its conduct. Christ can save the world only as He is living in the hearts of men and women. We talk glibly about the establishment of a Christian order of society through legislation and social engineering, as though we could bring it down from the skies, if only we worked hard enough. The Kingdom of God will never come that way. If the human race should suddenly turn to Christ, we would have immediately the possibility of a new Christian order. We could approach our problems in the framework of Christian understanding and brotherhood. To be sure, the problems would remain, but the atmosphere for their solution would be completely changed.

Jesus walked among the people. He was not afraid to come in contact with them—the best and the worst, the sick and the well, the high and the low. "There came a leper to him, beseeching him, and kneeling down to him . . . and Jesus, moved with compassion, put forth his hand, and touched him" (Mk. 1:40, 41). The dirtiest, the loneliest, the most forsaken person in the world at that time was the leper. Imagine what it must have meant to him for Jesus Christ to reach out and touch him in love and compassion. Probably no human hand had touched him since his disease became evident.

Any man who cares enough to want to bless the lives of people must somehow "sit where they sit." Wilfred Grenfell became the angel of Labrador because he went there to live with the people. David Brainerd lived with the Indians in Colonial America. William Booth lived in London's East End. William Seagrave became the famous and beloved "Burma Surgeon" because he lived his life out, sick or well, in a village in Burma. He refused to return to his home, which he loved, lest he die from illness or accident away from the people of Burma; and it was there he died on March 28, 1965, in a little village not many miles from the border of Communist China.

If we are going to touch the people of our communities, we too must know their sorrows, feel for them in their temptations, stand with them in their heartbreaks. Jesus Christ entered into the arena of our troubles, and He wept with them that wept and rejoiced with them that rejoiced.

This is the reason that I have such an interest in those who are working in the "intercity churches." It is probably the most frustrating ministry in America today—to face teeming multitudes of people, thousands of them unemployed, living in substandard housing. Religious ideas have little meaning for them. Their lives are totally disorganized. The intercity pastor faces all their frustrations and tries compassionately to enter into their problems. During the last fifteen years, the rush of white church members to suburbs has caused such a religious upheaval that a whole new urban ministry has emerged. Religious urban projects are springing up all over the country. To capture the attention of the changing, television-oriented city dweller living in an apartment house requires bold new techniques of evangelism and Christian leadership.

The Church's Mission

Yet here is where the tension in the church becomes acute. What is the church's primary mission? Is it redemptive or social—or both? There are those who hold that even evangelism should be reinterpreted along the lines of social engineering and political pressure. We are witnessing today the greatest emphasis on ecclesiastical organizations, resolutions, pronouncements and lobbying, to bring into being and enforce the social changes envisioned by church leaders as a part of the world where the church shall be the dominating influence. When most major Protestant denominations have their annual councils, assemblies, or conventions, they make pronouncements on matters having to do with disarmament, federal aid to education, birth control, the United Nations, and any number of social and political issues. Very rarely are any resolutions passed that have to do with the redemptive witness of the Gospel.

There are those who think always in terms of mass action. These groups have obligations, duties, and responsibilities. They feel that laws must be enacted that will compel the group to heed those responsibilities and that this is the major part of the Christian mission. There are others in the church who think that the mission of the church is not to give direction to society. Certainly, there is a sense in which the church is to advise, warn, and challenge by proclaiming the absolute criteria by which God will judge mankind—such as the Ten Commandments and the Sermon on the Mount—by proclaiming God's divine purpose through government in a fallen society, and by preaching the whole counsel of God, which involves man's environment and physical being as well as his soul. Yet there are those who disagree violently with this position. There is no doubt that the church is in danger of getting off the main track and getting lost on a siding. We have been trying to solve every ill of society, as though society were made up of regenerate men to whom we had an obligation to give Christian advice. We are beginning to realize that, while the law must guarantee human rights and restrain those who violate those rights, whenever men lack sympathy for the law they will not long respect it, even when they cannot repeal it. Thus the government may try to legislate Christian behavior, but it soon finds that man remains unchanged.

The changing of men is the primary mission of the church. The only way to change men is to get them converted to Jesus Christ. Then they will have the capacity to live up to the Christian command to "Love thy neighbor."

Also, I am afraid the church is trying to speak out on too many issues that really do not concern the church. There are certain issues we know to be wrong—racial injustice, crime, gambling, dishonesty, pornography. On these matters we must thunder forth as the prophets of God. However, I am not so sure that the corporate body of the church has a right to make political decisions. I am not sure that the leaders of the church have a right to speak, without consultation, for the whole membership of the church. There is no doubt that the American Protestant church came dangerously close in both the 1960 and the 1964 elections to getting involved in politics. Many church bodies openly opposed Mr. John F. Kennedy, and four years later many church groups passed resolutions against Mr. Barry Goldwater.

As a result of the church's straying off the main track of its ministry, many of its members are restive and dissatisfied. Some refuse to give any more money to the church. Many are looking elsewhere for spiritual food. One of the great labor leaders of this country recently confided to a friend of mine: "I go to church on Sunday, and all I hear is social advice; and my heart is hungry for spiritual nourishment." A President of the United States told me that he was sick and tired of hearing preachers give advice on international affairs when they did not have the facts straight. It is perfectly proper for a clergyman to give his own personal views on any subject as a citizen, but it becomes a different matter when the church speaks, as the church, on every social and political issue that comes along, especially when the issue is not a moral or a spiritual problem. Devout and spiritually minded men often take opposing sides.

I am convinced that if the church went back to its main task of preaching the Gospel and getting people converted to Christ it would have far more impact on the social structure of the nation than it can have in any other thing it could possibly do.

Christ's Ministry

There is recorded in the Gospel of Luke an interesting incident in the ministry of Christ: "And one of the company said unto him, Master, speak to my brother, that he divide the inheritance with me. And he said unto him, Man, who made me a judge or a divider over you? And he said unto them, Take heed, and beware of covetousness: for a man's life consisteth not in the abundance of the things which he possesseth" (Lk. 12:13-15).

Here was a test case. A man brought an economic problem to Jesus. In those days if a man had two sons, the father's property went to them in the proportion of two-thirds to the elder and the remaining one-third to the younger. In this case, perhaps, the younger son was claiming more than his third or maybe the older brother had seized more than his allotted two-thirds. It is not likely that this man would have faced Jesus with an unjust or unreasonable demand. We therefore give him the benefit of the doubt. His demand was just. And what did Jesus say? He replied: "Man, who made me a judge or a divider over you?" What a disappointing answer! Here is a man with a reasonable economic problem, and he is turned away by Christ. He probably went home to tell his friends that Jesus was not interested in social affairs. He probably said that Jesus was cold and indifferent to his material needs.

This was a genuine economic problem, one on which the church often speaks and passes many resolutions today. Did Christ look into the case and then pass a resolution? Did He study this economic question? No! He replied with apparent indifference: "Man, who made me a judge or a divider over you?" In other words, Jesus said He had not been appointed to this office of arbitrator in economic matters. The claims of the questioner may have been perfectly fair or they may not have been. Jesus felt that this was a matter for the authorities to decide.

Then Jesus turned to the main theme of his ministry and said: "Take heed, and beware of covetousness: for a man's life consisteth not in the abundance of the things which he possesseth." Here we see Jesus deliberately refusing to become enmeshed in an economic problem; He pointed to something far deeper. There was a more subtle complaint, a more deep-seated problem involved.

Social Injustices

There is no doubt that today we see social injustice everywhere. Looking on our American scene, Jesus would see something even deeper. He would say: "Beware of covetousness, beware of the spirit of perpetual discontent with what life offers, forever wanting more, forever looking at other people's conditions in life and never being content." Here is the social policy of Jesus. If only we in the church would begin at the root of our problems, which is the disease of human nature. However, we have become blundering social physicians, giving medicine here and putting ointment there on the sores of the world, but the sores break out again somewhere else. The great need is for the church to call in the great Physician who alone can properly diagnose the case. He will look beneath the mere skin eruptions and pronounce on the cause of it all—sin. If we in the church want a cause to fight, let's fight sin. Let's reveal its hideousness. Let's show that Jeremiah was correct when he said: "The heart is deceitful above all things, and desperately wicked" (Jer. 17:9). Then, when the center of man's trouble is dealt with, when this disease is eradicated, then and only then will man live with man as brother with brother.

Do not get me wrong. I believe in taking a stand on the moral, social, and spiritual issues of our day. I had not been preaching long before I decided that I would never preach to another segregated audience in any situation over which we had control. This was long before the Supreme Court decision of 1954. I lost many supporters. I had many threatening letters. I was called a radical, a liberal, and a Communist. Certain churches no longer would have me in their pulpits. However, I felt this was the Christian position and I could do no other.

In my Crusades, I have preached on every conceivable social issue. I have used my radio program *The Hour of Decision* to preach on every social issue of our day. I have talked on everything from bad housing to highway safety. However, the social issues of our day have not been the main theme of my preaching. My main theme has been the same as that of the early Apostles: "That Christ died for our sins according to the Scriptures; and that he was buried, and that he rose again the third day according to the Scriptures" (I Cor. 15:3, 4).

When Philip the evangelist was preaching to the Ethiopian nobleman on the hot desert road, the Scripture says: "He preached unto him Jesus." The African was probably being driven by slaves, and slavery was the greatest social injustice of that day. There is no record that Philip rebuked him for using slaves. He preached to him Jesus.

To the hungry, Jesus said: "I am the bread of life." To the thirsty, He said: "I am the water of life." To the tired, He said: "Come unto me all ye that labour and are heavy laden, and I will give you rest." To the guilt-laden person, He said: "Your sins are forgiven." Even to the dead, He said: "I am the resurrection."

There is another problem that has to do with social concern. The Apostle Paul said: "I have learned how to be content wherever I am" (Phil. 4:11, Moffatt). When the Apostle Paul wrote this, he was in a Roman jail. This is an astounding statement to come from one who was so dissatisfied with his own spiritual life that he called himself the chief of sinners, and on another occasion said he had not attained but was still pressing toward the mark. What did he mean? He meant that he had mastered the secret of being perfectly satisfied with any condition of life in which it pleased God to place him. He was not dependent upon circumstances for happiness. He did not cherish a grievance against life when he was short of money, or deprived of comfort or exposed to unfair criticism. He thought more of what he could give than of what he could get. He could say honestly: "For to me to live is Christ" (Phil. 1:21). In other words, life to Paul simply meant Jesus Christ; Christ to love and serve, and Christ to preach and worship.

True Values

Although Christ said that a man's life does not consist of the things he has, we in the church are very dangerously near to teaching the people that "things" are life's most important possessions. I live in Appalachia, which has been written up around the world as a poverty area in the United States. I know families who do not have as much as some families in New York and Philadelphia. They are considered poor by the standards of Wall Street. However, they have a joy, a radiance, and a peace rooted deep in their spiritual faith that gives them contentment and peace. I know millionaires in New York, Texas, and California who are almost ready to blow their brains out because they cannot resist the pressures of their lives. Which is the wealthier? Who is the richer? Paul could say from jail: "I am content." What could be worse than a cold, rat-infested Roman dungeon? We in the church are in danger of reversing the story of the prodigal son. Jesus said the prodigal son came to himself, left the far country, and went back to his father. Instead of trying to get the prodigal son out of the far country, we in the church are trying to make the prodigal son comfortable and happy in the world's pigpen.

Certainly, Paul suffered a spiritual discontentment that drove him on and on through every conceivable suffering that he might win men to Christ. Certainly, we as Christian citizens have no right to be content with our social order until the principles of Christ are applied to all men. As long as there is enslaved one man who should be free, as long as slums and ghettos exist, as long as any person goes to bed hungry at night, as long as the color of a man's skin is his prison, there must be a divine discontent.

Christian Responsibility

This sounds like a paradox, but it is not. We as Christians have two responsibilities. One, to proclaim the Gospel of Jesus Christ as the only answer to man's deepest needs. Two, to apply as best we can the principles of Christianity to the social conditions around us.

Jesus taught that the Christian is "the salt of the earth" (Matt. 5:13). Jesus used salt as an illustration because salt adds zest to food, and salt is a preservative. Some food would spoil without it. Our national society would become corrupt if it were not for the Christian salt. Greed and lust and hate would lead our nation into a veritable hell. You take all the Christians out of America and see what chaos would be created overnight. It is partially because the church has lost its saltiness that we have such appalling moral and social needs now. A pinch of salt is effective out of all proportion to its amount.

Christ also said: "Ye are the light of the world" (Matt. 5:14). The darkness of our world is getting ever darker. There is only one true light shining, the light of Jesus Christ, which is reflected by those who trust and believe in Him. Jesus Himself had come to shed light that men might see God through Him. His followers are to shine and to radiate His light. He said: "Let your light . . . shine before men" (Matt. 5:16).

Christ indicates that the world is the sphere where the light and the salt are to function. Present problems in our national life are serious, and every Christian has a definite responsibility. The Christian is a citizen of two worlds. In view of this dual citizenship, he is told in the Scriptures not only to pray for those in political authority but to participate in and serve his government. The Christian is the only real light-bearer in the world. The lives of the early Christians were their invincible witness. The world may argue against a creed, but it cannot argue against changed lives.

That is what the simple Gospel of Jesus Christ does when it is preached in the power and authority of the Holy Spirit.

Not only does the Christian follow Christ and learn of Him, but the Christian also must act. The world judges the Christian by his life, not by his belief. His acts are an indication of his faith. The Apostle James said: "A man may say, Thou hast faith, and I have works: show me thy faith without thy works, and I will show thee my faith by my works" (Jas. 2:18). An evangelist was once asked if he did not think the world was growing worse. He replied: "If it is, then I am determined it shall be in spite of *me*." We can paraphrase that: "If the world is growing worse, then it will be in spite of the Gospel of Christ and those of us who trust in Him."

18

The Fabulous Future

Nearly every American president of recent years has had a slogan to characterize the objectives of his administration. All of these slogans have held out to the people new hope and anticipation of a better life tomorrow. With Franklin D. Roosevelt it was "The New Deal"—Harry Truman, "The Fair Deal"—John F. Kennedy, "The New Frontier"—Lyndon Johnson, "The Great Society."

In spite of the darkening storm clouds on the horizon, man is preparing today for a fabulous future. The frontiers have changed from earth to space, from land to air, and from horsepower to nuclear power. Amazing scientific advances are rapidly leading to an era of unparalleled scientific wonders.

The anticipated projections of this fabulous future would have made Franklin D. Roosevelt stagger. We are told that the future belongs to the scientist. In transportation, time will shrink to almost nothing as rocket ships transport travelers from New York to London in less than an hour. We shall live in plastic houses completely open to the out of doors and heated by solar energy. Food processing will bring exotic delicacies from all parts of the earth. Communication advances will provide electronic telephones that we shall carry in our pockets and purses. Our newspapers will roll out of a facsimile machine and be available in our homes through television.

The planning for this fabulous future, however, has one fatal flaw! It is materialistic, secularistic, and humanistic. It does not take into account man's moral sickness and it has made little provision for God! The planners have not taken into account the words of Jesus: "Man shall not live by bread alone, but by every word that proceedeth out of the mouth of God" (Matt. 4:4). Today man eats continually of the tree of knowledge without partaking of the tree of life, and he is still under the Satanic delusion that he will become like God.

We base our hopes of this fabulous future on our present progressive and scientific educational process. The late Justice Robert Jackson said: "It is one of the paradoxes of our time that modern society needs to fear . . . only the educated man."[1] The reason for this fear lies in the fact that we are developing mentally without an equivalent morality.

Danger from Within

President Theodore Roosevelt said: "When you educate a man in mind and not in morals, you educate a menace to society."

Science is learning to control everything but man. We have not yet solved the problems of hate, lust, greed, and prejudice, which produce social injustice, racial strife, and ultimately war. Thus this fabulous future is threatened by many dangers, such as the nuclear destruction that hangs, like the sword of Damocles, over our heads.

However, the greatest danger is from within. Every other civilization before us has disintegrated and collapsed from internal forces rather than military conquest. Ancient Rome is the outstanding example of the fall of a civilization. While its disintegration was hastened by foreign invasions, in the opinion of Arthur Weigall, a world-famous archaeologist, it collapsed "only after bribery and corruption had been rife for generations." The Great Wall of China, which took

[1] William Buckley, *God and Man at Yale* (Chicago: Henry Regnery Co., 1951).

twelve hundred years to build, did not fall. It didn't need to fall. Three times the enemy walked through the gates simply by bribing the gatekeepers.

No matter how advanced its progress, any generation that neglects its spiritual and moral life is going to disintegrate. This is the story of man and this is our modern problem.

The Christian believes in a fabulous future, even though the present structure of modern society should disappear and all its progress should be wiped out by self-destruction as a result of man's failure and folly.

There is a sense in which the Kingdom of God is already here in the living presence of Christ in the hearts of all true believers. There is also, however, the ultimate consummation of all things, which is called the Kingdom of God. This is the fabulous future! It will be a future in which there will be no war. There will be no poverty. There will be happy and peaceful human relations. There will be full and ample opportunity to exploit all our abilities. There will be a state of complete reconciliation between man and God—between race and race—between nation and nation.

God's Intervention

The fabulous future that we Christians are looking for will not be the natural development of history. It will not come by political structuring. It will not be the result of education or science alone. It will come in the establishment of the Kingdom of God, by God's direct intervention!

There is a great emphasis in the churches on applying the principles of Jesus Christ to the social order in terms of a social gospel. It is thought worth trying to bring our democracy a bit nearer to the ideal of the Kingdom of God on earth. I firmly believe in the application of the Gospel to the social order, for the Gospel must relate to the social concerns of our day. In many respects, the best aspirations in modern life are a by-product of the Christian faith, but their Utopian objectives lack the means of achievement because they do not reckon with the unregenerate human heart. In fact, they often pursue a millennium on earth with no room for God or the fulfillment of His spiritual requirements. Even the clamor for social justice, which is a Biblical concern, seems today to seek an ideal mass society of highly privileged sinners who keep God at a great distance. But when the Kingdom of God is established, it will not be established by social reforms, democratic principles, or scientific achievement alone. It will be established by the hand of God in the midst of *the ruins* of our social and governmental institutions. This establishment is pictured in many places in the Bible. One of the most graphic is in the prophecy of Daniel, who saw the culmination of God's Kingdom on earth as an act of God and an event originating in heaven.

Daniel said the king had seen "that a stone was cut out without hands, which smote the image upon his feet that were of iron and clay, and brake them to pieces. Then was the iron, the clay, the brass, the silver, and the gold, broken to pieces together, and became like the chaff of the summer threshingfloors; and the wind carried them away, that no place was found for them: and the stone that smote the image became a great mountain, and filled the whole earth" (Dan. 2:34–35).

This great image represents the nations of the world. It was crushed by a stone. This is symbolic of the establishment of the Kingdom of God and it is "without hands" and from heaven. It is God's doing, not man's.

The reason for this divine establishment of the final phase of history lies in the nature of history itself. History is *not* infused with the factors and forces that can produce a glorious end. History does not carry its own happy fulfillment. The human equation is too evident. Man is too prone to depravity. This is not to say that God has no purpose in history between the fall of man and the second coming of Jesus Christ. His purpose is to reconcile man to Himself: "God was in Christ, reconciling the world unto himself" (II Cor. 5:19). Thus the message of every true Christian to his fellowman is, "Be ye reconciled to God" (II Cor. 5:20). All of God's plans and purposes are centered in His Son Jesus Christ. While God rules and overrules in history, the center of His activities is not in secular history *per se*, which is doomed by its spiritual revolt against the Lord of history.

The story of the Bible is the history of man at variance with God. Individual men are born in sin and alienated from God. Nations are at variance with God, and their glory is in ruins strewn across the highways of history. Their end will be a gigantic assemblage of nations, not to create the perfect state, but to receive the judgment of God for rejected truth. "For all nations have drunk of the wine of the wrath" (Rev. 18:3). Jesus taught it: "And before him shall be gathered all nations: and he shall separate them one from another, as a shepherd divideth his sheep from the goats" (Matt. 25:32). "And the nations were angry, and thy wrath is come . . . that they should be judged" (Rev. 11:18). According to the Scriptures, the world is heading toward judgment.

The Bible nowhere teaches that the church will ultimately convert the whole world to Jesus Christ. There has never been a generation in history, nor will there ever be a generation, in which the majority of the people will believe in Christ. Statistics indicate that the church is rapidly losing in the population explosion. There are fewer Christians per capita every day.

That Great Day

Throughout the Bible, there is an expression used many times by the writers. They refer to "that day," or "the day," or "the last days." When the Allied Forces invaded Normandy, it was called "D Day." When Japan surrendered to the American forces, it was called "VJ Day."

The writers of the Bible were looking for a climactic, which they called "that day." The early New Testament Christians continually talked about and looked forward to "that day." For example, the Apostle Paul says: "For I know whom I have believed, and am persuaded that he is able to keep that which I have committed unto him against *that day*" (II Tim. 1:12). The Apostle was saying that all of his past sins had been forgiven because of Christ, and that God was able to keep him until some climactic day in the future.

In II Timothy 4:8 the Apostle, referring to crowns and rewards the Christians will receive in the future for their faithfulness here, said: "Henceforth there is laid up for me a crown of righteousness, which the Lord, the righteous judge, shall give me at *that day*."

What kind of day were they looking for? What is this climactic day in history that the entire Bible talks about and to which almost every New Testament writer refers? What is this "D Day" of Holy Scripture? What is this "X Hour" the Bible promises the Christian and about which it warns the sinner?

Our political leaders warn us constantly of the danger of World War III breaking out with all of its terrifying nuclear destruction. Is the possibility of an all-out destructive war what the New Testament writers had in mind when they talked about "that day"? No, not at all. "D Day" and "X Hour" to the New Testament writers meant the glorious second coming of Jesus Christ to the earth again.

The Scripture says: "And to you who are troubled rest with us, when the Lord Jesus shall be revealed from heaven with his mighty angels, in flaming fire taking vengeance on them that know not God, and that obey not the gospel of our Lord Jesus Christ: who shall be punished with everlasting destruction from the presence of the Lord, and from the glory of his power; when he shall come to be glorified in his saints, and to be admired in all them that believe . . . in that day" (II Thess. 1:7–10). This does not sound as if education and science are going to triumph. Indeed, the Bible teaches the very opposite, that the world is heading toward destruction and judgment, but that out of the ruins God will establish Utopia.

Jesus Himself said: "But as the days of Noah were, so shall also the coming of the Son of man be. For as in the days that were before the flood they were eating and drinking, marrying and giving in marriage, until the day that Noah entered into the ark, and knew not until the flood came, and took them all away; so shall also the coming of the Son of man be" (Matt. 24:37–39).

Certainly no one would claim that the world was converted in the days of Noah. Yet as it was then, so shall it be when Christ returns.

The Apostle Paul wrote to young Timothy about those last days. "This know also, that in the last days perilous times shall come. For men shall be lovers of their own selves, covetous, boasters, proud, blasphemers, disobedient to parents, unthankful, unholy, without natural affection, truce-breakers, false accusers, incontinent, fierce, despisers of those that are good, traitors, heady, highminded, lovers of pleasures more than lovers of God; having a form of godliness, but denying the power thereof: from such turn away" (II Tim. 3:1–5).

Here is an explicit description of the condition of affairs immediately preceding the coming of Christ. There is nothing in any of these passages to indicate that the Kingdom of God is going to be brought to the world by natural causes.

Many people are confused by taking isolated passages out of their context and quoting them. For example, "Ask of me, and I shall give thee the heathen for thine inheritance, and the uttermost parts of the earth for thy possession" (Ps. 2:8). Or Isaiah 11:6, 9: "The wolf also shall dwell with the lamb, and the leopard shall lie down with the kid; and the calf and the young lion and the fatling together; and a little child shall lead them . . . the earth shall be full of the knowledge of the Lord, as the waters cover the sea."

A careful, contextual examination of the above-mentioned and similar prophecies will reveal that their fulfillment will be accomplished by terrible judgments. For instance, the things prophesied in Psalm 2:8 are thus introduced in the following verse: "Thou shalt break them with a rod of iron; thou shalt dash them in pieces like a potter's vessel." The context of Isaiah 11:6–9 indicates the same thing: "But with righteousness shall he judge the poor, and reprove with equity for the meek of the earth: and he shall smite the earth with the rod of his mouth, and with the breath of his lips shall he slay the wicked" (Isa. 11:4).

Secular writers have alluded to man's ultimate failure. In the preface to his *History of Europe*, H. A. L. Fisher wrote, "Men wiser and more learned than I have discerned in history a plot, a rhythm, a predetermined pattern. These harmonies are concealed from me. I can see only one emergency following upon another as wave follows upon wave."

T. S. Eliot expressed it another way in his poem, *The Hollow Men*:

> *This is the way the world ends,*
> *This is the way the world ends,*
> *Not with a bang but a whimper.*[2]

These men were right, but they were also utterly wrong! It will come, but as John Baillie said: "Not by any long road, not by any painless process of education, not by any natural evolution, not by any gradual and easy progress. All the facts give the lie to such Utopian dreams."[3] The world system of evil as we know it is going to come to a dramatic end—but this is not "the end." The longings and dreams of mankind will be fulfilled, as God establishes His glorious kingdom on earth for the enjoyment of mankind. Many students of the Bible and history believe that we have now entered the final phase of human history as a record of man at variance with God.

In the interest of self-preservation, the Charter of the United Nations said in its preamble: "We the people determined to save succeeding generations from war . . ." Can the United Nations save the world from war? The answer is No! It was conceived and created by statesmen who knew little of the significance of the

---

[2] *The Hollow Men* in *Collected Poems 1909-1962*.
[3] *A Reasoned Faith* (New York: Charles Scribner's Sons, 1963).

Biblical concept of history and the nature of man. When the perspective is wrong, the whole viewpoint will be wrong. When the premise is wrong, the logic will be faulty. I have supported the United Nations because it offered some hope at least of solving some problems and postponing some major hostilities. It is man's best attempt in generations, but the human equation is still there. The basic problem has not been touched. You cannot build a superstructure on a cracked foundation. The superstructure of the United Nations, in its gleaming building on the East River of New York City, has been built on the cracked foundation of human nature. At best, it is only a temporary stopgap.

For many centuries, every form of government, from family and tribal administration to despotic dictatorship and democracy, has been tried. No form of government has been able to establish righteousness, justice, and peace, the three elements without which we can never have continued national prosperity or international peace.

America has probably been the most successful experiment in history. The American dream was a glorious attempt. It was built on a religious foundation. Its earliest concepts came from Holy Scripture. God honored and blessed America as few nations in history. However, in recent years the nation has been moving away from its religious heritage. Whether it knows it or not, it is in deep trouble both at home and abroad.

The sinful, proud, rebellious heart of man can never, in its present constitution, muster intelligence enough to save the present world system. We may engage in delaying action by our international organizations and by disarmament, but we cannot produce lasting peace. Jesus Himself said there would be wars until the end of the age, and He indicated that these wars would get larger and more intense as "the end" draws nearer.

Cain lived not by God's design but by the law of tooth and claw, and we follow his pattern today. Civilization was born outside of Eden in the skepticism and immorality of a man who was self-willed, who chose to follow his own passion and reason rather than God's revelation. It was this man and this mood that produced civilization without God. And although we have added far higher forms of life to this early primitiveness, and although we have established far higher levels of civilization, we are still building with bricks without mortar. We are still moving in a direction away from God.

God Is No Absentee

As the Christian with the Bible in his hand surveys the world scene, he is aware that we do not worship an absentee God. He is aware that God is in the shadows of history and that He has a plan. The Christian is not to be disturbed by the chaos, violence, strife, bloodshed, and threat of war that fill the pages of our daily newspapers. We know that these things are the consequences of man's sin and greed. If anything else were happening, we would doubt the Bible. Every day we see a thousand evidences of the fulfillment of Biblical prophecy. Every day as I read my newspaper I say: "The Bible is true."

No matter how foreboding the future, the Christian knows the end of the story of history. We are heading toward a glorious climax. Every writer of the New Testament believes that "the best is yet to be."

As John Baillie has said: "The Bible indicates that the future is in God's hands. If it were in our hands, we would make a mess of it. The future is not in the devil's hands, for then he would lead us to destruction. The future is not at the mercy of any historical determinism leading us blindly forward, for then life would be without meaning. But the future is in the hands of One who is preparing something better than eye hath seen, or ear heard, or has entered into the heart of man to conceive."

The Psalmist said: "The Lord is my light and my salvation: whom shall I fear? The Lord is the strength of my life; of whom shall I be afraid?" (Ps. 27:1).

The story is told of a boy traveling alone in a railway compartment in England. At one of the stations an elderly gentleman engaged the boy in conversation, and the following dialogue ensued:

"Are you traveling all alone, Sonny?"

"Yes, sir."

"How far are you traveling?"

"To the terminus."

"Are you not afraid, taking such a long journey all by yourself?"

"No, I'm not."

"Why not?"

"Because my father is the engineer."

No wonder the boy had such great confidence and feared nothing. His father was in control, and his father knew his son was somewhere on the train. God, our Father, is in control of the world, and He knows "His own" on this planet in rebellion.

It is recorded that Oliver Cromwell's secretary was dispatched to the Continent on some important business. He stayed one night in a seaport town and tossed on his bed, unable to sleep. According to an old custom a servant slept in his room, and on this occasion slept soundly enough. The secretary, at length, awakened the man, who asked how it was that his master could not rest. "I am so afraid something will go wrong with this trip," was the reply. "Master," said the valet, "may I ask a question or two? Did God rule the world before we were born?" "Most assuredly He did." "And will He rule it again after we are dead?" "Certainly He will." "Then, Master, why not let Him rule the present too?" The secretary's faith was stirred. Peace was the result, and in a few minutes both he and his servant were in sound sleep.

History is going somewhere. The Christian says with David: "My times are in Thy hand" (Ps. 31:15). And we know full well that He who doeth all things well will bring beauty from the ashes of world chaos. A new world is being born. A new social order will emerge when Christ comes back to set up His Kingdom. Swords will be turned into pruning hooks, and the lion will lie down with the lamb. A fabulous future is on the way.

19

The Distant Trumpet

When I referred to the future that God is planning, a student at the University of Hawaii asked me: "Isn't this a form of escapism?" I said: "In a sense, yes; and before the devil gets through with this world, we are all going to be looking for the exit signs."

C. S. Lewis, in his remarkable little book *Christian Behavior*, said: "Hope is one of the theological virtues. This means that a continual looking forward to the eternal world is not, as some modern people think, a form of escapism or wishful thinking, but one of the things a Christian is meant to do. It does not mean that we are to leave the present world as it is. If you read history, you will find that the Christians who did most for the present world were just those who thought most of the next. It is since Christians have largely ceased to think of the other world that they have become so ineffective in this. Aim at Heaven and you will get earth thrown in. Aim at earth and you will get neither."

In the midst of the pessimism, gloom, and frustration of this present hour, there is one bright beacon light of hope, and that is the promise of Jesus Christ: "If I go and prepare a place for you, I will come again" (Jn. 14:3).

During the years of the Second World War, the words of General Douglas MacArthur echoed in the ears of the people of the Philippine Islands while they were under enemy occupation. He had promised, "I shall return," and he kept that promise. Jesus Christ has also promised, "I shall return," and He will keep that promise.

The whole nature of individual salvation rests squarely on the person and work of Jesus Christ. "For by grace are ye saved through faith; and that not of yourselves: it is the gift of God: not of works, lest any man should boast" (Eph. 2:8,9). "Not by works of righteousness which we have done, but according to his mercy he saved us, by the washing of regeneration, and renewing of the Holy Ghost; which he shed on us abundantly through Jesus Christ our Saviour; that being justified by his grace, we should be made heirs according to the hope of eternal life" (Tit. 3:5-7).

Likewise, the salvation of society in the reordering of man's social institutions, consistent with the abolition of social injustice, war, poverty, and disease, will be taken out of man's hands. It will not be achieved by education, evolution, politics, technology, military power, or science. Nor will it be achieved by a universal church that can influence legislation in the parliaments and congresses of nations, so as to produce such benevolent acts of men that all hate, evil, and sin will be abolished.

The salvation of society will come about by the powers and forces released by the apocalyptic return of Jesus Christ. It will be instrumented through the Kingdom of God in its principles of righteousness. It will be the prophesied fulfillment of redemption applied to every phase of human life and national existence. The second coming of Christ will be so revolutionary that it will change every aspect of life on this planet. Christ will reign in righteousness. Disease will be arrested. Death will be modified. War will be abolished. Nature will be changed. Man will live as it was originally intended he should live.

There is nothing on today's horizon or in contemporary thought that offers an alternate hope that is better. Someone has said: "No arrangement of bad eggs will give you a good omelet." These successive civilizations of the past have been different arrangements of human institutions, but we have never had a lasting, satisfactory, peaceful social order. It is impossible to build a peaceful world on the cracked foundation of human nature.

Jesus Christ Will Return

The importance of this hope of Christ's return is established by the frequency, extent, and intensity of its mention in the Bible. It is mentioned in all but four books of the New Testament. Christ constantly referred to His return, not only to His disciples, but to others as well. He said to the high priest, "Hereafter shall ye see the Son of man sitting on the right hand of power, and coming in the clouds of heaven" (Matt. 26:64). One out of every thirty verses in the Bible mentions this subject. There are 318 references to it in 216 chapters in the New Testament. One-twentieth of the entire New Testament deals with this subject.

It was predicted by most of the Old Testament writers: by Moses (Deut. 33:2); by Job (Job 19:25); by David (Ps. 102:16); by Isaiah (Isa. 59:20); by Jeremiah (Jer. 23:5); by Daniel (Dan. 7:13); by Zechariah (Zech. 14:4); and by many others. It was promised by Christ Himself: "Let not your heart be troubled: ye believe in God, believe also in me. In my Father's house are many mansions: if it were not so, I would have told you. I go to prepare a place for you. And if I go and prepare a place for you, I will come again, and receive you unto myself; that where I am, there ye may be also" (Jn. 14:1-3).

The fact of the coming again of Christ was proclaimed by all the Apostles in their preaching—by Peter (Acts 3:20, 21; I Pet. 1:7, 13); by Paul (Rom. 8:23; I Thess. 4:15-17); by John (I Jn. 2:28; 3:2); by James (Jas. 5:7-9); by Jude (Jude 14-15).

The hope of the second coming is found in the church's great creeds, such as the Apostles' Creed, the Nicene Creed, and the Athanasian Creed. The Thirty-Nine Articles of the Church of England say: "Christ did truly rise again from death and took again His body, with flesh, bones and all things appertaining to the perfection of man's nature, wherewith He ascended into Heaven, and there sitteth until He return to judge all men at the last day" (Article 4). Article 17 of the

Augsburg Confession deals at length with "Christ's return to judgment." The Apostles' Creed, repeated in many churches every Sunday, says: "From thence He shall come to judge the quick and the dead."

The Bible teaches it. The Apostles preached it. The church creeds affirm it.

However, the greatest and most telling testimony is from the lips of Jesus Himself. He said: "The Son of man shall come" (Matt. 25:31); "They shall see the Son of man coming" (Matt. 24:30); "Your Lord doth come" (Matt. 24:42); ". . . when he cometh in the glory of his Father" (Mk. 8:38); "Ye shall say, Blessed is he that cometh in the name of the Lord" (Lk. 13:35); "And ye now therefore have sorrow: but I will see you again, and your heart shall rejoice" (Jn. 16:22); "Hereafter you will see the Son of man seated at the right hand of Power, and coming on the clouds of Heaven" (Matt. 26:64, RSV).

Certainly, a predicted event that was the subject of such universal and frequent attention and such great promise is a worthy object for modern man's concern.

There are three Greek words used in the New Testament to describe the coming again of Christ. The first one is *parousia,* which carries with it the idea of the personal presence of Christ. In other words, when Christ returns, He will come in person.

The second Greek word is *epiphaneia,* which carries with it the idea of appearing. It is the appearance out of darkness of a star that has been there all day, hidden from view, and suddenly appearing at night.

The third Greek word is *apokalupsis,* which carries with it the idea of unveiling. It is the unveiling of one who has been hidden. Today the person of Christ is hidden from view, though His presence through the Holy Spirit is in our hearts. Today is the day of faith. In that day He will be revealed. In that day of His coming it will no longer be faith, but sight.

His first appearing was quiet—the shepherds, the star, and the manger. His second appearing will be with His dazzling warriors from heaven, to cope with any situation and to defeat the enemies of God until He has subdued the entire earth.

Thus, no Christian has the right to go around wringing his hands, wondering what we are to do in the face of the present world situation. The Scripture says that in the midst of persecution, confusion, wars, and rumors of wars, we are to comfort one another with the knowledge that Jesus Christ is coming back in triumph, glory, and majesty.

Many times when I go to bed at night I think that before I awaken Christ may come. Sometimes, when I get up and look at the dawn I think that perhaps this is the day He will come.

He Will Come Unexpectedly

The Bible teaches that the coming again of Jesus Christ will be sudden, unexpected, and dramatic. It will come as a surprise and take most people unawares. "For yourselves know perfectly that the day of the Lord so cometh as a thief in the night" (I Thess. 5:2).

When former President Eisenhower was vacationing in Denver a number of years ago, his attention was called to an open letter in a local newspaper, which told how six-year-old Paul Haley, dying of incurable cancer, had expressed a wish to see the President of the United States. Spontaneously, in one of those gracious gestures remembered long after a man's most carefully prepared speeches are forgotten, the President decided to grant the boy's request.

So one Sunday morning in August, a big limousine pulled up outside the Haley home and out stepped the President. He walked up to the door and knocked.

Mr. Donald Haley opened the door, wearing blue jeans, an old shirt, and a day's growth of beard. Behind him was his little son, Paul. Their amazement at finding President Eisenhower on their doorstep can be imagined.

"Paul," said the President to the little boy, "I understand you want to see me. Glad to see you." Then he shook hands with the six-year-old, and took him out to see the presidential limousine, shook hands again and left.

The Haleys and their neighbors, and a lot of other people, will probably talk about this kind and thoughtful deed of a busy President for a long time to come. Only one person was not entirely happy about it—that was Mr. Haley. He can never forget how he was dressed when he opened the door. "Those jeans, the old shirt, the unshaven face—what a way to meet the President of the United States," he said.

Of course the visit was unannounced, and under the circumstances it wasn't to be expected that he would be all dressed up in his best clothes. But all his life he will wish he had gotten up a bit earlier that day, shaved a little sooner, and at least put on a clean shirt before the President arrived. Readiness and watchfulness are all urged upon Christians, lest Christ's coming, taking us by surprise, should find us unprepared.

The second coming of Jesus Christ will be a series of events transpiring over a rather long period. There will be the rapture, the catching up of the believers to meet Him in the air (I Thess. 4:16,17). This is the next event on God's calendar, and it will involve the first resurrection when all the believers of all the ages will be raised from the dead and gathered together with the living believers. There is to be the marriage supper of the Lamb (Rev. 19:7), which is the moment of the coronation of Jesus Christ as Lord of lords and King of kings. There will be the great tribulation that Jesus referred to in Matthew 24:21 and 29. There is to be the rise of Anti-Christ (II Thess. 2:8–10; Rev. 13). There will be many other events that space does not permit me to discuss here. Some of these are clearly outlined in the Scriptures, and others are mysterious events about which we can only speculate.

When He Comes

However, some of the ultimate results of the coming of Christ are clearly outlined in the Bible:

Peace

First, peace will be established on the earth.

When Karl Barth, the Swiss theologian, visited the United Nations he said: "The international organization could be an earthly parable of the heavenly kingdom, but real peace will not be made here although it might seem as an approach. Peace will be made by God Himself at the end of all things."

Louis Mumford has said: "War is a specific product of civilization." It seems to be a characteristic that distinguishes man from beast, for man preys on his fellowman in a way not true of the beast.

Now with powers of total destruction that ancient man dared impute only to his gods, and with the practice of investing ever-increasing quantities of intelligence and energy in the building of even more dangerous absolute weapons, man has created the conditions that prepare for the return of Christ. The only solution to this problem of war is Christ's return and war's abolition. With all our military power, and with political alliances and military structures to preserve peace, we are coming at last to the end of the road. Our modern hopes for peace cannot rest on the practice of creating more war.

Pacifism will fail, for the pacifist acts as if all men are regenerate and can be appealed to through persuasion and goodwill. The pacifist also refuses to recognize the role of power in the preservation of justice, alongside the role of love. While disarmament might be desirable, unilateral disarmament would be folly in our present world. We must first disarm men's passions and change their hearts. War must be removed from men's hearts before it can be removed from the world's battlefields.

Isaiah the prophet, looking forward to that day of future peace, said, "His name shall be called . . . The Prince of Peace. Of the increase of his government and peace there shall be no end" (Isa. 9:6,7). Christ will establish permanent world peace.

Social Justice

Second, our social institutions will be reconstructed.

The present social institutions, which seek the establishment of justice for all, the abolition of poverty, the reduction of crime, and the prosperity of all men, cannot adequately achieve these results as long as these institutions ignore the basic problem of human nature. We can never secure total social justice by law alone. The Christian social reformer makes the mistake of expecting the existing social order to live up to the Christian ethic. Man does not have the capacity to live up to the Christian ethic. Christianity cannot expect the world to live the truths of the Gospel until it has the life that the Gospel provides in Christ. We Christians ought to be light and salt in the society in which we live. Christians have changed society for the better, but the ultimate and total solutions remain beyond us because of man's sinful nature.

Communists teach that by revolution and violence the perfect society shall be established here on earth and thereafter all men shall be wholly happy. Communism offers its panacea by compulsion and a forceful redistribution of property. However, all of these schemes are destined to fail and to create other conditions that only the return of Christ can solve.

In Isaiah 2:19, the Lord says He will "shake . . . the earth." I take this to include all social institutions.

Nature Restored

Third, Christ will restore nature to its original state.

Today all nature is in the minor key. Nature lives by the fang and the claw. Anyone who has seen a Walt Disney nature film knows that nearly all of the animal world is engaged in the survival of the fittest. This will all be changed. The prophets foresaw a time when the wolf would dwell with the lamb and the desert would blossom as a rose, when disease and death would be almost nonexistent, when the knowledge of God "would cover the earth as the waters cover the sea," when sin and its evil deeds would be limited and restricted. This constituted the prophetic dream of a golden age, a dream that became the promise of the Kingdom of God on earth from the lips of Christ Himself. Nature itself is to be transformed. The thorns and the thistles will be removed. The venom will be taken from the mouths of the serpents. All of nature will sing and shout to the glory of God.

International Righteousness

Fourth, Christ will make righteousness international.

"Nevertheless we, according to his promise, look for new heavens and a new earth, wherein dwelleth righteousness" (II Pet. 3:13). Human nature will be totally and completely changed. Righteousness will spring from the hearts of men. Moral good never comes from coercion. You can protect others by restraining the criminal, but the criminal himself is not improved. Man is improved only from the inside out.

President Eisenhower talked often about peace with justice. Such a period is coming permanently to the world, but only under the leadership of Jesus Christ. Perfect justice and righteousness are missing in our world. Now and then for brief periods in the ages of highest social achievement, and particularly under the impact of Christian ideals, such an era has been approximated, but only in a limited area for a limited time and in a limited way. The totality of evil and depravity existing in men is having its normal fruitage in a social order so complicated, confused, and corrupted that only the return of Christ can save it.

God's Will Done on Earth

Fifth, Christ will reproduce the will of God on earth.

This will be the time when the prayer He taught His disciples will be answered, "Thy kingdom come. Thy will be done on earth as it is in heaven." Heaven is heaven because God's will is its order. Earth will be heavenly when God's will is its order.

The Apostle John foresaw a time when a new heaven and a new earth will come into being. The chief characteristic of this new heaven and earth will be righteousness. The chief characteristic of our present earth is sin; hence its disorders, evils, disasters, injustices, disease, and death. When the new order of righteousness prevails, a new order of life will prevail.

When Christ came the first time, He dealt with evil as individual and hereditary. When He comes again, Christ will deal with evil as a practice. He will institute an age of such benevolence that evil cannot reign; and cruelty, oppression, and slavery will no longer exist. All of this will come to pass as a result of the personal reign of Christ following His return.

Marguerite Higgins, a war correspondent, received the much coveted Pulitzer prize for international reporting because of her coverage of the Korean struggle. She wrote an account of the Fifth Company of Marines, which originally numbered eighteen thousand, in their combat with more than a hundred thousand Chinese Communists:

"It was particularly cold—42° below zero—that morning when reporters were standing around. The weary soldiers, half frozen, stood by their dirty trucks eating from tin cans. A huge Marine was eating cold beans with his trench knife. His clothes were as stiff as a board. His face, covered with a heavy beard, was crusted with mud. A correspondent asked him, "If I were God and could grant you anything you wished, what would you most like?' The man stood motionless for a moment. Then he raised his head and replied, 'Give me tomorrow.' "[1]

For the true believer in Jesus Christ, the future is assured. We await the distant trumpet announcing the coming of Christ. The Christian has tomorrow. It is the Kingdom of God on earth.

---

[1] G. Curtis Jones, *What Are You Worth?* (St. Louis: Bethany Press, 1954).

20

Signs of the End

In 1860, the French chemist Marcelin Berthelot said: "Within a hundred years of physical and chemical science, man will know what the atom is. It is my belief when science reaches this stage, God will come down to earth with His big ring of keys and will say to humanity, 'Gentlemen, it is closing time.' "[1]

Not long ago in the *New York Times* Book Review Section there appeared an article by Michael Amerine entitled "Literature of Doom." It began: "Fantasy and fantastic fiction are merely handwriting on the wall compared to today's true literature of doom." Some of the current books listed in the article were:

MUST WE HIDE?
THERE WILL BE NO TIME
MANUAL FOR SURVIVAL
FEAR
WAR AND THE BOMB
MUST DESTRUCTION BE OUR DESTINY?
AFTER DOOM, WHAT?
LITTLE WORLD GOODBYE.

One day on the Mount of Olives when the disciples were alone with Jesus, they asked Him three very important questions: "Tell us, when shall these things be? and what shall be the sign of thy coming, and of the end of the world?" (Matt. 24:3). The disciples had accepted the fact that Jesus would return, and now they wanted to know when. They wanted to

---

[1] Walter B. Knight, *Knight's Treasury of Illustrations* (Grand Rapids: Eerdmans Publishing Company, 1962).

know, too, if there would be any signs preceding His coming. They knew that the Old Testament Scriptures were filled with the signs of His first coming and that these Scriptures had prophesied accurately the details of that coming.

If only the world had studied the signs of the Old Testament, they would have known that Jesus was coming and they would have welcomed Him. But their ignorance and blindness concerning the teaching of the Scriptures led them to fail to recognize Him. Hundreds of years before Jesus was born, the Old Testament revealed that:

—He would be of the tribe of Judah (Gen. 49:9, 10)
—He would be born in Bethlehem (Mic. 5:2)
—He would be born of a virgin (Isa. 7:14)
—He would be called out of Egypt (Hos. 11:1)
—He would come as a prophet (Deut. 18:18, 19)
—His own people would reject Him (Isa. 53:3)
—He would make a triumphal entry into Jerusalem (Zech. 9:9)
—He would be betrayed and sold for thirty pieces of silver (Zech. 11:12, 13)
—He would be put to death by crucifixion (Ps. 22)
—His hands and feet would be pierced (Ps. 22:16)
—Soldiers would cast lots for his clothing (Ps. 22:18)
—He would be raised from the dead (Ps. 16:9, 10)
—He would ascend into heaven (Ps. 68:18)

Jesus told His disciples that there would be signs for which they could watch, but He warned them on two occasions to beware of setting dates. "But of that day and hour knoweth no man, no, not the angels of heaven, but my Father only" (Matt. 24:36). "It is not for you to know the times or the seasons, which the Father hath put in his own power" (Acts 1:7). Although He warned them about speculating on the exact time of His return, He did assure them that there were signs throughout the Scriptures, as well as in His own words, which would make it appear to those who have "eyes to see" that the time is near. "When these things begin to come to pass, then look up, and lift up your heads; for your redemption draweth nigh" (Lk. 21:28).

The New Testament uses the word "sign" in various ways. In some instances it is a "wonder" in the form of a miracle to establish the divine claims of Jesus that He was the Son of God. One time Jesus referred to the "signs of the times" to rebuke the Pharisees for their inordinate demands that He produce proofs of His Messiahship. However, there are uses of "signs" that serve as evidences in the Biblical revelation.

Jesus said there would be a future generation with certain characteristics to indicate that the end is near. In other words, there is an "X generation" at some point in history where all the signs will converge. Those whose hearts have been transformed by Jesus Christ, whose minds have been enlightened by the Holy Spirit, will be able to read the signs of that day and to warn the people as Noah did. Today it would seem that those signs are indeed converging for the first time since Christ ascended into heaven.

WHAT ARE SOME OF THESE SIGNS?

1. The Mental State of the World

Jesus said two things would characterize the mental state of the world just before His return. First, "upon the earth distress of nations, with perplexity" (Lk. 21:25). To be distressed is to be oppressed or under pressure. Perplexity means "bewilderment." In other words, He said the generation before His return would be under severe pressure from every point of view and there would be no apparent way out. This sounds very much like something written by Sartre, Camus, Huxley, Hemingway, or some other modern writer. In fact, Jean-Paul Sartre wrote a book called *No Exit*.

Jesus said the world would reach a state of international impasse when nations would go down one blind alley after another, only to find that each was a dead-end street. "Men's hearts failing them for fear, and for looking after those things which are coming on the earth" (Lk. 21:26). There will be worldwide frustration, stalemated wars, and great abundance together with millions starving. As men contemplate the future, He said, they will be not only afraid, they will be terrified.

Second, He said: "And then shall many be offended, and shall betray one another, and shall hate one another" (Matt. 24:10). There has never been a time when people were so on edge, so easily hurt and offended. The psychiatrists are so busy that they themselves have nervous breakdowns as they try frantically to patch up our jangled nerves. Homes crumble under the devastating pressures of modern life. In some parts of the world as the pressures build up, families are actually being betrayed by their own members. We are surely in danger in this generation of psychological breakdown.

2. *The Moral State of the World*

In the time of Noah, it is written: "And God saw that the wickedness of man was great in the earth, and that every imagination of the thoughts of his heart was only evil continually . . . And God said unto Noah, The end of all flesh is come before me; for the earth is filled with violence through them; and, behold, I will destroy them with the earth" (Gen. 6:5,13). Jesus said: "As it was in the days of Noah, so shall it be also in the days of the Son of man. They did eat, they drank, they married wives, they were given in marriage" (Lk. 17:26,27). Despite God's warnings through Noah, they were so occupied with themselves and with their wickedness that they "knew not until the flood came, and took them all away" (Matt. 24:39).

Jesus also said: "Likewise also as it was in the days of Lot; they did eat, they drank, they bought, they sold, they planted, they builded; but the same day that Lot went out of Sodom it rained fire and brimstone from heaven, and destroyed them all. Even thus shall it be in the day when the Son of man is revealed" (Lk. 17:28–30).

Never has there been a time when men tried so desperately to have fun as they do today. We are sated, banal, and bored. In *The Future of Man,* Teilhard de Chardin wrote: "The great enemy of the modern world, 'Public Enemy No. 1,' is boredom . . . I repeat: despite all appearances, Mankind is bored. Perhaps this is the underlying cause of all our troubles. We no longer know what to do with ourselves."[2] We are even tired from our vacations. It is not just that television programs are so bad, but we have become sick from too much. Long ago Job said: "The triumphing of the wicked is short, and the joy of the hypocrite but for a moment" (Job 20:5). The Bible says: "Even in laughter the heart is sorrowful" (Prov. 14:13).

The world is on a moral binge such as was not known even in the days of Rome. We have at our fingertips every pleasure that man is capable of enjoying, and man has abused every gift God ever gave him, including sex, until he no longer finds joy and satisfaction in them. *Time* magazine[3] reported recently on a "Festival of Free Expression" in a Paris youth center, where young men and women performed before audiences immoral acts of such depravity that they cannot be recounted here. This is man, doing what he wants to do. This is human nature, without God, expressing itself. And it is a sign of the end.

3. A Falling Away

Jesus said: "And many false prophets shall rise, and shall deceive many" (Matt. 24:11). "Now the Spirit speaketh expressly, that in the latter times some shall depart from the faith, giving heed to seducing spirits and doctrines of devils" (I Tim. 4:1). The Apostle Paul warned: "For the time will come when they will not

---

2 Pp. 145, 146.
3 June 4, 1965.

endure sound doctrine; but after their own lusts shall they heap to themselves teachers, having itching ears; and they shall turn away their ears from the truth and shall be turned unto fables" (II Tim. 4:3,4). This all seems to point to a time of widespread hypocrisy when multitudes of people will be herded into the church without having had a personal experience with Jesus Christ. Sects will grow. False teachers will infiltrate the church. The Bible will be under severe attack.

The strategy of Satan has not changed since he asked Eve in the Garden of Eden: "Yea, hath God said?" There are some teachers of religion who try deliberately to destroy the authority of the Scriptures and the faith of the church. They are the wolves in sheeps' clothing about which Jesus warned His followers. They are leaders of the "falling away," which is to characterize the church at the end of the age.

"For there are certain men crept in unawares, who were before of old ordained to this condemnation, ungodly men, turning the grace of our God into lasciviousness, and denying the only Lord God, and our Lord Jesus Christ" (Jude 4). The word translated "crept in unawares" is an unusual Greek word occurring only in this place. Literally translated, it means to "creep in sideways" like a burglar in the house. This burglar has come not to steal our material possessions; he has come to rob us of our faith in God, His Son, and His Word. When faithful men of God raise an outcry against the presence of the burglar, they are accused of disturbing the peace. Old forms of error, known in earlier times, exert themselves again under such labels as "the new morality," "the new theology," and "religionless Christianity."

The Apostle Paul said: "That day shall not come, except there come a falling away first, and that man of sin be revealed, the son of perdition" (II Thess. 2:3). "Falling away" refers plainly to an abandonment of belief. Many passages of Scripture speak of this. The prophet Amos wrote: "Behold, the days come, saith the Lord God, that I will send a famine in the land, not a famine of bread, nor a thirst for water, but of hearing the words of the Lord: and they shall wander from sea to sea, and from the north even to the east, they shall run to and fro to seek the word of the Lord, and shall not find it" (Amos 8:11–12). There will come a time when people hungering for the truth will seek it where it is supposedly disseminated, such as books and churches, but they will not hear the Word of the Lord. Instead of receiving a message to satisfy their spiritual longings, they will hear a sermon on some current political or social problem, or a sermonette on art and literature. And so they wander from one place to another, going from hope to despair, and eventually they give up. "Now the Spirit speaketh expressly, that in the latter times some shall depart from the faith, giving heed to seducing spirits, and doctrines of devils; speaking lies in hypocrisy; having their conscience seared" (I Tim. 4:1, 2).

4. An Increase in Lawlessness

Jesus said: "As lawlessness spreads, men's love for one another will grow cold" (Matt. 24:12, NEB). "This know also, that in the last days perilous times shall come. For men shall be lovers of their own selves, covetous, boasters, proud, blasphemers, disobedient to parents, unthankful, unholy, without natural affection, truce-breakers, false accusers, incontinent, fierce, despisers of those that are good, traitors, heady, high-minded, lovers of pleasure more than lovers of God; having a form of godliness, but denying the power thereof: from such turn away" (II Tim. 3:1–5). Notice that this passage teaches explicitly that these are the characteristics of the last days. Our newspapers are filled with accounts of the rebellion of youth, the overthrow of governments, and riots in almost every country on earth. We have only to quote the crime records to show that lawlessness is increasing at a frightening rate around the world. Jesus taught that just before the end, lawlessness would be worldwide. He said: "Ye shall hear of wars and commotions" (Lk. 21:9). This word "commotions" carries with it the idea of rebellion, revolution, and lawlessness, indicating that this is a sign of the approaching end of the age.

5. The Coming of Scoffers

"There shall come in the last days scoffers, walking after their own lusts, and saying, Where is the promise of his coming? for since the fathers fell asleep, all things continue as they were from the beginning of the creation" (II Pet. 3:3,4). Many professing Christians say this is a false teaching since the second coming of Christ did not take place as the early church expected. They say, "Why hasn't Christ already come? Did not Jesus say: 'Surely I come quickly'?" However, that promise literally translated says: "I am actually on the way."

In our skyscrapers many offices are as high as seventy or eighty stories. An executive on the top floor calls to the basement garage and says: "I am on my way. Get my car ready." This does not mean that he has actually arrived at the garage, but that he is on the way and by the time the car is ready, he will be there. This is the meaning conveyed to us in the words: "I come quickly." Those Christians who are now in the basement or the grave shall be raised first; and when they reach the ground floor in a moment, in a twinkling of the eye, we shall be taken up together to meet the Lord in the air.

Those who believe in the inevitability of human progress find it hard to believe in the return of Christ. If we believe that man is going ahead by himself, we will never accept the promise of Christ that He will return and bring an end to sin itself.

Also, there are those who refuse to believe in His coming again, because it would cut across their plans and dreams. They want to eat, drink, and be merry without any interference in their self-centered lives. This is why the scoffers in Noah's time refused to believe in the flood of which He tried to warn them.

6. Widespread Persecution

"Then shall they deliver you up to be afflicted, and shall kill you: and ye shall be hated of all nations for my name's sake. And then shall many be offended, and shall betray one another, and shall hate one another" (Matt. 24:9, 10).

"But take heed to yourselves: for they shall deliver you up to councils; and in the synagogues ye shall be beaten: and ye shall be brought before rulers and kings for my sake, for a testimony against them. . . . the brother shall betray the brother to death, and the father the son; and children shall rise up against their parents, and shall cause them to be put to death. And ye shall be hated of all men for my name's sake" (Mk. 13:9, 12, 13). Notice the emphasis Jesus puts on "for my name's sake." Thousands of Christians compromise their faith in Jesus Christ by denying Him. Even some clergymen neglect or deliberately refuse to close a public prayer in the name of Jesus for fear of offending an unbeliever. They cannot endure the persecution that may follow an acknowledgment of Jesus Christ. This, too, is another sign.

7. Affluence

"Go to now, ye rich men, weep and howl for your miseries that shall come upon you. Your riches are corrupted, and your garments are moth-eaten. Your gold and silver is cankered; and the rust of them shall be a witness against you, and shall eat your flesh as it were fire. Ye have heaped treasure together for the last days" (Jas. 5:1–3).

While millions starve, other millions grow richer. A few years ago, when we heard of a millionaire, we thought of him with awe. Today in the Western world there are thousands of millionaires. No longer is a man with a hundred thousand dollars considered wealthy. There is nothing wrong with being wealthy if the wealth was acquired honestly. However, neglect of the stewardship of one's resources is a sin in the sight of God. The Apostle Paul warned: "The love of money is the root of all evil" (I Tim. 6:10). Jesus said: "Beware of covetousness" (Lk. 12:15). Samuel Johnson said: "The lust of gold, unfeeling and remorseless, is the last corruption of degenerate man."

This is, of course, one of the great appeals of Communism. Disciples of Marxist materialism have gone into the poverty-stricken areas of the world and called the people their comrades. This appeals to those who live in substandard conditions while at the same time they see pictures of prosperous, wealthy nations. The Apostle said this would be one of the signs of the end.

8. The Preparation for Armageddon

"And ye shall hear of wars and rumors of wars" (Matt. 24:6). The Bible indicates that toward the end, wars will become more widespread, more devastating, and more frequent.

There is no doubt that the nations of the world are setting the stage for the enactment of one of the most terrible scenes in the drama of human strife, and the whole world is hurtling toward a war far greater than anything known before. In the Scriptures it is called the "battle of Armageddon" (Rev. 16:14–16; Joel 3:9–14).

Modern war is the most highly developed of all sciences. We have perfected our weapons but failed to perfect the men who use them. There have been men such as Hitler who would have used any means whatsoever to conquer the world. Can we assume that no such man lives now?

9. Knowledge and Travel

"But thou, O Daniel, shut up the words, and seal the book, even to the time of the end: many shall run to and fro, and knowledge shall be increased" (Dan.

12:4). The meaning of Daniel's words could not possibly have been understood until this generation. Indeed, the Scripture says that they are "closed up and sealed till the time of the end" (Dan. 12:9).

Today we know well what Daniel meant. This is surely the age of speed and travel and knowledge. Human knowledge doubles every fifteen years, and man has gone from the horse cart to missiles in less than two generations. Walter Reuther, the American labor leader, told me recently that we will gain more knowledge in the next ten years than we acquired in the past two hundred years. Until the coming of the automobile and the airplane, it was hard to understand what Daniel meant when he said that "many shall run to and fro." But now there are millions of cars on the highways and countless planes in the air at all hours of every day and night.

This passage could mean, also, that knowledge of the prophetic Scriptures will increase, and this is certainly true today. There is a greater interest in, and more study of, the prophetic Scriptures on the part of many Christians than perhaps at any time in history. New archaeological and scientific discoveries have brought prophecy into sharper focus. For the first time since the Scriptures were written under the inspiration of the Holy Spirit, we can understand many parts of them in the light of current world events.

10. Peace Conferences

"For when they shall say, Peace and safety; then sudden destruction cometh upon them, as travail upon a woman with child; and they shall not escape" (I Thess. 5:3). Never has there been so much talk of peace. The world longs desperately for peace, but no peace seems to be in sight.

In the second Psalm David asked: "Why do the (nations) rage?" Because they do not know which way to turn in this age of violence and threat of destruction. In that same Psalm David said: "The kings of the earth set themselves, and the rulers take counsel together, against the Lord, and against his Anointed, saying, Let us break their bands asunder, and cast away their cords from us." This "take counsel together" speaks of the desperate effort on the part of the world's leaders to establish peace, but God is left out of their planning. The Prince of Peace is never consulted about peace. Foolish man pursues his own program, claiming boldly that he can solve his problems by himself without God.

11. The Coming of the World Dictator

There are so many interesting references in the Bible to a future world government to be ruled by a great Anti-Christ that space does not permit discussing all of them here. It is obvious that the world's acceptance of one-man rule must be preceded by a period of preparation. At a recent peace conference in Washington, speaker after speaker referred to the necessity and the possibility of a world government. In the Gideon Seymour Memorial Lecture at the University of Minnesota, Arnold Toynbee said: "Living together as a single family is the only future mankind can have now that Western technology has simultaneously annihilated distance and invented the atomic bomb." He added: "The alternative to the destruction of the human race is a worldwide social fusion of all the tribes, nations, civilizations, and religions of man."

During the past decade, it has been realized that no nation can live to itself, for what affects one country affects all. There is also the trend toward dictatorship in many of the emerging nations and this means a breakdown of democracy. Government in the hands of a large group has often failed to function adequately, partly because of widely differing views. Endless differences, debates, and discussions nullify the value of the counsel of many. I once asked the dictator of an African state why they did not have democracy in his country. He replied: "Before democracy can work you must have an informed and intelligent electorate. We will not be ready for democracy for a hundred years."

In the Bible we read: "For God hath put in their hearts to fulfil his will, and to agree, and give their kingdom unto the beast, until the words of God shall be fulfilled" (Rev. 17:17.) Another revealing passage says: "For the mystery of iniquity doth already work: only he who now letteth will let, until he be taken out of the way. And then shall that Wicked be revealed, whom the Lord shall consume with the spirit of his mouth, and shall destroy with the brightness of his coming: Even him, whose coming is after the working of Satan with all power and signs and lying wonders, and with all deceivableness of unrighteousness in them that perish; because they received not the love of the truth, that they might be saved. And for this cause God shall send them strong delusion, that they should believe a lie: that they all might be damned who believed not the truth, but had pleasure in unrighteousness" (II Thess. 2:7–12). This tells us clearly that there has been a lawless power at work through the ages, and that toward the end of this age when people "have pleasure in unrighteousness," the restrainer, who is the Holy Spirit, will restrain only until the believers are taken away.

Then this superman who will be the incarnation of Satan, called Anti-Christ in the Scriptures, will be permitted to have world control. The Bible teaches that the world will reach a point where it will set up a world government, and a world dictator or president will emerge. Television cameras will no doubt be on the scene, and the news will be flashed around the world that a man of peace, a universal ruler, has been chosen.

The word "beast" in Revelation 13 is used to express the idea that this will be a man of great strength and ability to force his will upon the world. The term "beast" is not meant to indicate repulsiveness. On the contrary, the Scripture says that this man will be admired, feared, and worshiped. He will dominate the world scene with a cleverness the world has never known. He will temporarily put down war that has been devastating the earth. He will devise brilliant economic methods with immediate results. Prosperity will return, money will be plentiful everywhere, and the fear that has gripped every part of the world will give way to hope. The world will stand in awe and wonder at his superlative genius and power, as millions actually worship him as a god. He will regiment all humanity, demanding that before food can be purchased his subjects shall be stamped with his mark (Rev. 13:17). The age of the computer will contribute to his ability to control the life of every person on the globe. He will be the very incarnation of evil. His one dream, one desire, one ambition will be to destroy even the thought of God on the face of the earth. He will blaspheme God and will exalt himself beyond any kind of god the world has ever known.

In 1902, *Harper's* magazine carried an amazing portrait of the coming ruler. The editors of *Harper's* said: "There will arise 'the man.' He will be strong in action, epigrammatic in manner, personally handsome, and continuously victorious. He will sweep aside parliaments and demagogues, carry civilizations to glory, reconstruct them into an empire, and hold it together by circulating his profile and organizing further successes. He will codify everything, galvanize Christianity, he will organize learning into meek academies of little men and prescribe a wonderful educational system, and the grateful nations will deify a lucky and aggressive egotism." The Bible says of this world ruler: "And through his policy . . . he shall cause craft to prosper in his hand; and he shall magnify himself in his heart" (Dan. 8:25). The Bible teaches that some of his early followers will be Christians in name only.

12. Worldwide Evangelism

"And this gospel of the kingdom shall be preached in all the world for a witness unto all nations; and then shall the end come" (Matt. 24:14).

In the year 1500, the Bible had been printed in only fourteen languages. By 1800, it was in seventy-one languages, and by 1965 it had been printed in more than 1,250 languages and dialects. Add to this the media of radio and television, as well as the accelerated missionary programs of the churches since World War II. There are very few places in the world today where the Gospel cannot be heard. Because of modern travel, communications, and techniques, it is possible that the prophecy of Matthew 24:14 is being fulfilled in our generation for the first time.

There are many other signs of the end revealed in the Bible that space does not allow me to mention. But this we know, Jesus Christ will come. I do not know when. I do not know the hour, the day, the month, or the year. It is wrong and unscriptural to try to set the date of Christ's return. God alone knows when He will come. Yet the Bible says that He will come back to this earth. There is no possibility that the nations of the world can solve the problems of human nature until He comes again.

One thing we do know, the coming of Christ is nearer than when we first believed. It may be that many of these events will transpire before this generation has passed away. The poet Campbell said: "Coming events cast their shadows before." What we see happening today may well be a preparation for God's intervention in human affairs with the coming of Jesus Christ. Paul told the Christians to "comfort one another with these words" (I Thess. 4:18).

What Should You Do?

For the Christian, all is not hopeless unless his affections are centered on the things of this world. If you have been living a life dedicated to God, laying up treasures in heaven, with your affections on things above, then you have no cause for despair and discouragement. This could be the hour before the dawn when Christ shall return.

In view of these rapidly moving events, what should your attitude be?

1. PREPARING WITH URGENCY

Jesus said: "Therefore be ye also ready: for in such an hour as ye think not the Son of man cometh" (Matt. 24:44). Are you ready to meet Him if He should come today? In many places, the Bible warns us to be ready. You may say that this is an appeal based on fear. "By faith Noah, being warned of God of things not seen as yet, moved with fear, prepared an ark to the saving of his house" (Heb. 11:7). That word "fear" could be translated "terrified." Noah was terrified at the prospect of the coming events, and it was this fear that drove him to build the ark.

2. WAITING WITH PATIENCE

"For ye have need of patience, that, after ye have done the will of God, ye might receive the promise. For yet a little while, and he that shall come will come, and will not tarry" (Heb. 10:36,37). The promised birth of Isaac to Abraham and Sarah was long delayed; but God's promise did come to pass, even when it seemed impossible.

3. WATCHING WITH ANTICIPATION

Matthew Henry wrote: "To watch, implies not only to believe that our Lord will come, but to desire that He would come, to be often thinking of His coming, and always looking for it, as sure and near, and the time of it uncertain."

"We are waiting with longing expectation for the coming . . . of the Lord Jesus Christ" (Phil. 3:20, Weymouth). The Apostle Paul wrote to Titus: "Looking for that blessed hope, and the glorious appearing of the great God and our Saviour Jesus Christ" (Tit. 2:13). After hearing a minister preach on the second coming of Christ, Queen Victoria said: "I wish He would come during my lifetime so that I could take my crown and lay it at His feet."

4. WORKING WITH ZEAL

"Blessed is that servant, whom his lord when he cometh shall find so doing" (Matt. 24:46). Some people have the idea that if Christ is coming, then why must we carry on? Why not quit working and watch? This was one of the problems of the Thessalonians to whom Paul wrote to affirm that Christ was coming. He explained some of the details of the last days, and he urged them to get to work. The hope of the coming of Christ should make us work all the harder so that we shall "not be ashamed before him at his coming" (I Jn. 2:28).

To the Christian, the coming of Christ will be a glorious moment. To those outside of Christ, it will be the greatest of all calamities, a tragic separation, an unbelievable disappointment. But to those who are ready, what a glorious consummation! Almost the last words of the Bible are "Surely I come. Amen. Even so, come, Lord Jesus."

21

The Coming Judgment

One of the most colorful agnostics in American history was Robert G. Ingersoll, who gave dramatic lectures throughout the nation, questioning the Bible and the existence of God. One night when he was addressing an audience in a small town in New York, he proclaimed eloquently his doubts about a future judgment and hell. When he was finished an old drunkard stood up in the rear of the hall and said with thick tongue: "I sure hope you are right, Brother Bob. I'm counting on that."

Modern man does not like to think of God in terms of wrath, anger, and judgment. He likes to fashion God after his own preferences and give God the character- istics he wants Him to possess. He tries to remake God to conform to his own wishful thinking and make him- self comfortable in his sins. This modern "god" has the attributes of love, mercy, and forgiveness without jus- tice. This means an absence of judgment and punish- ment for sin. God is reconstructed along the lines of tolerance, all-embracing love, and universal goodwill. The Biblical view that righteousness is as ultimate as love in the divine nature is abandoned. In this picture of God there are no laws that demand absolute obedi- ence and no standards to which man must adhere. For example, more than nine hundred clergymen and stu- dents gathered some time ago at Harvard Divinity School to ponder the so-called "new morality" and its significance for the church. One professor of divinity said that premarital sex between engaged couples was all right, that God would understand. A professor at another theological school thought that no sexual relationship should be absolutely condemned by the church. Thus many church leaders continue to reconstruct God according to the secular and humanistic trends of our time.

However, this kind of "god" would make an impossible world. It would be chaotic, irresponsible, and self-destroying. It would be impossible for man to live with certainty and happiness. To have meaning, man's life must be based upon law and a lawgiver. The Psalmist said: "The law of the Lord is perfect, converting the soul; the testimony of the Lord is sure, making wise the simple. The statutes of the Lord are right, rejoicing the heart: the commandment of the Lord is pure, enlightening the eyes" (Ps. 19:7, 8). The Bible warns that "evil men understand not judgment" (Prov. 28:5). Jesus himself put His stamp of approval on the law when He said: "It is easier for heaven and earth to pass, than one tittle of the law to fail" (Lk. 16:17). The Law of Moses and the Sermon on the Mount are standards that can never be changed. No clergyman has a right to lower these standards in the name of God, lest he be in danger of defiling the law, blaspheming God, and becoming guilty of heresy.

God Will Judge Every Man

The Bible teaches that God is indeed a God of judgment, wrath, and anger.

If the Bible teaches anything, it teaches that God is going to judge man. Time after time Jesus warned of judgment: "It shall be more tolerable for Tyre and Sidon at the day of judgment, than for you" (Matt. 11:22). "Every idle word that men shall speak, they shall give account thereof in the day of judgment" (Matt. 12:36). "The Son of man shall send forth his angels, and they shall gather out of his kingdom all things that offend, and them which do iniquity; and shall cast them into a furnace of fire: there shall be wailing and gnashing of teeth" (Matt. 13:41). "For there is nothing covered, that shall not be revealed;

neither hid, that shall not be known" (Lk. 12:2). "For the Father judgeth no man, but hath committed all judgment unto the Son" (Jn. 5:22).

The Apostles taught throughout the New Testament that there would come a time of judgment: "He hath appointed a day, in the which he will judge the world in righteousness by that man whom he hath ordained" (Acts 17:31). "But after thy hardness and impenitent heart, treasurest up unto thyself wrath against the day of wrath and revelation of the righteous judgment of God; who will render to every man according to his deeds" (Rom. 2:5). "To you who are troubled rest with us, when the Lord Jesus shall be revealed from heaven with his mighty angels, in flaming fire taking vengeance on them that know not God, and that obey not the gospel of our Lord Jesus Christ" (II Thess. 1:7,8). "It is appointed unto men once to die, but after this the judgment" (Heb. 9:27). "A certain fearful looking for of judgment and fiery indignation, which shall devour the adversaries" (Heb. 10:27). "Who shall give account to him that is ready to judge the quick and the dead" (I Pet. 4:5). "The kings of the earth, and the great men, and the rich men, and the chief captains, and the mighty men, and every bondman, and every free man, hid themselves in the dens and in the rocks of the mountains; and said to the mountains and rocks, Fall on us, and hide us from the face of him that sitteth on the throne, and from the wrath of the Lamb: for the great day of his wrath is come; and who shall be able to stand?" (Rev. 6:15-17).

These are only a few of the hundreds of passages that could be cited to point to a time of judgment yet to come, in which every man who has ever lived will be involved and none will escape! If you took all the references to judgment out of the Bible, you would have a much smaller Bible.

Justice, Mercy, and Love

There are many who say that judgment is not consistent with justice, mercy, and love. This is because they do not understand the nature of God. They have refused to accept the revelation of God's nature from the Bible.

Judgment is consistent with *justice*. Justice demands the balancing of the scales, and without judgment this would be impossible. When Jeremiah said "a King shall . . . execute judgment and justice in the earth" (Jer. 23:5), he put these factors in juxtaposition. Justice is impossible without judgment. Law cannot exist without a penalty. Reason would tell us that there will be a time when the Hitlers, the Eichmanns, and the Stalins will be brought to an accounting. Otherwise, there is no justice in the universe. Thousands of evil men have lived and practiced their evil upon others without seeming to pay a penalty in this life. Reason tells us that there will be a time when the crooked places will be made straight (Isa. 45:2).

Judgment is consistent with *mercy*. The God who would be merciful must move in mercy according to the standards of justice and righteousness. Judgment in no way conflicts with mercy; for if mercy is to be extended, judgment must be a part of the divine order. To be merciful without being just is a contradiction.

The judge who administers justice must base his acts upon law. The breaking of law demands penalty. To show mercy in the face of broken law is to destroy order and create chaos. Mercy is a quality that cannot forget or neglect the principle of law. If it is not a universal attitude in all cases of broken law, it is destructive of order.

A number of years ago I was stopped for driving too fast through a speed zone, and in the courtroom I pleaded guilty. The judge was not only friendly but rather embarrassed for me to be in his court. The fine was ten dollars. If he had let me go free, it would have been inconsistent with justice. The penalty had to be paid either by me or someone else!

Judgment is consistent with *love*. A God of love must be a God of justice. It is because God loves that He is just. His justice balances His love and makes His acts of both love and justice meaningful. God could not consistently love men if He did not provide for the judgment of evildoers. His punishment of the evildoer and His separation of the righteous is a manifestation of God's great love. We must always look at the Cross on the dark background of judgment. It was because God's love for man was so intense that He gave His Son so that man would not have to face the judgment.

Judgment is necessary as a spur to conscience. Man needs the incentive of reward for goodness and the threat of punishment as a deterrent against evil. In the present composition of his moral nature, punishment is a necessary "goad" to his conscience. He requires this threat and its warning to prevent the doing of evil. This may not be the highest motive for doing good, but it is necessary in the imperfections that have existed in the moral nature of man since the Garden of Eden. We must take man as he is, not as he ought to be, and predicate our opinions of justice, mercy, love, and judgment on the character of God and the present imperfect nature of man. The "absolute ideal" does not exist except in the unreasoning fancy of the modern philosopher who spins his philosophical theories without consideration of the Biblical revelation of God and of man's spiritual disease.

Suppose in any country that there were no police forces at all. There would be chaos overnight. Suppose there were no courts to straighten out the wrong. What a mess the country would be in. No one would be safe anywhere. In some cities, people are not safe despite police protection, and on some streets even the policemen are in danger. And now and then a policeman is himself arrested for infraction of the law. The evil passions of men, even with law enforcement, are only slightly restrained. To this the daily newspaper testifies with its stories of crime.

The Last Great Conflict

The Bible teaches that man is so rebellious against the laws of God that someday he will mass his armies against God Himself. This will be the last great conflict, Armageddon. "And he gathered them together into a place called in the Hebrew tongue Armageddon" (Rev. 16:16). This will be the final war, the last convulsive effort of fallen man against the law of God. What will be God's answer? A show of mercy? A display of tolerance? *No!* It will be judgment. The only alternative to mercy, spurned and rejected, is judgment. God has offered His love and mercy and forgiveness to men. From the Cross, God has said to the entire world, "I love you." However, when that love is deliberately rejected, the only alternative is judgment.

The Different Judgments

Contrary to popular opinion, the Bible knows nothing of a general judgment in which all men appear before God at the same time. The Bible lists a number of different judgments. For example, there is one judgment of the righteous at the judgment seat of Christ (II Cor. 5:10). There is another judgment of the nations (Matt. 25:31–46). There is also a judgment of the unrighteous dead at the great white throne (Rev. 20:11–15). These judgments of different groups, at different times and for different reasons, form the composite picture of judgment in the events disclosed in the prophetic Scriptures.

The Judgment for Sin

This judgment took place at the Cross. The Scripture says: "For he hath made him to be sin for us, who knew no sin, that we might be made the righteousness of God in him" (II Cor. 5:21). Because of this, the Scripture teaches: "There is therefore now no condemnation to them which are in Christ Jesus" (Rom. 8:1). In other words, the judgment for sin that I deserved is already past. Christ took my judgment on the Cross. Every demand of the law has been met. The law was completely satisfied in the offering that Christ made of Himself for sins. "The Lord hath laid on him the iniquity of us all" (Isa. 53:6). "Who his own self bare our sins in his own body on the tree" (I Pet. 2:24). "But this man, after he had offered one sacrifice for sins for ever, sat down on the right hand of God" (Heb. 10:12).

The law had said: "The wages of sin is death" (Rom. 6:23), and "The soul that sinneth, it shall die" (Ezek. 18:4). I deserved judgment and hell, but Christ took that judgment and hell for me. Christ himself said: "Verily, verily, I say unto you, he that heareth my word, and believeth on Him that sent me, hath everlasting life, and shall not come into condemnation; but is passed from death unto life" (Jn. 5:24). No statement could be any plainer, that the true believer in Jesus Christ shall not come into judgment. That judgment is past. "For thou hast cast all my sins behind thy back" (Isa. 38:17). God said through Jeremiah the prophet: "I will remember their sin no more" (Jer. 31:34).

We shall never understand the extent of God's love in Christ at the Cross until we understand that we shall never have to stand before the judgment of God for our sins. Christ took our sins. He finished the work of redemption. I am not saved through any works of merit of my own. I have preached to thousands of people on every continent, but I shall not go to heaven because I am a preacher. I am going to heaven entirely on the merit of the work of Christ. I shall never stand at God's judgment bar. That is all past.

Once while crossing the North Atlantic, I looked out my porthole when I got up in the morning and saw one of the blackest clouds I had ever seen. I was certain that we were in for a terrible storm. I ordered my breakfast sent to my room and spoke to the steward about the storm. He said, "Oh, we've already come through that storm. It's behind us."

If we are believers in Jesus Christ, we have already come through the storm of judgment. It happened at the Cross.

The Judgment of the Believer

From what I have just said, this sounds like a contradiction. It is not judgment in the sense of condemnation, but of evaluation. It is the time when Christ will give rewards to His own. "For we must all appear before the judgment seat of Christ; that every one may receive the things done in his body, according to that he hath done, whether it be good or bad" (II Cor. 5:10).

While the true believer in Christ cannot work for his salvation because it is "not of works, lest any man should boast" (Eph. 2:9), and because it is "not by works of righteousness which we have done, but according to his mercy he saved us" (Tit. 3:5), nevertheless we can work for a reward. The Scripture says: "For other foundation can no man lay than that is laid, which is Jesus Christ. Now if any man build upon this foundation gold, silver, precious stones, wood, hay, stubble; every man's work shall be made manifest: for the day shall declare it, because it shall be revealed by fire; and the fire shall try every man's work of what sort it is. If any man's work abide which he hath built thereupon, he shall receive a reward. If any man's work shall be burned, he shall suffer loss: but he himself shall be saved; yet so as by fire" (I Cor. 3:11–15).

Any work done by a follower of Christ to the glory of God is "gold, silver, precious stones." But if any follower of Christ works with any self-interest or personal ambition involved, it will be "wood, hay, and stubble" and will be burned.

This is not a question of salvation, but of "works" after salvation. In these passages, the believer in Christ is represented as building a superstructure of service or works that is to be tested by fire. Thus, every Sunday school teacher, every youth worker, every social worker, every clergyman, every Christian is going to pass through the fire which will test every believer's work.

The Apostle Paul was constantly concerned with being "approved" of God (II Cor. 10:18). He was not concerned about his personal salvation, for that had been settled at the Cross. However, he was afraid that his works might be disapproved, if he was not extremely careful about how he worked for God.

Believers in Christ are going to receive a reward at this judgment seat of Christ. This reward is sometimes mentioned in the Scriptures as a "prize" (I Cor. 9:24). Sometimes it is called a "crown" (I Cor. 9:25; Phil. 4:1; I Thess. 2:19).

Believers in Christ owe nothing to God in payment for salvation, which is bestowed as a gift. But they do owe God a life of undivided devotion and service. Even a cup of cold water given in the name of Christ shall not go without its reward. This becomes an incentive to love one's neighbor and to show this love by becoming involved in his troubles and needs. When a woman in New York City had a baby on the street and screamed for help, scores of persons passed her by. They would not even call a doctor or the police. They said that they did not want to get involved. One of those who did not want to get involved was a professing Christian, who later was filled with such remorse and conviction that he went to his pastor tearfully to blurt out his sin. Certainly, this man lost a reward that day.

The Great White Throne Judgment

This is recorded in Revelation 20:11–13, where the Apostle John says: "And I saw a great white throne, and him that sat on it, from whose face the earth and the heaven fled away; and there was found no place for them. And I saw the dead, small and great, stand before God; and the books were opened: and another book was opened, which is the book of life: and the dead were judged out of those things which were written in the books, according to their works. And the sea gave up the dead which were in it; and death and hell delivered up the dead which were in them: and they were judged every man according to their works."

Here is the judgment toward which every person outside Christ is headed. The date has already been set by God. All men of all races and nationalities, both past and present, will be there. It will be the day for which all other days were made. You may make and break appointments in this life—but this is one appointment you will keep.

Modern skeptics and scoffers will laugh at and ridicule the idea of a coming judgment. They laughed at Noah's prediction of the flood. They laughed at Jeremiah when he predicted the destruction of Jerusalem. They laughed at Lot when he warned the men of Sodom that God was going to rain fire and brimstone. They laughed at Amos when he warned Israel of coming judgment. But all these judgments came true. "God . . . now commandeth all men every where to repent: because he hath appointed a day, in which he will judge the world in righteousness" (Acts 17:30, 31).

In that day "The Books" will be opened. These books contain the records of every man's life from the cradle to the grave. In the Chapel of St. George in London's Westminster Abbey, is a memorial of World War II. It consists of four bound volumes, which contain the names of the sixty thousand civilians who were killed by enemy action in the city of London. One volume lies open on the shrine and a light shines down upon the typescript names that appear on the opened pages. Each day a page is turned.

Thus will the names of those who were rich or poor, titled or common, old or young, healthy or ill, sound of body or crippled, famous or infamous, stand together to be revealed in the light for all to see on the pages that are kept so accurately by God. It is a book of death. What a terrifying moment for millions when "The Books" are opened.

Dr. Wilbur Penfield, director of the Montreal Neurological Institute, said in a report to the Smithsonian Institute: "Your brain contains a permanent record of your past that is like a single continuous strip of movie film complete with sound track. This film library records your whole waking life, from childhood on. You can live again those scenes from your past, one at a time, when a surgeon applies a gentle electrical current to a certain point on the temporal cortex of your brain." The report goes on to say that as you relive the scenes from your past, you feel exactly the same emotions that you did during the original experience. Could it be that the human race will be confronted by this irrefutable record at the judgment bar of God when "God shall judge the secrets of men by Jesus Christ"? (Rom. 2:16).

There are many warnings in the Scriptures concerning that great day that is to come, that day of judgment. This will be the day prophesied in Proverbs 1:24–31: "Because I have called, and ye refused; I have stretched out my hand, and no man regarded; but ye have set at nought all my counsel, and would none of my reproof: I also will laugh at your calamity; I will mock when your fear cometh; when your fear cometh as desolation, and your destruction cometh as a whirlwind; when distress and anguish cometh upon you. Then shall they call upon me, but I will not answer; they shall seek me early, but they shall not find me: For that they hated knowledge, and did not choose the fear of the Lord: They would none of my counsel: they despised all my reproof. Therefore shall they eat of the fruit of their own way, and be filled with their own devices."

In that great day, men will call upon God for mercy, but it will be too late. In that day, men will seek God, but they will not be able to find Him. It will be too late.

This is the day Jesus referred to in the Sermon on the Mount when He said: "Not every one that saith unto me, Lord, Lord, shall enter into the kingdom of heaven; but he that doeth the will of my Father which is in heaven. Many will say to me in *that day,* Lord, Lord, have we not prophesied in thy name? and in thy name have cast out devils? and in thy name done many wonderful works? And then will I profess unto them, I never knew you: depart from me, ye that work iniquity" (Matt. 7:21–23).

There will even be people who did the work of the Lord. They were busy in the church. They had done many wonderful works. But Jesus Himself says, "I never knew you." What a dreadful thing. They thought their own good works would save them. It should sober us into the realization that someday Jesus Christ will be the Judge. "For the Father judgeth no man, but hath committed all judgment unto the Son" (Jn. 5:22).

When he was a young man, Judge Warren Candler practiced law. One of his clients was charged with murder, and the young lawyer made the utmost effort to clear his client of the charge. There were some extenuating circumstances, and the lawyer made the most of them in his plea before the jury. Moreover, there were present in the court the aged father and mother of the man charged with murder; and the young lawyer worked on the sympathies and emotions of the jury by frequent references to the God-fearing parents.

In due course, the jury retired for deliberation. When they had reached a verdict, they returned to the jury box. Their verdict read: "We find the defendant not guilty." The young lawyer, himself a Christian, had a serious talk with his cleared client. He warned him to steer clear of evil ways and to trust God's power to keep him straight.

Years passed. Again the man was brought into court. Again the charge was murder. The lawyer who had defended him at his first trial was now the judge on the bench. At the conclusion of the trial, the jury rendered its verdict of "GUILTY."

Ordering the condemned man to stand for sentencing, Judge Candler said, "At your first trial, I was your lawyer, today I am your judge. The verdict of the jury makes it mandatory for me to sentence you to be hanged by the neck until you are dead."

Today Christ is our Lawyer, our Savior, willing to forgive and to cleanse and to forget. However, there is coming a fearful day when He will be our Judge.

22

The World on Fire

A friend said to Mark Twain: "I am worried. The world is coming to an end."

"Don't be worried," replied the famous humorist. "We can get along without it."

Mark Twain may not have known it, but he spoke the truth. We can get along without it, because God has arranged to fashion a new world by fire. The Apostle Peter wrote: "But the day of the Lord will come as a thief in the night; in the which the heavens shall pass away with a great noise, and the elements shall melt with fervent heat, the earth also and the works that are therein shall be burned up" (II Pet. 3:10).

This time of burning was foreseen by the prophets as the great and terrible day of the Lord when the earth would quake, the heavens tremble, the sun become dark, and the stars withdraw their shining. It would be a day, said the prophet, when "a fire devoureth" and "a flame burneth." Over and over again, the prophets used the word "fire."

Many times in the Bible the word "fire" is not the fire of combustion as we commonly know it. The Bible teaches that God uses fire as a cleansing and purifying agent. When we read that the Holy Spirit came as "tongues of fire," we do not suppose these were literal fires but rather a representation of the character of the Holy Spirit as a cleansing agent. Fire can be considered also an agent of purification. When the prophets speak of fire in the world's judgment, or when Peter mentions fire at the end of the age, it is not likely that they refer to the fire of combustion. It could be the fire of fission, the release of nuclear power by the splitting of the atom. This is only speculation, of course, but it could be the elemental and creative form of fire used in the beginning, and to be used again in the "new beginning" to bring into being a new earth.

The Fire of Judgment

Certainly it will be a fire of judgment upon the wicked world. The book of Revelation is occupied largely with details of these judgments, centering on the unloosing of the seven seals (Chapter 6), the blasting of the seven trumpets (Chapter 8), and the pouring out of the seven vials (Chapter 16). These are no doubt symbolic representations of the series of judgments that conclude the present age. It is when these judgments are over that Christ is to come in all His splendid glory. His coming is likened to a flash of lightning (Matt. 24:27) and to chariots like a whirlwind (Isa. 66:15). His eyes are likened to a flame of fire (Rev. 1:14), and His voice to that of a roaring lion (Joel 3:16). It is called in the Bible "the great and terrible day" when men shall creep into clefts and ravines and call for the mountains and rocks to "Fall on us, and hide us from the face of him that sitteth on the throne, and from the wrath of the Lamb: for the great day of his wrath is come; and who shall be able to stand?" (Rev. 6:16, 17). It is interesting to note that the last prayer of mankind will be, not to the true and living God, but to the rocks and the mountains. Even then, man's heart will be in such revolt against God that he will turn to idols instead of to God.

The Purifying Fire

However, it will be not only a fire of judgment but a fire of cleansing and purifying. Among the vast number of promises in the Bible is the promise of a new world. This is the promise that wrong shall be made right, evil shall be made good, the corrupt shall be made clean, and the curse shall be changed into a blessing. The fulfillment of this will be in the new heavens and the new earth. This is what Peter described when he wrote:

"We, according to his promise, look for new heavens and a new earth, wherein dwelleth righteousness" (II Pet. 3:13). But we are in danger of being robbed of the comfort of this promise by two things, according to Peter. *First,* by the presence of the unending cycle of evil, disappointment, sickness, injustice, and death, which could obscure this great hope for a new world. So the Apostle said: "I stir up your pure minds by way of remembrance" (II Pet. 3:1). *Second,* by the presence of scoffers who ask: "Where is the promise of his coming?" This scoffing is based on their contention that "since the fathers fell asleep, all things continue as they were from the beginning" (II Pet. 3:4). The scoffer says this is a world of natural law, therefore divine intervention is unlikely. But the scoffer is guilty of monumental ignorance in his supposition that "all things continue as they were from the beginning of the creation."

God intervened in human affairs through the flood in the past, and He will intervene in the future. God intervened in human affairs by the Cross of Christ, to let the world know of His great love for man, "not willing that any should perish," and He will do so again in the events surrounding the second coming of Christ. In the past, the instrument of intervention was water, but in the future it will be fire.

The Threefold Change to Come

In II Peter 3 the Apostle described a *threefold change* to occur at that time. *First,* "The heavens shall pass away with a great noise." This probably refers to the atmosphere surrounding the earth. It does not mean they will pass out of existence, but that they will change. It means displacement, not destruction, for in their place will come a new atmosphere and a new earth. They will be reconstructed for the habitation of the new man who will have a new body. Even the climate will change to accommodate this new man.

Second, Peter says: "The elements shall melt with fervent heat." Here "elements" means that which is rudimentary, or the first step. When it applies to matter, as it does here, it refers to the rudimentary structure of matter in terms of atoms. All matter consists of atoms. All elements can be changed by heat. It is commonly supposed that this is the heat of combustion or burning, but it could be the heat generated by separating the proton and neutron in the nucleus of the atom, thereby releasing the tremendous heat energy in nature by which the present heaven and earth will be changed into the new heaven and new earth. We really do not know. We can only conjecture in the light of the knowledge of modern science.

In dealing with the future in terms of Biblical prophecy we are not entitled to make dogmatic assertions. We are entitled, however, to make reasonable assumptions in the interpretation of future events. With the incredible amount of information available to a modern interpreter, he is in a position to make these reasonable assumptions, which promise to bring great enlightenment in his understanding of the Scripture. Thus today we are in a position to understand such Scriptures as Peter's description of the new heavens and earth to an extent that was not possible a generation ago.

The *third* change Peter describes is in the earth. He says: "The earth also and the works that are therein shall be burned up." Whatever is not suited for the new life of the new world will be destroyed. This is what some call the end of the world, but the world will never end. It will only be changed into a better world.

The process of change that will produce the new heavens and earth is seen in these words: "Seeing then that all these things shall be dissolved, what manner of persons ought ye to be in all holy conversation [manner of life] and godliness, looking for and hasting unto the coming of the day of God, wherein the heavens being on fire shall be dissolved, and the elements shall melt with fervent heat?" (II Pet. 3:11, 12).

It is remarkable that two thousand years ago a divinely inspired writer should have used the term "dissolve," which has become suddenly fraught with modern meaning through contemporary science.

"Dissolved" was the same word Jesus used when Lazarus stood before Him in front of his burial tomb, bound in grave clothes. Jesus said: "Loose him, and let him go" (Jn. 11:44). And when the things of nature "shall be dissolved," they shall be loosed from their grave clothes of disease, death, and poverty. All nature will be let go into a new and glorious state of existence.

Every one of us has dissolved a tablet in a glass of water. What took place? The tablet disappeared, but it was not destroyed. Instead of a solid, it became a liquid. It changed its appearance but not its substance. It assumed another form of existence. This happens every time you take an aspirin.

Some such dissolving as this will take place—not destruction or extinction, but a change into new forms, conditions, and occurrences. The catalyst could well be a fire, such as that of nuclear fission. Great geological, zoological, chemical, and astronomical changes will take place, but what is of even greater importance is the new order of things. Great moral and spiritual changes will occur because it will be a new world "wherein dwelleth righteousness."

What is wrong with the world is sin in human nature and the curse in physical nature. "Cursed is the ground for thy sake . . . thorns also and thistles shall it bring forth to thee; and thou shalt eat the herb of the field: in the sweat of thy face shalt thou eat bread" (Gen. 3:17–19). This will all be changed! The dissolving, loosing process will produce the change in physical nature as well as the change in human nature. Righteousness will be the determining characteristic of the new world.

The Bible says: "Behold, I make all things new" (Rev. 21:5). God will do this by means of fire. This leads us to ask these questions: Why new heavens and a new earth? Why fire? Why judgment? Why cataclysmic change? Why not instead of these things the continuation of human progress producing a golden age?

The answer lies in the fact of sin and God's redemptive purpose. Sin cannot be destroyed or changed by any scientific process. Just as there had to be a Cross

and its Golgotha to end sin in the heart, so there must
be another divine event to end evil in the world. There
is no easy way for redemption to be accomplished.
Man, as well as God, must suffer. Man must feel the
awful price paid for sin. This time it will be worldwide
in both physical and human nature. The new heavens
and earth will emerge from a world on fire. Every
vestige of sin and corruption must be destroyed. Even
matter will be purified. Every aspect of the primeval
curse of sin must be obliterated. The world must be let
loose and freed from the restrictions and limitations
imposed upon it by the curse of sin. There must be
universal riddance of all evil in man and nature, so that
no handicaps are carried over into the structure and
composition of the new world.

Preparing for the Future

The future belongs to those who prepare for it, and
we are instructed to prepare for it. Peter wrote: "Seeing
that ye look for such things, be diligent that ye may be
found of him in peace, without spot, and blameless" (II
Pet. 3:14).

The Bible says: "The world passeth away, and the
lust thereof: but he that doeth the will of God abideth
for ever" (I Jn. 2:17). Recently, I talked with a famous
architect who said that his buildings would last for
eternity. I had to smile, for he has built only for an
hour. Our world will disappear like a child's castle of
sand on the beach. The pride of power, the pomp of
wealth, the beauty of art, the cunning of skill—all will
go. The sea of flame will overwhelm and devour everything without exception. The whole world will become
again one molten mass.

Then God will take the molten mass and reshape the
earth and the heavens into His own design.

Meanwhile the Bible teaches that Satan will first be
bound, then released, and cast into the lake of fire. "And
he laid hold on the dragon, that old serpent, which is the
Devil, and Satan, and bound him a thousand years" (Rev.

20:2). "And the devil that deceived them was cast into the lake of fire and brimstone, where the beast and the false prophet are, and shall be tormented day and night for ever and ever" (Rev. 20:10). In this manner, the originator of evil and sin will be forever banished from God's universe, never to trouble man again.

I believe the earth will be consumed by fire because God said it. And we have seen science demonstrate the awesome power of atomic energy. Pliny said that it was a miracle to him that the world escaped burning for a single day.

The Bible teaches that all of this will happen when it is little expected. The dread hour will come as a thief in the night. It was not expected in Noah's day that the world would be destroyed by water. The people argued with Noah, saying that all things had continued as they were from the days of their first father Adam, and so they would always be. They thought Noah was a fool, going up and down the land proclaiming judgment to come and frightening the people.

Man has not changed. Man still rejects the testimony of the Scripture. He continues in sin and rebellion against God. He will do so up to the very moment when the sound of the trumpet will convince him that the Lord is come and that the day of judgment for ungodly men has arrived.

Today our world is mad in its obsession with pleasure, sex, and money. Its ear is too dull to hear the truth. Most men's eyes are blind. They do not want to see. They do not want to hear. They hurry to their doom. "When they shall say, Peace and safety; then sudden destruction cometh upon them, as travail upon a woman with child; and they shall not escape" (I Thess. 5:3).

Yet God longs for men to be saved. "The Lord is . . . not willing that any should perish, but that all should come to repentance" (II Pet. 3:9). God is at work to get men to stop their downward plunge in sin. He has sent His Holy Spirit to convict, His preachers and prophets to warn. His Word is printed in nearly every language. Man is without excuse.

23

The World of Tomorrow

The General Electric exhibit at the New York World's Fair of 1964 and 1965 had as its theme song, "There Will Be a Bright Tomorrow." No doubt the producers used this song with tongue in cheek considering the precarious condition of the world. But when the Christian says, "There will be a bright tomorrow," he has no reservations, for God has promised it and "there hath not failed one word of all his good promise" (I Kings 8:56).

The Christian hope is based on two worlds—this world and the next. When these two worlds are in view, we are adequately prepared for a full life here. The Christian has the hope of a life of joy, peace, and outgoing love in the midst of a world of trouble. The Christian has the hope of better living conditions as a result of Christian influence in any society or community. However, the Christian's great and ultimate hope is in the world to come. It is true that a person is not prepared to live until he is prepared to die. Emil Brunner says: "What oxygen is for the lungs such is hope for the meaning of human life." Dr. R. McNair Wilson, a cardiologist, wrote in his autobiography: "Hope is the medicine I use more than any other."[1]

Everywhere in the Bible it is assumed that there will be a next world. The Bible does not argue for its existence or elaborately explain it. Gordon Allport says: "The future is what concerns people most of all."[2] In

1 *Doctor's Progress* (London: Eyre and Spottiswoode, 1938).
2 *The Individual and His Religion* (New York: The Macmillan Co., 1960).

describing the future of the Christian, the Apostle Paul once said: "Eye hath not seen, nor ear heard, neither have entered into the heart of man, the things which God hath prepared for them that love him" (I Cor. 2:9).

Once the Apostle Paul had a vision of heaven when he saw things "unlawful to utter." This indicates that he could not explain it adequately in language that would be understood. We cannot comprehend the wonders of the next world or correlate its knowledge to that of this world. To do so would be beyond our present capacity to understand. At the close of the Bible it is written: "And I saw a new heaven and a new earth: for the first heaven and the first earth were passed away" (Rev. 21:1).

A New Creation

Everything in respect to heaven will be new. It is described as a new creation in which we shall move in new bodies, possessed of new names, singing new songs, living in a new city, governed by a new form of government, and challenged by new prospects of eternity. The paradise that man lost will be regained, but it will be much more. It will be a new paradise, not the old one repaired and made over. When God says, "Behold, I make all things new," the emphasis is on "all things." We shall live in a brand-new world.

The traditional concept of the "heaven-dweller" is a caricature. We often think of heaven as a place where people sit at a harp, with wings sprouting from their shoulder blades. We have seen pictures of a jewel-studded halo on a man's head, an angelic look on his face, golden streets under his feet, the dazzling beauty of gates of pearl to fill his eyes. This, of course, is not the true nature of the heaven-dweller. He does not live in a static form of life.

Someone has said that on the door of heaven is inscribed: "No admission except on business." Heaven is not all rest. It is labor, adventure, excitement, employment, and engagement. The Scripture says concerning the people in heaven, that "his servants shall serve him" (Rev. 22:3). It will be much like the present life with labor and leisure, but missing all the imperfections that have destroyed the full and true meaning of life.

According to Jesus, life in the future world is related to "many mansions," a term variously understood to mean many places of sojourn, many homes, or many planets to visit. We can read much into this statement of Jesus, but to me it means active, creative, adventuresome living.

Ian McClaren wrote: "Heaven is not a Trappist monastery. Neither is it retirement on pension. No, it is a land of continual progress." Heaven will have many opportunities for endless adventure and abundant creative living.

Time magazine once described the house of the future, calling it "the New Age House." This house was "like none ever built before. Its roof was a honeycomb of tiny solar cells that use the sun's rays to heat the house, furnish all the electric power. Doors and windows opened in response to hand signals; they closed automatically when it rained. The TV set hung like a picture, flat against the wall—so did the heating and air-conditioning panels. The radio was only as big as a golf ball. The telephone was a movielike screen which projected both the caller's image and voice. In the kitchen the range broiled thick steaks in barely two minutes. Dishes and clothes were cleaned without soap or water. The house had no electrical outlets; invisible radio beams ran all appliances. At night, the walls and ceilings glowed softly with glass-encased 'light sandwiches,' which changed color at the twirl of a dial. And throughout the house, tiny, unblinking bulbs of a strange reddish hue sterilized the air and removed all bacteria."[3]

This was written years ago, and some of this dream has already come to pass in many homes. However, the

3 April 29, 1957.

houses of heaven will be far more spectacular. They will be beyond the fondest dream of any housewife.

Sometime ago, I visited Rocket City in Texas. It is one of the most fantastic developments in America. It is the place where the astronauts live and train. They showed me some of the capsule food which has been developed for spacemen to use when they go to the moon. One of the scientists laughingly said: "Maybe this is going to be the food of heaven!" The Bible does teach that there will be some kind of food peculiarly adapted to the bodies of those who will live in heaven, for the book of Revelation speaks of "a tree of life which bore twelve manner of fruits."

Jesus Christ Will Be There

However, the most thrilling thing to me about heaven is that Jesus Christ will be there. I will see Him face to face. I will have the opportunity to talk directly to Him and to ask Him a hundred questions that I have never had answered.

A little boy was riding alone on a train on a hot day when the travelers were extremely uncomfortable, and the scenery was not too interesting as they passed through the desert of Arizona. A lady sitting beside the boy asked him: "Are you tired of the long ride?" The little boy smiled and said, "I'm a little tired, but I don't mind it much. You see, my father is going to meet me when I get to Los Angeles."

Sometimes we get a little tired of the burdens of life, but it is exhilarating to know that Jesus Christ will meet us at the end of life's journey. The joy of being with Him forever is beyond the ability of any writer to describe. The Apostle Paul was so anxious to see Christ that he was "willing . . . to be absent from the body, and to be present with the Lord" (II Cor. 5:8).

The Bible teaches that the throne of God is in heaven. "Heaven is my throne, and earth is my footstool" (Acts 7:49). His kingdom is the universe and there is no limit or end. Scientists tell us that space is infinite and that we live in an expanding, not receding, universe. Our telescopes have never found the limits of outer space. When we get to heaven we will not be limited to one particular space. The universe will be our empire. And what is true of space is true of what we now call time, for time will be succeeded by eternity, and we will move on into the endless eons of the future, exploring the endless reaches of the universe.

A Place Being Prepared

Heaven is more than just a state of mind or a condition of life. It is a place being "prepared," meaning that it is to be suited to the habitation and use of the people who have been reconciled to God by Jesus Christ.

All this leaves us with the conclusion that heaven will be as expansive as the universe itself. It will be as wonderful and beautiful as only the creator God can make it. Everything for your personal happiness and enjoyment is being prepared. Every longing and every desire will have perfect fulfillment.

One of the descriptions of heaven is that found on the Bible's concluding pages where it says: "And I John saw the holy city, new Jerusalem, coming down from God out of heaven, prepared as a bride adorned for her husband" (Rev. 21:2). There is nothing more universally beautiful than a bride. Think of all the anticipation, care, and preparation of a bride. Her dress, her hair, her bearing, her smile, and her transparent joy all combine to make her wedding moment the most transcendent event of her life. I have never seen an unlovely bride, and the Bible uses this beauty to describe heaven. On the morning of my oldest daughter's wedding I had a private talk with her. I had never seen such a combination of anticipation, joy, and happiness on her face before.

The Apostle John, who was given a glimpse into eternity, said: "And God shall wipe away all tears from their eyes; and there shall be no more death, neither sorrow, nor crying, neither shall there be any more pain: for the former things are passed away. And he that sat upon the throne said, Behold, I make all things new" (Rev. 21:4, 5).

One night a young girl taking a walk with her father was very quiet for a long time. Finally, her father asked what she was thinking about. "I was just thinking," she said, "if heaven with its stars is so beautiful wrong side out, how wonderful it must be on the right side."

Perfection

Heaven will be the perfection we have always longed for. All the things that made earth unlovely and tragic will be absent in heaven. There will be no night, no death, no disease, no sorrow, no tears, no ignorance, no disappointment, no war. It will be filled with health, vigor, virility, knowledge, happiness, worship, love, and perfection.

Heaven will be more modern and up to date than any of the present-day constructions of man. Heaven will be a place to challenge the creative genius of the unfettered mind of redeemed man. Heaven will be a place made supremely attractive by the presence of Christ.

One of the almost unmentioned wonders of heaven will be the varied kinds of beings represented in its population. Some are called princes, others potentates, others rulers, for there will be thrones, principalities, and powers to be occupied by various ranks of celestial princes. There will be seraphim and cherubim, angels and archangels, Gabriel and Michael, plus the innumerable myriads who tread the celestial courts and palaces. These will surround God on His throne to recognize His Majesty, ever attentive to His orders, watching over the inhabitants of the celestial worlds.

When we have compressed the Bible's descriptions of heaven into a composite picture, we find it to be a new heaven and a new earth crowned by "a city whose builder and maker is God." In the book of Revelation, John pictures it as having trees, flowing fountains, fruits, robes, palms, music, crowns, precious stones, gold, light, colors of the rainbow, water, knowledge, friendship, love, holiness, and the presence of God and His Son. This and much more will be heaven!

The Apostle Paul said: "We . . . are citizens of heaven, and from heaven we expect our deliverer to come, the Lord Jesus Christ" (Phil. 3:20, NEB). The Bible teaches that we Christians are aliens here. We are strangers, foreigners, pilgrims, and sojourners on the earth. "Here we have no continuing city" (Heb. 13:14). We desire a better country, which is heaven.

Citizens of Heaven

No exemption is granted the Christian from the common lot of the human race. We are born to trouble even as others and have tribulation like the rest. When depression comes, we may be out of work. When war rages, we are in danger. We are exposed to the same diseases and many of the same psychological problems as others. Thus we must take an interest in the present world. We must do all we can to help our neighbors with whom we dwell, be they believers or not.

However, it is true that even in this world the Christian has certain privileges as he anticipates heaven. As Charles Spurgeon used to say: "All the legions of hell cannot compel us to do the devil's work." The prince of this world may make his servants serve him, but he cannot raise a conscription among us "aliens." The true child of God claims an immunity from all the commands of Satan. In actuality, we are the only ones who are completely free. There are those today who say that we must do as others do, that we must conform to our world, that we must swim with the tide, that we must move with the crowd. But the believer says: "No, do not expect me to fall in with the evil customs and ways of this world. I am in Rome, but I will not do as Rome does. I am an alien, a stranger, and a foreigner. My citizenship is in heaven."

We are tuned to a different world. The Scripture says: "If any man love the world, the love of the Father is not in him" (I Jn. 2:15). Be willing rather to be sneered at than to be approved, counting the Cross of Christ greater riches than all the treasures of Washington, London, Paris, or Moscow.

To aliens, the treasures of this world will not be attractive. Our treasure is in heaven "where neither moth nor rust doth corrupt, and where thieves do not break through nor steal" (Matt. 6:20). Neither the American dollar, the British pound, nor the German mark can be spent in heaven. When we get to heaven we shall wish that we had laid up more treasure in its banks. I would far rather be rich toward God than before men.

As citizens of heaven, we also share in heaven's glory. The Bible teaches that even the angels are our servants. The great saints of the past are our companions. Christ is our Brother. God is our Father. And we will receive immortality. "Beloved, now are we the sons of God, and it doth not yet appear what we shall be: but we know that, when he shall appear, we shall be like him; for we shall see him as he is" (I Jn. 3:2).

Only One Door to Heaven

There is one more thing of tremendous importance concerning heaven, and that is how to get there.

There are restrictions to entering heaven. The Scripture says: "There shall in no wise enter into it any thing that defileth, neither whatsoever worketh abomination, or maketh a lie: but they which are written in the Lamb's book of life" (Rev. 21:27). This says plainly that certain people will not be allowed to enjoy the glories and joys of heaven. They are the ones who neglected to have their names written in the Lamb's book of life. They are the ones who rejected God's offer of love, mercy, and grace. They are the ones who said "No" to Jesus Christ. Jesus Himself said: "Enter ye in at the strait gate: for wide is the gate, and broad is the way, that leadeth to destruction, and many there be which go in thereat: because strait is the gate, and narrow is the way, which leadeth unto life, and few there be that find it" (Matt. 7:13, 14).

Have you, by faith, entered that narrow gate? Do you now walk on that narrow road that leads to eternal life? Or, are you among the masses of humanity who are on the broad road leading to destruction? What is your destination? Which road are you taking? Not every person will be found in heaven.

A man in a car stopped to ask a pedestrian the way to a certain street. When the man told him the way, the driver asked doubtfully: "Is that the best way?" The man replied: "That is the only way."

There is only one way to heaven. Jesus said: "I am the way, the truth, and the life: no man cometh unto the Father but by me" (Jn. 14:6).

The last invitation of the Bible says: "And the Spirit and the bride say, Come. And let him that heareth say, Come. And let him that is athirst come. And whosoever will, let him take the water of life freely" (Rev. 22:17).

This is still the age of grace. God's offer of forgiveness and a new life still stands. However, the door will one day be closed. Someday it will be too late. This is why the Bible continually warns and challenges: "Now is the accepted time" (II Cor. 6:2).

When the flood came, Noah was safe and secure in the ark. He had been foolish enough to trust God and to take Him at His word. When the world goes up in flames, you can be safe and secure by believing and accepting the "foolishness of God." This makes little sense to this dying world, but to those of us who are saved, it is the power of God unto salvation.